# Also by Michael Fre

For Beth, Ellie, Ben, Jamie, Jacob and Sam

Just to let you know where you come from
And to express my love, which couldn't be stronger

# Confessions of a Serial Biographer

## Michael Freedland

*For Sandra
Warmest best wishes

[signature]

2005*

VALLENTINE MITCHELL · LONDON

First published in 2005 in Great Britain by
VALLENTINE MITCHELL
Suite 314, Premier House, 112–114 Station Road,
Edgware, Middlesex HA8 7BJ
and in the United States of America by
VALLENTINE MITCHELL
c/o ISBS, 920 NE 58th Avenue, Suite 300,
Portland, OR 97213 3786

Website: www.vmbooks.com

British Library Cataloguing in Publication Data:
A catalogue record for this book has been applied for

ISBN 0 85303 619 5 (cloth)
ISBN 0 85303 620 9 (paper)

Library of Congress Cataloging-in-Publication Data:
A catalog record for this book has been applied for

Typeset by FiSH Books, London
Printed in Great Britain by MPG Books Ltd, Bodmin, Cornwall

# Contents

# Prologue: Father's day

It was a dreary day in November 1999. But perhaps no more than you should expect from a Sunday in November. In fact, I imagine the weather had been just like that a hundred years before when my father, David Freedland, was born. The world had changed beyond recognition in that century. In 1899, horses pulled carts, streets were lit by gas (and frequently not lit at all) and communications amounted to sending a letter – which, totally unlike the situation a century later, would sometimes get to its destination on the day it was posted. Two world wars had come and gone, with consequences no one could possibly have predicted. A Holocaust had wiped out six million of his people. On the other hand, remarkable advances in science had brought miracles that cast common killer diseases like diphtheria, smallpox and what used to be known as infantile paralysis (polio) back into the dark ages. You could fly from one side of the globe to the other in a day.

If almost everything else had changed in those hundred years, so had David Freedland's family. It was easy to realise that day in 1999 when we were celebrating what would have been his centenary.

David had been born in London's East End – dark, smoky, noisy and in the shadow of where, not long before, Jack the Ripper had gone about his business. We were marking the hundred years since then in Hertfordshire. It was lush and suburban. Dad liked greenery and loved his family. He would have been pleased to know that both were in evidence that day, 16 years after his death – although, in truth, I never liked to think of it as that. I have always hated euphemisms, not least that one about people 'passing away'. Yet, when I thought about it then and think about it now, my father had remained with us ever since he died. Not a day went by, or still does, without my thinking about him – and usually with a smile. I hear a joke and I think of him. Like the one about the Jewish man in the cinema queue. As he stands there, a big man of a different faith stamps on his foot. 'Mister,' he says, 'are you doing this for a joke or on purpose?' 'On purpose,' replies the thug. 'Good,' says the man. 'That sort of joke, I don't like.'

I told that joke on the day of our family reunion. And mentioned my mother's favourite *bête noire*, his pipe. We missed my mother, Lily Freedland, that day, too. She would have enjoyed the tribute to her partner of 54 years, the other half of one of the happiest marriages I knew. But she had been dead for six years by then.

The people we would have expected were all there – my wife, Sara, of course, our children, Fiona, Dani and Jonathan, their spouses and their children, David's great-grandchildren. Sally, his last surviving sister, her children and various other cousins were there, too. Sixty of us. But it was those *various* other cousins who made the impact. Lovely people – whom we had never met before. One was the midwife who came to visit Fiona after the birth of her second baby, Ellie. She saw the name 'Freedland' in the hospital records. It was her own name and she wondered if we were related. We were. It turned out that her great-grandfather had been my father's eldest brother – whom I never knew. His name was Michael. The fact that , in breach of Jewish custom, I was given the same name as his during his lifetime, gives some idea of the relationship he had with the rest of the family. But I had once met his son, the grandfather of this young lady, Hannah, who was delightful. She, also, not Jewish.

Then there were the children of yet another brother, Izzy, whose existence I had heard of once when I was about 9 years old – and heard not a word about since. His daughter Sylvia wrote to me when she had heard one of my radio programmes. She explained the relationship – her father had been cut off by his father, my grandfather Nathan Freedland, when he ran off with the family cook. A cook! Plainly, things had improved for the Freedlands since David was born in the East End. But not in family terms. Nathan might have been touched by so many of his descendants assembling for a family reunion. He may have been less than happy to know that Sylvia's lovely family were Jehovah's Witnesses. It was the first time I had met them – and the first time I had come across a Jehovah's Witness who didn't remain on the front doorstep.

It was, in so many ways, the Jewish story. I've always felt part of that story. It has always been a part of my life. My three lives. The personal one, the Jewish communal one and, more and more, the one that introduced me to the great and the near great – and the bloody nuisances who were neither, but thought they were both.

# LIFE ONE

# 1  The old folks at home

I always believed my grandfather, Barnet Mindel, had blue legs. I was quite five years old before I discovered that he simply wore blue long johns and that when he lifted his trouser legs they were what I saw.

I wish I had asked him about those. Now, after all those years and following a series of events neither I nor anyone else could have predicted, I also wish I had asked him more about his and the family's origins. When he was about 10, my son Jonathan was given an assignment to produce a family tree. He was proud that he could go back 70-odd years. His teacher wasn't impressed. The boy next to him could date his family line to 1066. That, too, is the Jewish story.

Stoke Newington was the family home. Or at least the home of the Mindels, of whom I always felt one, despite my surname. I think my father felt at least as much a Mindel as a Freedland, since the family welcomed him as my mother's choice and, as far as I know, loved him more than his own had done.

It was not difficult to love my parents, or, from my point of view, my grandparents, who were among the greatest influences in my early life. And so was their home, which, as a child, I thought quite palatial, with high ceilings and leather furniture. Actually, it was just a flat above a shop, but I wasn't aware of that at the time, any more than I was aware that Stoke Newington wasn't exactly Hollywood – or Hampstead Garden Suburb. My mother got to calling it 'Smoke Newington', and I suppose she had a point. When Barnet and Annie Mindel, who were to become my grandparents, moved there in the first decade of the last century, it was considered upmarket, the first stage of the Jewish exodus from the very East

End where my father had been born. By the time I came along in the last fortnight of 1934, it was established as a centre for middle-class London Jewry.

My beloved Aunt Sylvia, my mother's younger sister, was born there and stayed for the next 80 years – her husband, Mick, made it his home, too.

Something neither Sara nor I have fully come to understand is why two of our children have subsequently chosen Stoke Newington as the site of their own homes. The place the Mindels took 80 years to leave has become 'yuppie', and they and their own children are all as happy there as monkeys surrounded by banana trees.

The Mindels' story and that of the Freedlands, to whom I shall come soon, was one which would be recognised by everyone who rejoices in the contribution made by immigrants to the British way of life – and, I like to think, be appreciated by them. Barnet, then Berel, came to the country at the age of 16 and arranged for his parents and his four brothers to follow. They found accommodation in some East End hovel, described vividly by Barnet's youngest brother Lou to me shortly before his death at the age of 103. 'We slept in a tiny, damp room, lit by gas. On our first night there, my mother wanted to turn off the lights and so blew out the flame. I was 9 years old, but I knew better. Otherwise, there would have been no Mindel family in London.'

Home for them had been Dunilovich, a tiny village in what is now Belarus but was but a stone's throw from the Lithuanian capital of Vilna (now Vilnius). It was the centre of Jewish learning in Eastern Europe, known as the Jerusalem of Lithuania. Berel's father, who rejoiced in the Hebrew name Yehuda Yidel (Judah the Jew; I now have a grandson with the name Judah, who I am pleased to say doesn't need to be reminded that he is a Jew), was a tailor who had had, and probably always had, rough times. My great-grandfather, like his own contemporaries and fellow citizens of Dunilovich, was strictly Orthodox, which was probably not difficult in a *shtetl*, one of the *Fiddler on the Roof* villages where virtually everyone else was Jewish – apart, that is, from the constable, the priest and a group of gentiles who couldn't understand why they should have been picked to have so many 'foreigners' among them, although, truth to tell, the Jews had been there longer than they had themselves.

As I said, I knew little more of the family history than I knew about my grandfather's blue legs. Uncle Lou told me about two other brothers. Both had been the studious type and had gone to *yeshivot*, or Talmudic colleges. At one, Sam, the eldest of the tribe, had got into a fight of sorts (yes, they even had fights at Talmudic colleges) and a fellow student threw a pen in his direction. It hit an eye and, as a result, he was partially blinded – which might or might not have been the reason for his not seeing the joys of a home in London and going to live in America. That was also the Jewish story. Another brother, Levi Yitzhok, fared much worse. Someone hit him over the head with a sacred book, which might have been said to have put him off for religion for life – that is, if it hadn't put him off life itself first. Levi Yitzhok died of the injury. Uncle Lou told me that the first he knew of the death was when his father came home unexpectedly. 'He came into our house, threw off his boots and sat on the floor. That's how I knew my brother had died.'

There was also a sister, Leah, who died – how, I have no idea. But it was in Dunilovich. My mother, born in 1906, was named after her.

This was a compassionate family. When they emigrated to Britain, the Mindel passport included the brothers, Sam, Barnet, Simon, Nat, Lou – and Leah. The assumption is that they smuggled a little girl out of Dunilovich by giving her the name of my dead great-aunt.

Simon was slightly younger than Barnet and, like him, went into the tailoring business. Then there was Nat, the most brilliant of the brothers. Within months of coming to Britain in 1901, he had won a scholarship to the famous Grocers Company School, later Hackney Downs Grammar. He went on to London University, became a schoolteacher and was then called up into the army. There is a wonderful picture of three brothers, Barnet, a lance-corporal, Lou, an aircraftman in the Royal Flying Corps and Nat – a captain in the Camel Corps.

With his brother Berel, he went to Egypt and then on to Palestine. After the war, he returned there to become a Mandatory Government official and before long was Commissioner for Migration. Not an easy job for a Jew at a time when immigration to the Promised Land was severely limited. When he doubted he should remain in office, Chaim Weizmann begged him to stay. The first president of Israel presumably believed that having one's own controlling the books was better than someone on the other side of the fence. Later, he worked for the 'Joint', the American Jewish Joint Distribution Committee, formed at the end of the war to try to help 'DPs', the displaced persons, the survivors of the Nazi death camps. As such, he became the first Mindel in 50 years to go back to Dunilovich. 'There was nothing there,' he told me. Later, he became a senior official in the Israeli government. He was not universally accepted. After working for the Mandate in such a senior position, and always determined to show his admiration for British ways and British manners – his son, Yehuda, was educated at the Perse School, Cambridge – the Israelis regarded him as too British. To the British, he was a Jew.

My grandparents never had any such difficulty. They were very Jewish – and very honoured to have become British. Grandpa proudly always said he voted Liberal. He was also very proud of the fact he had served his king and country in the war. It was necessary, he always told me, to repay what his country had given him. As a ladies' tailor, he was an internationally recognised craftsman. On the wall of his workshop at the back of the High Street flat (I assumed that anyone whose business was at home couldn't possibly be said actually to *work*; how I later suffered from people thinking just that about me) was a letter from an official at the White House, thanking him for the great suit Grandpa had made his wife.

But the greatest achievement of my grandfather was meeting my grandmother, the matriarch of the family who seemed too young to die in 1960 at the age of 80. She was always the most vibrant person in the family, and I adored her – to the extent that there are days when I still cannot believe she is no longer here.

They had met in her Latvian home town of Libau (the only reference to Libau I have ever seen was at the back of the ship taking Barbra Streisand away from her own *shtetl* in the movie *Yentl*), where he had gone for one of his first tailoring jobs, sleeping on the work table. Annie Micket was 16 and apparently they fell in love. I have always liked the idea of their falling in love. Both came from Orthodox families, but not so Orthodox that the only marriage they could consider would be one arranged by their elders and betters.

Grandma also knew that there was no future for her in Latvia and took off for Cardiff, where she had an uncle. She was 16. Grandpa followed her and they married in London in 1905. Lily, my mother, was to be the eldest of four – her brother Jack arrived the following year, in 1907. (He became a tie manufacturer, spoke beautifully and was something of a snob. He married an heiress to the Lyons food empire, but it did him no good. He was the first member of the family to divorce, and he married well a second time.) Then came Sylvia, who has always been a rock and a comfort – she was the one I would go to whenever I had problems. Doris, the youngest Mindel child, for whom I have great love, was 18 years younger than my mother – her daughter, Linda, used to joke that she was actually Lily's love child. I am sure, knowing my mother, that it could never have been the case. But it *is* a good story.

Grandma was an elegant woman. Sara always said she was like Queen Mary – without the pearls and, certainly, without the klepto-mania. She was loved because she was warm and comfortable. She was not one of those grandmothers who smothered her grandchildren with hugs and kisses. She was matter of fact. She was loving, but she never had to say so. She was also exceptionally sensible. Grandma knew what was going on in the world and what was going on in her family. If you had problems, you went to her and, like a judge summing up a complicated court case, she gave an instant review of both sides of the argument. It was no coincidence that when I went into the army, it was to the Stoke Newington flat that I went when I was on leave – or when I stole a weekend off to which I wasn't entitled.

She also had the ability to think laterally and develop ideas. For my twentieth birthday, she decided she wanted to give me something that I really wanted. 'He loves records,' said my mother. I knew she had said that and looked forward to a new Al Jolson LP. That wouldn't have been good enough for Grandma – and she proved it. She went off to Selfridges and made a record. There were few tape recorders then, and neither she nor I had one. To my shame, I remember being disappointed. But in the years since, I have come to be so very grateful for her intelligence and her brilliant sense of doing something different. To hear her voice again is a privilege granted to few grandsons almost half a century after their grandmother's death. I have to say, even now, I can't always manage to do that without emotion. And it was not just because she began with the words: 'I want to tell you what I think of you. I think you're wonderful.' (I haven't had too many reviews like that since then.)

My wish is that I had had the sense to ask her for more stories about the years before she came to Britain. I can recall only two anecdotes – that, as a child, she used to wash herself in the snow, and then the one story that I know about previous generations. It appears that her grandfather – until then, I didn't think my grandparents actually had grandparents of their own, which, thinking about the age expectancy of the early 1800s, is perhaps not surprising – had a son who emigrated to Texas, an unusual thing in itself. Even more unusually, he got on a boat from Libau and went to pay them a visit. He was introduced to his daughter-in-law, who offered him chicken – which she proceeded to smother in butter. He left for home the next morning. But that left new questions: was the woman Jewish? Was the chicken otherwise kosher? And if so, how would he know? Or was he just offended by the Jewish injunction against the combination of milk and meat?

Going to my father's family in the north-west London suburb of Brondesbury was always a very different experiment. There, I was showered with love, hugs and kisses and great concern for my welfare. Everything I said seemed to be regarded as brilliant. Yet somehow, the restrained love evident in the High Street seemed more natural.

My father's father, Nathan Freedland, was a widower, born in a village close to Kovno (now Kaunus), which, from 1920 to 1939, would also have its time as the capital of Lithuania. He and Elizabeth, his wife, my paternal grandmother, had come to Britain a few years before the Mindels. Elizabeth died when Dad was 16. She was a diabetic and suffered greatly in an age before the discovery of insulin. My father missed her, I think, right up to his own death at 84. His relationship with his father during his own childhood was rather more fraught. He always said that Nathan favoured his daughters (two of whom had been killed in a fire before Nathan and Elizabeth left Lithuania) above their sons. There were four surviving girls: Betty (Rebecca, known to the family adults as Beckie), Hetty (Henrietta), Leila (Lily) and Sally (Sarah).

Betty was the one who made the most fuss of me, and yet she was the most difficult to know. She was in her early thirties when she married 'well' – in terms of the 1920s when she and her father's friend

Abram Levin stood under the *chuppah*, the bridal canopy. He must have been at least 35 years her senior. He didn't speak very good English – in fact, he didn't speak much of anything. He growled. And what I remember most about him was the way he never said hello or goodbye, just 'good luck', which I have to believe he meant. Betty called him 'Money,' which I was told was Yiddish for 'husband'. But since he had a lot of the stuff, 'Money' could have been an apt description for him. Auntie Hetty was very different. She married late and due to a totally unnecessary 'accident' – a so-called friend pulled a prank and let down a deckchair in which she was sitting – she damaged her spine and was from then on virtually crippled. She could walk, but painfully. I loved her very much, but for reasons I have never understood was left out of her will – which my parents, my brother and my cousins were not.

Leila was probably the most sophisticated of the sisters. She had an artistic touch that she conveyed by her home, her clothes and everything about her. I knew her less well than the others because she went to live in America a few weeks after my bar mitzvah in 1947. When I made my first trip to the States in 1966, I was the first member of the family she had seen in 19 years and, things being as they were, she hadn't even spoken to anyone on the phone. (Actually, she had broken that rule just a week before when she heard of Betty's death.) Later, when she made numerous visits, I got to know her better and I was glad to do so. I still think of her when I look at my bookshelves. As a child, she bought me a book every birthday and I still have most of them.

Sally, the last surviving Freedland sibling of that generation, is a delight with a wicked sense of humour. She was at one time an actress – at RADA with Charles Laughton, she reminded us on numerous occasions – but didn't exactly become a star. Nevertheless, there is still a lot of the actress in her.

Nathan was proud of her. He actually had quite a lot to be proud of himself. He had come over to England without much more than his wife and his name – although whether it was Freedland in those days no one can be sure. There are census records of the Lithuanian village revealing a family called 'Freundland'. Was that *my* family? And why the spelling? People still write 'Friedland', which upsets me only when it appears as a newspaper or magazine byline. (Since my son Jonathan became much more famous than I, it has happened rather less.)

Nathan pulled himself and his family up by his bootstrings – a cliché, but I will always remember the boots he wore. I also remember the glass eye he had. For years, I could never understand why there was always a big dent behind his left eye, but was always too polite to ask. I also loved the way he clicked when he ate. Who knew about false teeth? As a 4-year-old, I tried to find ways of clicking, too.

He had settled in the East End in Newark Street – which, remarkably, was on the corner of the road where Sara lived when we first met – but plainly came into better circumstances as the first years of the twentieth century passed. My father's boyhood was spent in Amhurst Road, Stoke Newington – a fair step ahead of the nearby High Street, where the Mindels lived. Next door was Lord Amhurst of Hackney, who had his own coach and four, and next to him, a man whom my father envied. The day Dad started school at nearby Sigdon Street, this neighbour retired. Dad said he couldn't wait till he did, too.

When he started work at 14, it was with a china company. His first job was to deliver a load of cups and saucers which he decided was much too heavy for him. The solution to his problem came when he had to cart his load via a railway bridge – he threw the lot over the top and wasn't surprised when he was told to look for another job.

Life wasn't that much fun for him – but my grandfather appeared to flourish. He was a diamond merchant and seemed to do well enough at it. In fact, he was still going to sales at the age of 90. But those weren't his glory days any more, the time when he had moved to Brondesbury and bought a house in Dartmouth Road that seemed to my childish mind a veritable palace – with a spiral staircase, no less, and room for two maids who worked from a kitchen that had indicators to show from which room a bell was being pushed. That very much impressed me. But I drove through Dartmouth Road some 30 years after he had moved from there with Rosa, his second wife, whom everyone called 'Auntie' (actually I'm not really sure if she was officially his wife; a rumour has since gone round the family that they never did marry, but I never thought of Grandpa Freedland being a swinger). The house was in the process of being converted into a welfare hostel and the front door that I remember so well was open. The staircase and the hallway were much smaller than I recalled, but it was big enough for them, for their daughters when they came to stay and for us, too, when we called.

There was also space for Mr Erb, a lodger, which makes me think that when the two maids had left things weren't quite so good. Then there was a lady I remember suddenly appearing on the scene, a Miss Cohen. Years later, Miss Cohen would be responsible for my admiration for my grandfather being increased a hundred-fold. Miss Cohen was a German refugee and Nathan had agreed to sponsor her as a domestic – a frequent way of helping Jews escape from Nazi persecution. Miss Cohen arrived on the Dartmouth Road doorstep, mentally ready to pick up the nearest mop and broom. But that wasn't Grandpa Freedland's idea at all.

'I don't need a domestic,' he told her, 'but you need a home. You stay here until you are able to find a job and a home of your own.' I don't know how long it took her to do just that, but she was in the house for a very long time.

My grandfather was a former immigrant who not only believed that by being a good citizen he was giving a little back to the country which had provided him with a home, but appreciated the difficulties others had when they arrived here. The fact that he had also helped save a life earned him the admiration of everyone who knew about it. Truth to tell, there were not many of those. He was not a man who boasted about anything, good deeds included.

He hit hard times later, sharing flats with his daughters Betty and Hetty, and ended up with a terrible life in a home for the blind. But his reputation was unsullied. In the 1980s, I happened to mention that my paternal grandfather was in the diamond business to the secretary of the diamond bourse at Hatton Garden, Sammy Fisher (Lord Fisher of Camden), who was also President of the Board of Deputies of British Jews. He rang me the following Sunday morning. 'Your grandfather, Nathan Freedland, joined the bourse in 1924 and remained a member for the rest of his life. I can tell you, you should hold your head up high. In all that time, not a single complaint was ever made about him.'

There was another reason why I hold him in such affection. At the age of 16, I worked for the Post Office as a temporary Christmas postman. Grandpa sent me his usual birthday card – but this time with the message: 'I'm pleased that you have become a man of letters.' Not bad for an immigrant who had to teach himself to read and write English.

If it is true, as I suspect, that my father and grandfather took quite a time to get to know each other better, it was, or should have been, to the regret of both of them. My father was the sweetest man I have ever known. He was devoted to his wife and she to him, although I have always thought that she would have preferred him to have had more ambition. He never had any riches in the traditional sense, but was exceptionally endowed with one of the greatest gifts open to man – contentment. He asked no more of life than that his family be happy and well, that he could smoke his pipe, read his paper, play his Mantovani tapes and watch television, sitting in a comfortable armchair in a house with a garden where he could grow his peas and marrows (which had a habit of coming up in the garden of the house next door).

In the mid-1920s, he was manager of B. Mindel and Co., the then menswear shop of the man who was to be my other grandfather. Lily Mindel worked in the shop, too. Before long, it became obvious that Dad was leaving work later than even the requirements of pre-Depression retail trading dictated. He and Lily fell in love and he'd go home (sent home by Barnet Mindel, by all accounts) to his bedsit in Finsbury Park, stopping on the way at one of the mobile coffee stalls which were then as much a feature of London life as the barrel organs and fogs.

None of that should give the impression that either Lily or Dave were fast movers (what man would like to think of his mother being a fast mover?). He didn't propose until he had got himself a better job in nearby Bethnal Green. They were engaged in 1928 and married two years later. I came along on 18 December 1934.

# 2  Me

I was born at the Hackney Downs Nursing Home, not far from the ancestral pad in Stoke Newington, and named Michael, ostensibly because Freedland family folklore decreed that either a great-grandfather (Nathan's Hebrew name was Natan ben Meir – Meir is often the Hebrew for Michael) or a great-uncle had been called that and he had lived to the age of 114. I'm not sure whether anyone ever believed it, but I couldn't quarrel with the motives behind the naming idea. Since the traditional greeting to a Jewish child is that he should live to be 120, 114 was plainly considered to be well on the way.

My parents were loving. My father couldn't wait to get home on Thursday afternoons, his early closing day, to play with me and I couldn't wait to be with him. My mother loved me deeply, I know. But she could be very strict and was not beyond using her hands for punishments that she assured me hurt her more than they hurt me. I could never quite understand the logic of that. On the other hand, I never doubted that love; indeed, I took it for granted and when I think of the lengths to which she went to assure my welfare, I can only be grateful.

I cried for her (and for Sylvia) when, aged 3, I was taken to the London Jewish Hospital to have my tonsils out, and ran into her arms when she came to collect me.

I have to say that hospitals were playing a big part in my life at that time. Not that I was ever seriously ill, but I think taking me to see one doctor after another at an unlimited number of hospitals and consulting rooms seems to have been her favourite occupation. We would be going to the laundry and end up at Great Ormond Street, the children's hospital. There was a trip to the market and I found myself back at the Jewish hospital. She told me we were going to the library, but it was to see a stern gentleman with a light on his head on Harley Street.

I know I had flat feet. The Harley Street consultant told me I had acidosis. But none of that seemed to my juvenile mind (or does now to my ageing one) to be reason for this constant tourism to places where I was more scared of the smell than the possibility of more serious remedies. Mum decided my chest needed expanding (she should only see it now), so I had to do exercises. She thought I looked pale, so I had sun-ray treatments, sitting on a mat, wearing goggles and exposing myself to what today would be regarded as near-lethal doses of ultraviolet rays. (Being fitted for shoes must have been equally dicing with something terrible; before either mum or the shop assistant could be sure a shoe fitted, I had to place my feet in an X-ray machine and wiggle my toes, which were seen in excrutiating detail on the screen of what I now realise was like an ancient 'What the Butler Saw' machine.)

It got so that I was frightened of going out with my mother to buy bread or a chicken. I was convinced the baker or butcher would turn out to be a specialist in some disease I had no idea existed. The consequences of all that have turned out to be quite serious. Today, I will do anything in my power to avoid going to a doctor – or even visiting people in a hospital, although I have had to do far more of the latter than I would have wished, as will become clear later on.

I have just one happy memory of those hospital visits. I must have been 4 years old and sitting on my mother's lap on the bus taking us to the one in Stepney. As I looked out of the window somewhere near Shoreditch, the adjoining seat was suddenly taken. I looked round and saw it was my dad sitting there. Whether he had deliberately caught that particular bus or it was sheer coincidence I have no idea. To this day, I can still summon up the exquisite excitement of that moment.

At 5, I was given a red cap and told I was going to school. It was Princess May Road, just across from the shop in the High Street – which by now was selling women's shoes. This was one of those horrific places that had the word 'institution' stamped all over it – high walls, tiled corridors and dusty floors. All I remember of that first day at school was sitting on that floor and being told to try on gas masks. The teacher, tall, gangly, bespectacled and suffering from bad breath, told us we had to be careful with the masks since the London County Council had spent a great deal of money on them. What was the London County Council? This 5-year-old had no idea.

I think it was being carried down to the shelters that evening which changed all our lives. My parents decided that the time had come to leave London. As many people, including my own wife, who suffered incredibly from the experience, have told me, I was very lucky not to have been separated from them during the war years. I wasn't being evacuated alone.

The fact is that we ended up at St Pancras station and Dad booked two and a half tickets for Luton. I think he chose it simply because Luton was the destination of the next train. Had there been one to Bedford, we might well have gone there. 'You'll like Luton,' he told me. 'Lots of toyshops.' I don't ever remember seeing any, but that was a white lie I understood – even then.

# 3    *Luton*

My father's family told me they believed I had had pickled herring in my bottle. They couldn't understand how my mother could feed me delicacies of this kind, how a little smoked salmon had gone a long way into my juvenile stomach, how chicken soup featured so considerably in my diet. Thinking about that, perhaps that's why I had acidosis. But then everything would change in Luton, where you couldn't get pickled herring or pickled cucumbers (the taste and smell of which I remember from those pre-Luton Stoke Newington days; it has never quite been replicated).

No longer would there be the regular Sunday afternoons at Brondesbury, where I would jump on to a worn green couch and call 'Ah main', which I had picked up from going with my grandfather to the Shacklewell Lane synagogue, where occasionally they would let me sit in the choir. I later realized what a rare privilege that had been – with my voice, I think choirs actually advertised for me not to apply for membership.

Luton was going to be different – and I resented it. We arrived on a cold, dark evening in October 1940. I think to me that arrival symbolised the war. It was miserable, the way getting a sudden cold is miserable. It was as if everybody was sneezing. Luton was a town that was sneezing and had no handkerchief. I hated it from the first moment we got off the train and was engulfed in a cloud of smoke from the train's engine. Somehow, I thought that the couple of days we would be there would be all covered in smoke, too. I have two other memories of that arrival – getting on a dark red single-decker bus and the conductress in a funny hat telling me to hold on tight. I had never seen a woman collecting fares before. The other distinct memory is that of a sign on the railway bridge as we walked through those dismal streets – 'Thursday is Newsday'. I could have had no idea how vitally significant that advertisement for the local newspaper would be quite a few years later.

School was Denbigh Road, which is today almost 100 per cent Asian; a school that in 2004 featured in the national news when a Muslim girl was not allowed to wear her long gown; there were no Asians in the Luton to which I arrived, the nearest thing there was to an ethnic group were Jews like us). It was wartime and teachers were as scarce as smoked salmon and bagels. There were 56 children in a class and, actually, I do remember learning to read, to write, to study the elements of history, which I lapped up. I even learned mental arithmetic, which these days, when I could be talked out of two and two making four, I find incredible. The teachers, in short, were remarkable.

I started in the infants' school, where there was a breakdown in communications between myself and my teacher, Miss Oliver (who, strangely, later became head teacher of my younger brother Geoffrey's school). She ordered me not to talk, which has always been an impossible task where I'm concerned. 'Michael Freedland, you've got a long tongue,' she said, using a term I had never heard before. 'No, I haven't,' I protested. 'Look.' At which I put out my tongue and had my knuckles wrapped with her ruler.

It was there that I made my first friends, particularly a fellow of my own age called John Smith – a name I thought at the time was about as unusual as icecream. We became very close, but were later involved in the only serious fight meek little Michael ever had while at school. He made some remark about my mother and I rounded on him to the extent that he fell to the ground and I was pronounced the winner – no wonder I have never forgotten it. As it so happened, my mother arrived on the scene to witness my triumph. 'What was it all about?' she asked. 'Did he say something about Jews?' I didn't want to say that I was defending her honour – I suppose I was upset about the names she had been called. For the rest of her life, she would tell the story of the fight – and say it was all about my defence of the faith.

I was always very proud of my mother when she came to call for me at school. She cared much more about her appearance than did most of the other mothers. We had little or no money – I can remember her crying because there wasn't enough to pay for the groceries – but her father had made her a couple of suits, or costumes, as they were called in those days, and she always wore lipstick and had her hair nicely styled.

She also introduced me to the cinema, for which, along with so much else, I shall also be grateful. On Saturday afternoons, we would queue up for a ninepenny seat at the Savoy, the Odeon, Palace or Union for a film that was deemed to be 'suitable'. Then, when I got a little older, our Thursday evening treat was another trip to the 'pictures'. Nobody knew anything about babysitting in those days and I loved the adventure of it all – a joy and a habit, to say nothing of a career foundation, that has stayed with me ever since.

War touched us as it did everyone in very different ways. Dad's sister Sally came to stay with us for a time. Her husband, Louis, was in the army and every day or so she wrote to him about life in 'Luton By The Sink' and about the progress of their 4-year-old son David. As she wrote, she had a dictionary by her side. After days of watching this ritual, my father could take it no more. 'Why don't you just send him the dictionary?' he asked her.

It was a gentile world we lived in in those days. I had few Jewish friends. They were as difficult for me to find as boys not called Smith. One, though, was a nice lad called Brian Helps, with whom I was invited to the home of another boy – I'll call him Jack Cohen. The Cohens were better off than we were. Mr Cohen owned a hat factory and they had a car and lived in a big house in a posher residential road than the one in which we resided. We were invited to stay for tea. The maid – see, I said they were rich – brought in glasses of fruit squash, bread, butter and jam. And icecream. I was amazed. I hadn't seen icecream for three or four years. My mouth watered, particularly when I saw Jack's family enjoy it to the full and Brian and I were left with our watering mouths open wide – for nothing more than a slice of bread and raspberry jam. At 10 years old, I was smothered in embarrassment for my gentile friend, who was even poorer than we were. I remember going home, telling my mother about it and thinking even then that that was how anti-Semitism started.

In a town like Luton, the Jewish community was keen to show that it was part of the fabric of the local community. Accordingly, one Rosh Hashanah, as the community marked the start of the Jewish New Year with services held at the town's Methodist Central Mission Hall, the minister, the Reverend Harry Ritvo, played the 'goy' card as one desperate effort to get the congregation to behave itself, to do the un-Jewish thing and be quiet during the service. 'We are about to be honoured by the presence of the mayor of Luton, Councillor Roberts,' he announced solemnly. 'Please show some decorum.' From that moment on, it was as if one of the needles used by any of the dozens of tailors in the community had been dropped. Not a sound. When the service was over, Dad asked the minister what had happened to the mayor. 'Does it matter?' said the then 40-something 'Reverend', shrugging his shoulders and giggling through his beard. For the record, Councillor Roberts hadn't been mayor for three years, but that didn't matter to him.

A lot of the fun has gone out of the High Holydays since those days – particularly Yom Kippur, the 25-hour Day of Atonement, which begins at dusk with the sacred Kol Nidre service, solemn prayers and an appeal for local funds and, these days, for Israel. There was no Israel in my childhood, but there was an appeal.

It was the best show of the year. Ritvo, in his white robe and kippar skullcap, stood in the pulpit and invited donations. 'Mr Greenberg, £5 ... Mr Cohen from Stopsley [there were Mr Cohens from New Bedford Road, from London Road and all over the town, but this was Mr Cohen from Stopsley], Anonymous, £20 ... ' It was marvellous to see who gave what. We would compare notes from the previous year, to see who was up and who was down. And we always tried to work out who was 'Anonymous'. One year, it was Mr Levy, Modern Gowns and Fashions in George Street, '£20, anonymous.' And there was always 'Mr Gimelfarb, £5.' My friends and I waited for Mr Gimelfarb's fiver. But I never found out who Mr Gimelfarb was.

In the early 1940s in the street where we lived, Cranleigh Gardens, we *weren't* the only Jewish family in the neighbourhood. Four doors away lived the Bakers, who were plainly better off than we were – they had chicken to eat on Shabbat. But they also managed to buy an extra quarter, which they sold on to Mum and from which she made a meal for three and a little soup. The Bakers also had a fridge and used to allow us to store our perishable food in it. This was my job. I used to take the Freedland food to the Bakers to put in their fridge. But one week, it landed me in more trouble than I had ever previously experienced. For there was one other disfigurement to our road, in addition to the smokescreen machines which had been placed on the kerbside in case Field

Marshal Goering decided to attack Cranleigh Gardens: a collection of iron bins, like dustbins, into which food waste was to be put. The waste was to go to feed pigs – which was no reason for us not to use them. That was another one of my jobs: to take the food waste and put it in the 'pig bins'. The problem was that my mother wrapped both the waste and the food for the Bakers' fridge in similar newspaper parcels. Friday arrived and I was deputed to collect our quarter of chicken. What Mum unwrapped was an ice-cold package of tea leaves, potato peelings and fish bones. I don't know if she ever remembered the look she gave me that Friday or what we had for dinner that night, but I do. There was a small tin of salmon in the larder and that was our feast.

It was just one of the problems of wartime existence. I didn't know at that time how easy I had it. Unlike other children (like the little girl who would become my wife), I was not evacuated alone, I was not left motherless as she would be, I was not bombed out of my house. And, most significantly of all, we were not victims of the Holocaust. My grandmother's family were all wiped out in Latvia – her parents, her brother and his children, had tried life in London, but had decided to go back to Libau. It took no investigations to realise they had perished when the Nazis arrived.

Denbigh Road was where I first came to grips with the fact that I hated sports. I also hated swimming – ever since I was thrown in the deep end in an effort to teach me. But I can recall things that I did learn there – surprising things, now that I come to think of it. It was at Denbigh Road that I first heard of Tel Aviv being a wholly Jewish city. I was very proud to know that. I heard about the Spanish Inquisition – although nobody thought to mention that there was any Jewish involvement in that.

The household changed radically in 1944 when my brother Geoffrey arrived. More than nine years younger, he wasn't the company I would have loved and as the years moved on, I wasn't exactly the playmate he might have hoped for. In some ways, I suppose I was like a third parent, laying down the law when it was none of my business. As the years have gone by, we have become much better friends – and when our children were small he was a lovely uncle and great babysitter.

His circumcision was at our home. Harry Ritvo, a man whom I had already deemed to be Luton's own Dracula, came to perform the ceremony, the gory details of which I learned for the first time when Uncle Lou took me and my cousin David into the garden to explain what it was all about.

My mother wouldn't have wanted to do that. When I first discovered that before babies were born the father had some unknown action to perform, I asked her about it. 'Ask your teacher,' she said. It was a very sheltered life. Mum had a close friend called Mrs Cohen. One day she came to tea and opened a parcel. 'I've just bought this brassiere,' she said, taking out a pink garment – as pink as my face. I rushed out of the room swamped in embarrassment.

But that didn't mean that my mother neglected her son, although the visits to the doctor got slightly less frequent. She was content with the school clinic, to which I was assigned all too frequently. I would go there to have teeth out, under gas. One day, I was recovering from the operation, with two nurses holding me over a metal sink, blood pouring from my mouth. 'My mummy,' I remember saying haltingly between tears and fights for breath, 'my mummy says she's going to take me to the pictures.' 'Oh yes,' said one of the very kind blonde nurses, 'what are you going to see?' '*Blood and Sand*,' I said.

Then there were the visits to a consultant called David Levi, who studied my flat feet and addressed me as 'child'. Meanwhile, he ordered my parent: 'Mother, tell the child to walk over here.' I didn't exactly adore this man. Perhaps 35 years later, I stopped a very elderly gentleman to ask if he had change for a parking meter. As his arthritic hands fumbled for coins, I thought I realised who he was. At a discreet distance, I followed him to Wimpole Street. When he went through an imposing black door, I kept watch. When the door was closed, I looked at the brass plate on the wall. As I expected, the name on the plate was 'David Levi'. He died soon afterwards. I now wished I had introduced myself as 'child'.

At the back of the synagogue was a tiny 'committee room', where the top class in the local Hebrew school met. It was also where, in times of peace, children would go for their allocation of sweets on the 'Rejoicing of the Law' holiday, Simchat Torah, which celebrated the completion of the weekly readings from the scrolls of the Torah, the Five Books of Moses, and the start of a new cycle all over again. But this was the time of sweet rationing. You couldn't get the sweets to distribute, let alone the boxes of chocolates that had gone, I was told, to children attending the smarter United synagogues, like the famous one at Egerton Road in Stamford Hill, then one of the most prestigious establishments of its kind. But the people from Stamford Hill had gone to places like Luton. What they had been used to could not be replicated. There was no unrationed confectionery. But there were cough sweets, which were handed out with abandon and with no health warnings on the side. The lucky ones got chocolates – or at least chocolate-laced ExLax. I suppose someone thought that sitting on the loo would give us plenty of opportunities to think of God. I seem to remember that being repeated year after year. Why no one thought of doing something about it, I'll never know. Perhaps no one thought it wrong. Chocolate was chocolate and we would always run to get that – if maybe a little too often during those first weeks of autumn.

Saturday mornings were always devoted to the synagogue. I took it as much for granted as I did going to school and I never thought much about it. It was my ambition – and that of my parents – for me to be included in the number of boys who went there, too, on Saturdays, wearing a a new school uniform with a cap badge of gold and red. This was the regulation attire of Luton Grammar School. But when the 11-plus examination results were announced, I was not one of the youngsters down for a place there, the only such establishment in a town of some 100,000 people.

My mother wouldn't accept that. Had I not come fourth in the class, which was not bad in a roll of 56? So she told the tale to the headmistress, Mrs Brooks, who the previous week had caned me two days in succession for crimes to which I still plead not guilty.

Mrs Brooks was a stern-looking bespectacled woman whom I had disliked ever since the time she, in the company of a nurse, had taken all the boys in the class up to what we considered the school's secret room – and ordered us to take off our trousers. We were never told why and I have regarded it since as a case of child sexual abuse. But when it came to the subject about which my mother was calling, she came up trumps. She wrote a letter to the local education authority and the following Saturday morning, a brown envelope came to tell me I had passed. That was reason to thank Mrs Brooks. Above all, it was thanks to my mother.

There was another feature of what could lightly be called my education. Wednesdays after school, Saturday afternoons and

Sunday mornings, I was subject to the admonitions of the Reverend Harry David Ritvo. One of my classmates had dared to say that she hadn't been there on Shabbat afternoon because her parents had taken her to London. Ritvo's face grew to the colour of the beetroot-mixed chrane or horseradish that we could not get in war time Luton. 'You mustn't go to London on Shabbos,' he decreed. 'It is not permitted to travel. If your mother says she is going on the train, you will say, 'I WILL NOT go. You can take me in chains, but I will not get on that train.' It was the first of a dozen or more incidents involving this extraordinarily good-looking black-bearded man who inspired fear in me and in most of my pals – but who actually heard a wolf whistle or two from young maidens of a different persuasion as he paraded through the streets of Luton, a cravat around his neck, an extra-large hat on his head.

There were times, however, when he got to become just too much of a nuisance to the normal, peace- loving life I wanted to lead. That was when I, with red-haired Hershel Basofsky (now Harold Bass and still one of my dearest and closest friends) decided to take action. Harold is now what is known in Yiddish as a *gutta neshamah* – a man with a good soul – who will walk the traditional million miles until he can find a good deed to do. He is extraordinarily religious, but in those days he used to spend the two shillings his father gave him as fees for the *cheder* classes on hiring a rowing boat on the local park lake. He and I came up with an idea to demonstrate our revenge (in the hope, no doubt, that our saintly teacher would never discover who it was who was actually doing the revenging). We put orange peel in Ritvo's petrol tank – and then watched as 'the Reverend' tried and failed to start his black Vauxhall.

Life at the grammar school was harder than Denbigh Road – and not just the work there. I was always proud of going to that school, but I can't say I enjoyed it. The fellow who said that schooldays were the happiest days of his life must have had a pretty lousy life since then.

It was an ultra-modern art deco building – which Dad always said looked like a ship. It was eight years old when I joined it, but was already in need of an internal coat of paint. It had murals of Luton life, including one I remember of the dark-red painted single-decker buses that plied its streets. The teachers looked as if they could do with a brush-up, too. I thought they were terribly old – until, in

2004, I read a history of the school. Most of them were in their thirties.

Learning? There was a smattering of French, a bit of history which I supplemented by my own voracious reading of the subject and precisely no mathematics whatsoever. I once got 5 per cent in an exam. These days, I now realise that a good teacher would have taken me aside and asked, 'Now what is it that you don't understand? Let me see if I can help you.'

Instead, the teacher, a Mr May, sneered. He happened to be our form master. When it came to assembling our term-end reports, he sniggered: 'I was surprised to see, Freedland, that you're not the moron I thought you were.' Small comfort, but better than one other incident in which the two of us were involved. I think I must have been talking, which was not the sort of behaviour the master found to his liking. He said nothing. Instead, all there was to hear was the swish of his chalk-marked gown as he charged down the form room, followed by the sound of an explosion in my left ear. He had slapped it – with the force of a steam shovel.

He saw the bewildered, much pained look on my face. My ear was numb. 'I suppose you are going to start snivelling,' he said. 'You people always do.' I wasn't sure which hurt more, the pain of the assault or of the insult. On principle, I didn't 'snivel' and, alas, I didn't tell my parents either. A visit to the headmaster wouldn't have gone amiss. I am sure my mother, who rationed such visits to the office of K. B. Webb, the head whom she regarded as 'charming' to an extraordinary degree, would have acted and in the twenty-first century the man would have been fired. So would the super-annuated master who wondered why I had finished my physics end-of-year exam early – and then decided the best thing would be for him to tear up my paper and order me to start again, with just ten minutes to go. Webb did get a maternal visit after that and he allowed me an average mark – which was a pity, since I knew more answers that time than was usual.

I never knew how to take Mr Kenneth Burgess Webb. I think I quite admired him. He came from a working-class background and had become headmaster while still in his thirties, which was quite an achievement. When he was about 80, I was invited to be the guest speaker at an old boys' reunion. I was very proud to be asked – except that Webb was less than generous to me. 'I gather you write books,' he said. 'Haven't read any of them. Don't suppose I ever will.' When it came to making my speech, he heckled me throughout. I recalled Mr Cyril Godfrey, the second master, saying that a ruler had to be called a 'scale'. As he explained, 'I'm the only ruler here.' I thought it funny. 'It wasn't Mr Godfrey who said that,' he interrupted. 'It was Mr Sanderson.' I later sent him two books. 'If you don't like them, send them on to someone you hate for Christmas,' I wrote. He never replied.

The incident with May, however, was of a different order. It was the first brush with anti-Semitism in the school. Yes, there were the odd remarks from fellow pupils, but not many and not serious. As a sop to those of us who kept the kosher dietary laws, school dinners amounted to sharing the delights of one thin slice of indifferent cheddar on a bed of mashed potato (boiled potato without the benefits of milk, cream or butter, although there was a little salt, which we could sprinkle on it to our hearts' desire).

We wore our caps for the daily prayers. 'Take your hats off,' shouted a master who wandered into what he considered his form room during our service. 'We can't, sir,' we explained. 'Take 'em off,' he repeated and left the room, at which we continued the service and kept our caps on. The following day, he came in again. 'Still wearing your hats?' he said. 'Take 'em off.' We continued to wear them and after a third try, he left us alone. Was that anti-Semitism, too? I've often wondered.

There was also one other master who was no lover of my people. This became clear when I had to look for my first job. I had dearly wanted to go to university, but, since it was unlikely I would get a scholarship, my parents couldn't afford it. They couldn't rustle up the money for the fees or afford to do so without the pittance of a salary I might otherwise be able to bring home. It was something that caused not a little resentment on my part, and it took years before I became reconciled to the fact that I would have to depend on the 'university of life'.

Rex Clayton was supposedly the chemistry master, but spent most lessons describing his days cuddling his teddy bear in the trenches during World War One and telling us how badly people in Luton spoke – which, on the whole, they did. He was also careers master, which meant he was supposed to advise on the jobs we were going to do when we left school. I had this fantasy of being an ambassador, which was quite reasonable, I thought, for the kid from Stoke Newington. He plainly did not. He laughed. 'I suggest banking,' he said. Banking? For a boy who had scored 5 per cent in maths? I saw the look on his round face and I worked it out: Jews and banking! A Jew in the diplomatic corps? Do him a favour. I did him a favour by not asking him anything again.

There was one particular exception to that list of rather inferior schoolmasters. His name was Mr C. W. Parry, who taught French. Mr Parry was Welsh and you knew it from listening to his voice as he struggled for breath. He had only one lung. Whether this was from working in the mines or possibly a war injury, he never told us. He was much too modest for that. He once told a Jewish friend of mine: 'Never go away from your faith. You have a great heritage.' I wish I had known him better and had had him teaching me for longer. When I left school, he sent me a delightful letter.

The establishment of the State of Israel was one of the great moments in my early life. We heard about the great achievement at one of those Sabbath morning services at Moor Path. The elders rejoiced at the news that had just come over the wireless – for once, no one quarrelled with the idea of listening to the radio and so breaking a Sabbath commandment – that not only had David Ben Gurion announced the establishment of the state, but America had recognised it. My dear friend Gerald Sunshine and I left the *shul* and bought an *Evening Standard* with the headline that Egyptian planes were bombing Tel Aviv.

I suppose it was that that made me a lifetime Zionist – and was the reason Gerald and I established a group we called the Social Zionists, socialist and Zionist. I think we dreamed of one day standing for Parliament, if not the Knesset, and forming a government. We used to meet at first in the marble hall of the local reference library – until we were told to be quiet.

As it was, I had my career to think of. And it is without the slightest shred of a doubt that the way it took off was my mother's doing.

# 4    The *Luton News*

At 16, I left school and, like a group of friends from the Grammar, decided to look for a summer job. I didn't want to deliver any more letters or break my back as I had the year before, picking potatoes – 'spud bashing'. So I wrote to the *Luton News*, the local newspaper. The editor, an impressive man of about my father's age, gave me an interview and offered me a job – full time.

My mother did something that I hated her for at the time, but for which I have been grateful ever since. She went to see that editor, Mr John Sargeant, actually the editor-in-chief of the *Luton News* parent company, Home Counties Newspapers, the man I had seen myself.

He convinced her it was going to be a hard slog, but thought I had shown promise when he spoke to me. But, he said, it would take time. First, I had to go into what he temptingly called the Black Hole of Calcutta. Not an inappropriate term. But I took the offer – of the grand total of 37s 6d a week. I would be in the Black Hole for a year before I could become a reporter. It was the corner of the noisy composing room, where the lines of type, produced by the even noisier Linotype operators, who sat at another corner of the huge factory, were assembled. It was there that I would be a 'copy-holder', reading the original reporters' and advertiser's typing to a 'reader' who would check my voiced words against the printed proofs.

My entry through the front door of the *Luton News* building was greeted with near dismay by the elders of the town's Jewish community, who were now family friends. One man put the case forcibly to my mother: 'Tell me,' he said, 'will he ever own his own newspaper?' 'Yes,' I said when the story was relayed to me. 'I've just brought an *Evening Standard*.' Or did I say '*Evening News*' or '*Star*'?

In that terrible 'reading room', there was virtually no heating and no air – except from a giant window, which when shut made this section of the place unbearable and when opened would make being there seem like being in a wind tunnel, with paper flying from one table to another.

I arrived on 3 September 1951 – the fact that it was the anniversary of the outbreak of war was not lost on me.

John Sargeant took me to the Black Hole personally and introduced me to the head reader, whom we'll call Mr Harrison, who told me that I would be reading with his wife, who hadn't yet arrived. My testosterone level was at its height and I thought that might be an enticing prospect. Until at 10.30 Mrs Harrison arrived in a cloud of . . . not the perfume I had imagined, but sweat. She was a middle-aged woman (how middle-aged, I never knew) untidy and with dirty teeth. She persisted in calling me 'Mick', which I hated, but I didn't have the courage to tell her to desist. She arrived at 10.30 every morning, an hour and a half later than I, and insisted on saying every time I tried to find a little air to breathe, 'Come on Mick, we've got work to do.' I resented that then and still do – for some ridiculous reason. I wasn't any more keen when I discovered that I was invited to go on the print shop annual outing. I had to go, but I wasn't thrilled about the pre-war motor coach that took us to London to see . . . *Rose Marie On Ice.*

It was really hard work, and I'm not just referring to sitting on a hard, cold seat at Earls Court, watching *Rose Marie On Ice*. On Wednesdays, press day, I had to get in at 8.30 in the morning and not leave until 8.30 that night. It was not what I considered to be journalism. I had to read stories about church fetes, advertisements for suits and trousers and, occasionally, the fun ads, like the one that offered a 1934 Austin for £10 – 'complete with tow rope'. Every now and again, there would be the report of an indecent assault case at the local courthouse. That was another reason why I wished that I wasn't in partnership with Mrs Harrison.

And then, finally, came the day when John Sargeant came in and told me I was about to be 'released from bondage'. I didn't have to tell him how terrible it had been – he knew. The following Monday I was being promoted to the reporters' room.

I was lucky that George Smallman was chief reporter. He was in his early thirties, but he had the kindness of a favourite uncle.

'You'll do very well,' he assured me. I was happy to take his word.

The first job I was given was, he explained, one of the most vital a local reporter had to do. I didn't say that I really wanted to be a *national* reporter – it was early days yet. 'You have to get to know the people in this town. Some of the most important are the clergymen. I know you know Rabbi Ritvo . . .' the Luton synagogue minister was a mere 'Reverend' but I knew he wouldn't have minded the promotion. 'but you must know the others, too. Here's the number of the Catholic priest.' I made the call. A lady answered. 'I'm afraid Father Murphy isn't here at the moment,' she told me in a thick Irish brogue. 'OK,' I responded, 'when your husband gets back, ask him to give me a ring.' The sound of the chortling from my colleagues still rings in my ears every time I think of it.

A couple of weeks later, George Smallman had me down in the big office diary to cover the centenary celebrations of the local Co-operative Society, an important event in the life of one of the only two department stores on George Street, the main Luton drag. The other store was called Blundells.

They were both old-fashioned establishments, with long glass-covered mahogany counters and, above the heads of the assistants, a railway that never ceased to fascinate me. You paid £2 for an item costing £1 7s 6d and the assistant would place your money in a container which, by means of a catapult, would race along the railway to a booth where a cashier would take out the cash and the bill – and then substitute the required change, which would then whiz back to the assistant. It was to one of those assistants that I announced my presence. 'I have come from the *Luton News* to cover the centenary celebrations,' I declared. 'Oh,' said the lady, again of indeterminate age, 'you had better see Mr Hayne. He's upstairs on the fourth floor.'

'Thanks,' I said and started to walk up the stairs. Mr Hayne's name was on the polished door. A secretary came out to greet me. 'You're from the *Luton News*? Just wait here and Mr Hayne will be out soon.'

In the meantime, she offered me a cup of tea. This, I now knew, was the grown-up world. I had finally arrived. No longer a copyholder in the Black Hole of Calcutta. Not a nonentity at Luton Grammar School. I was in the home of big co-operative business and old enough to be offered tea. I must say I was impressed by this place. My mother shopped at the Co-op and even had a number to ensure the 'divi' to which she was entitled. I remember it still, 25875. Funny that, I don't remember my current building society account number, my passport number or virtually any other to which I have been assigned. But the Co-op . . . I was grateful for that welcome I was getting at the Co-op.

Mr Hayne was a former mayor of Luton, which was a sinecure handed round to the borough councillors like a box of chocolates. Every now and again, the good citizens of the town found one with a soft centre. Hayne was certainly that. He was superbly dressed with silver grey hair cut to provide 'wings' over his ears. This was a consummate politician, who would have looked ideal sitting in Prime Minister Harold Macmillan's cabinet. I was 17 and didn't bother to wonder what he was doing in a place like the Co-Op.

'How are you?' he asked in a kindly voice that made me think he really wanted to know. 'Would you like another cup of tea?' The secretary was buzzed and within minutes, so quickly she must have known the request was going to come, in she walked with a silver tea set, two beautifully thin cups and saucers and what looked like a delectable fruit cake, undoubtedly the Co-Op's best. I couldn't help thinking that my mother's divi was going to be worth having, perhaps even enough to buy a packet of the tea I was being served at that moment.

'Tell me,' said Mr Hayne, who I later discovered was given the nickname 'Daddy' by the older boys at the office, 'how long have you been on the *Luton News*?'

'Two weeks, sir,' I said, ignoring the period in bondage in the Black Hole, which didn't count as journalism. He seemed impressed. Perhaps not many reporters called him 'Sir', but I had been well brought up.

'Do you like it?' he asked and before I could answer, said: 'Have some fruit cake. It's my favourite.'

'Thank you, Sir,' I said.

'It's a very good paper,' he went on. 'Very fair. Would you like another cup of tea?' I said thanks. 'Now tell me what you are here for.'

'Well, sir,' I replied somewhat mystified that he had not been properly briefed. But then I had been told that people of a certain age are not always totally aware of the things they should be aware of and was ready to be charitable. I reckoned that if I played my cards right, I might get another slice of fruit cake.

He read my mind, even if I wasn't reading his. 'Have another slice of cake,' he said, before pressing the point.

'Well, sir,' I began again, 'I've come to write about the centenary of the Co-operative Society (I thought it best not to call it the Co-Op, not to a borough councillor who wore a good suit).'

'Yes,' he said, 'a wonderful organisation. Have another slice of cake.'

I couldn't insult the man, so I accepted. 'Yes,' he repeated,' a wonderful organisation... by the way, you do know you are in Blundells, don't you?'

Retire an embarrassed young reporter, his face as red as the cherries on the top of the fruit cake. I hadn't begun to wonder what a former Tory mayor was doing at the Co-Op.

The Americans learn their journalism in college. Today, a bright ambitious youngster can walk into a national paper job straight from university. In my time, the local paper was the only acceptable entry point. It was, in truth, the best education I ever had – although I was treated to something called the Journalists' Proficiency Certificate, the first ever course. I in fact became an apprentice, signing articles just like the youngsters in the printing shop. It wasn't a brilliant idea. One day and two evenings a week we had to spend at the local technical college, an antiquated building which had been the first home of my old school.

I didn't enjoy being at school there – taking advanced English and British life and institutions was interesting. But for a whole day I was doing shorthand and typing – in a class made up of aspiring young secretaries, sending off letters acknowledging 'receipt of yours of the 21st inst, in regard to the dispatch of 100 pairs of ladies' knickers...'

It wasn't for me. I hated shorthand almost as much as I hated being one of the girls. It wasn't as if any of those young women I found attractive. It was as if entry for females to this college precluded good looks, or that a pretty woman wouldn't dream of becoming a shorthand typist in Luton

Actually, my shorthand writing wasn't bad. It was my shorthand reading that I couldn't get to grips with. I never really learned to trust it – even though I still find myself thinking in shorthand in the midst of a speech or a conversation that otherwise holds little interest.

Typing was different. For that alone, I remain grateful for that course. I learned to touch-type. In my last years on the paper, my typing was so fast that, on Saturday afternoons, I was deputed to take down a running commentary on Luton Town's Division Two football matches. For the first time in my life, I got to know a little about sport. But not enough to spoil my well-earned reputation as a soccer ignoramus. When I was sent to actually *cover* a football match, I barely knew what a ball looked like – and had the goal keeper scoring twice. No, it was not for me. But I did get my proficiency certificate – including a 100 per cent mark for interviewing ability. 'How anyone can get 100 per cent at anything, I don't know,' wrote a director of Home Counties Newspapers, congratulating me. At least, that was what I think he was doing. The whole process allowed me to be deferred from National Service for two years.

In truth, local newspapers performed an invaluable service in their communities and for a journalist there was no better professional education than working in one. The *Luton News* was a wonderful training ground and, even if I soon realised I was getting into a rather too comfortable rut, I appreciated it. I got to know the clergy, I got to know the grocers and their battles against green stamps and I got to know the politicians. I knew from the beginning that this was going to be the best part of all for me, especially since I had ambitions to be an MP and had been fascinated by Daddy Hayne and his colleagues.

The current mayor, Tom Skelton, was a very different character. A former factory worker, he was Labour's choice and was a delight. He lived close to our home in Cutenhoe Road – his was a terraced house in a neighbouring street – but he enjoyed all the fripperies of office, not least the official limousine.

Understandably, this car was a Vauxhall, made in Luton, but with fittings you couldn't buy in a showroom. I got to know those fittings because we had lunch at the same time every day and he used to arrange for his chauffeur to give me a lift home, sitting next to him on the back seat. When the local Jewish ex-servicemen took a coach to their own remembrance service and parade (a marvellously patriotic occasion that continues today, a mix of British and Jewish like no other event – the Chief Rabbi prays and the massed band of the Brigade of Guards plays) in 1951, the mayor, both gentile and gentle, marched at the front of the Luton contingent, his gold chain bouncing as he walked.

That parade and Tom Skelton's part in it played an important part in my career. I wrote about it for the *Jewish Chronicle* and they paid me ten shillings and sixpence for my trouble. I brandished the cheque in front of my friends' eyes. I am not sure how impressed they were. Gerald Sunshine dismissed it as 'unearned income'. I didn't have the presence of mind to point out that the half guinea was very well earned indeed.

It was, in fact, my first freelance payment. I didn't have any idea just how important freelance work would be in my life. The senior reporters on the paper ran what was known as a 'lineage pool'. They would send local stories to the national press and split the proceeds among themselves. If mere junior reporters like me managed to stumble on a good story, we were given half the amount earned. It was iniquitous, but that's the way things were and I wasn't in the business of rocking the boat.

There were obituaries to write – mainly of nice, ordinary local men who had been employed all their lives in the hat trade or at Vauxhall Motors. When there weren't obits to write, there were weddings – stories beginning 'Honeymooning on the romantic island of Jersey are...' All very different from the stuff I was sending to the *JC*.

But none of the stories I sent to what was then known as the Organ of British Jewry compared with the one in 1953 which the paper chose to run in a panel in heavy black type. This had come about as a result of a Sabbath morning service.

Towards the end of the sacred prayer recital, Harry Ritvo mounted his new pulpit. 'I have to tell you something very serious has happened,' he reported to his startled congregation. 'There has been an act of sacrilege.' The worshippers were stunned. But it got worse as he went on. 'Someone has broken into my room – and [our breaths were bated by now... his voice getting even more solemn]. bashed in my hat.'

Everyone loved the story, but Harry Ritvo wasn't thrilled. 'You have made me an object of ridicule,' he pronounced. 'I have treated you like a son... and you do this to me.'

As much as I would have liked to, I didn't point out that had he not made his solemn announcement I wouldn't have had the opportunity to write about it. As for myself, I believed I had a sacred duty to publish and be damned – to coin the title of the then newly published memoirs of the ex-*Daily Express* editor, Arthur Christiansen. It was my first confrontation with the subject of a story. It would not be the last.

Ritvo was not the only clergyman with whom I had a close relationship. Strangely, I was also on first-name terms with a local Methodist minister. The Reverend William Gowland was the town's industrial chaplain and, in his own movement, a national figure, one day to be president of the Methodist Conference, which I liked to think of as their Chief Rabbi. He was always good for a story – after all, any churchman who said that his pews were for 'people who sweat and swear' was usually able to rent me a quote or two. Dozens of them made the early editions of the *Evening Standard* or the *Star* or the *Evening News*.

Not all the stories I filed as 'lineage' under the catchline 'Smallman, Luton' (George Smallman, as chief reporter, was the nominal head of the lineage pool) were as much fun. There was the disappearance of a young girl named Anne Noblett, daughter of a wealthy businessman. Eventually, she was found in a deep freeze near her home at Harpenden.

It was my first murder story. I didn't enjoy murders or much crime, although a day at the borough court often produced gems – like the time a greengrocer who was thought to be Jewish (he wasn't) was handed the Old Testament. The court clerk told him to cover his head. He agreed – and placed the Bible on top of his bald pate. Then the magistrate asked him his first question. Was he driving his car on the day it collided with a horse and cart? 'Yes, Your Majesty,' he answered. Anyone answering like that couldn't have been considered all bad, and he was let off with a caution.

What I really enjoyed writing about was local politics. Or rather national politics emanating locally. Our own MP was a character who was, I since realise, about the best constituency member I have ever met. Dr Charles Hill was already a national figure when he won the 1950 election as Luton's 'Liberal Conservative' MP. He had been in the forefront of the fight against the National Health Service, as general secretary of the British Medical Association, the BMA, a battle he had soundly lost. But he was even better known, much better known, as 'the Radio Doctor'. Every Friday morning, he would sum up the nation's ills. 'When you hear the rhythmic sound of a storm brewing inside, you have to expect what's coming next – a belly ache'. He gave his Labour opponents a belly ache all the time.

Hill looked like an overgrown Just William, with a pudding-basin haircut and a cherubic face, frequently obscured by a huge pipe. He was an extraordinary man, who had been brought up in a London slum by a widowed mother, had worked his way through medical school and yet had become a confirmed Tory. But he didn't sound like one. His fruity voice still had a great deal of cockney about it – which, of course, endeared him to the grandees, who thought that they appealed to all social classes. Of course he was brilliant – which was why he almost immediately got office, first as a parliamentary private secretary, then as Postmaster-General (we joked about getting our letters on time) and finally as Chancellor of the Duchy of Lancaster, in charge of the government's information services at a time when it needed them very badly. Ultimately, he became one of the victims of Harold Macmillan's famous Night of the Long Knives – the wholesale sacking of cabinet ministers, which the onetime Liberal leader Jeremy Thorpe famously said was a case of a man 'laying down his best friends for his life'.

Charlie Hill later became Lord Hill of Luton and then chairman, first, of what was then the Independent Television Authority and soon afterwards of the BBC (ironically accused of being there as a spy by Harold Wilson, who thought the corporation were ganging up against him). I knew him best when he was Luton's MP, a representative who understood wonderfully how to get on with his electorate. He lived in a beautiful house in the nearby and posher Harpenden, to which he drove from London in a big Rover – in the days when that was a prestigious marque. But when he went to Luton it was in a clapped-out Morris Minor. I remember covering a meeting of what was then called the Spastics Society. It was held in a pub. The chairman was somewhat nervous. 'What would you like to drink, Dr Hill?' he asked. 'A pint of bitter,' said Hill, who certainly did not drink that in the Members' Bar at the House. It was precisely what his audience liked to hear.

When I bumped into him in the town's main shopping centre in George Street on a Saturday, there was usually the greeting, 'Morning, Michael, what lies are the paper telling this week?' We both laughed at this, but he did later sue the paper for libel (not for anything I had written, I hasten to say, but because he objected to a leader written by the editor; I seem to remember it was settled less than amicably). Because it was the intelligent thing to do, Hill kept up a good relationship with the local reporters. Every Christmas, he sent us a bottle of the best Haig Dimple whisky.

The real joy in an election campaign – in the days when election campaigns were really that; live people spoke to live people, not to a TV camera – was to attend one of Hill's political rallies. That was a lesson in dealing with hecklers, the like of which I hadn't heard before or have heard since.

There was the man whose voice sounded like a piece of metal rubbed against sand paper. 'What we want', he shouted, 'is more Marshall Aid, what we want is a better Health Service, what we want...'

'What you want, chum,' responded the candidate, 'is a cough drop.'

And then there was this about testing the bomb. 'The Socialists say we shouldn't do it. But if we do have the bomb, for God's sake let's make sure we've got a good 'un.'

He had a marvellous gift for language. 'I'm pleased nobody is raising the issue heard at the last election – that not one single mother's son should have to give his life in battle...as if an election was the time to talk about the morality of single mothers having sons.' That was perhaps more a laughing matter in the 1950s than in the twenty-first century.

# 5   Defending my country

I myself was called to the colours in May 1956. A brown envelope contained instructions to report to the Royal Army Service Corps depot in Farnborough, Hampshire. It included a travel warrant and details of the train I should catch.

This was not good news. I didn't want to be a soldier. My career was catching up with itself. Not only did I know Dr Hill and his coterie, I was a film critic. My love of the cinema had finally borne fruit and I was writing about the movies – the ones shown at the same Savoy, Union (by then the Ritz), Palace (it had become the Gaumont) and Odeon cinemas to which my mother had taken me all those years before.

The call-up meant that I was going to lose the column on the Tuesday *Pictorial* that I was just getting into. That meant no afternoons happily scribbling away about my favourite subject, but also no chance of taking my current girlfriend to the pictures for free.

Mum's influence was, however, paying dividends that I didn't at first appreciate. Because of the flat feet for which I had been regularly treated at the school clinic, I was told I was grade three, which meant that, medically speaking, I had just scraped into Her Majesty's Royal Army Service Corps by the skin of my callouses. I could have done without the singular honour I was being paid.

I was even more honoured when I heard the very next day that the government for which I had not voted had decreed that grade threes were no longer going to be taken. But, no, it didn't mean that those who were already in the service would now get out.

I sat and cried on my bunk, especially when, that first night, I couldn't get my locker laid out properly and couldn't 'bull' my boots and webbing with the polishes the army had so kindly agreed to sell me from my first 'wage' of 10s 6d (yes, they gave us the money and then ordered how we immediately had to spend it). There was a group of rough Glasgow youngsters in the same barrack room, who insisted on singing 'Scotland the Brave' at every conceivable opportunity. They were very good at bulling boots. 'Dinnae worry,' said one, 'I'll help ye with yours in the mornin.' But when the 'mornin' came, he was more interested in the prospect of a mug of bromide-laced tea and seemingly all the bacon and fried bread he could eat. Inwardly, I was crying again, but I don't think I let on.

We went marching the first day. There was a Jewish boy walking next to me. As we tried to keep in step with the other, far more keen, troops on parade, he read a letter he had just received from his mother in Leeds. 'Have you got a nice room, darling?' she asked. If I hadn't hated the lovely room I shared with 25 other malodorous men who wanted desperately to show they could take it – providing they had their comics to read and their sexual fantasies relieved in the usual way – I would have laughed then as much as I do now at the memory. The kid from Leeds, incidentally, is now a crown court judge.

I liked marching almost as much as I liked that barrack room. My mother sent me a salami every week – the Americans had a song about that: 'Send a Salami to your Boy in the Army', written by Hal David, the same guy who later produced 'Anyone Who Had A Heart' and 'Raindrops Keep Falling On My Head' and all those other standards with Burt Bacharach.

The sausage was a welcome supplement to the diet I was offered. As I ate only kosher, there was little that I could get through at meal-times – the days when the Ministry of Defence considered it a duty to cater for ethnic minorities hadn't yet arrived. I kept it in my locker, until various non-commissioned officers started wondering about the smell emanating from my portion of the room, close to the big black enamel stove. It wasn't the stove. It wasn't even my feet. They never did discover the origins of the peculiar aromas. By that time, I had begun to be a little fed up with the salami myself. I sent Mum a note saying, 'I vursht you wouldn't keep sending it to me.'

This was the time I met a young man called Apfelbaum, who was having trouble with his bowels. Or at least he claimed he was. I had been in the army for three weeks when he alleged he had not 'been' for three months. The cry from the other beds in the room never varied whenever he walked in, usually looking paler than the last time he had braved the room: 'Been yet, Apfelbaum?' He went to see the medical officer at least twice a week and was always sent away with a flea in his ear, if not with a suppository for placement further down.

Plainly, he was trying to 'work his ticket', as we said in those days. I had no such idea, although it wouldn't have been totally against my wishes. But one day I broke the habits of a youthtime, (and later adulthood) and went to see the doctor. The truth of the matter was that every time I went marching, my feet hurt more than they ever had before.

'I'll give you a chit, excusing you from marching,' he said. 'And another excusing you from wearing boots.' I said thank you and added that I was suffering from bad hay fever and could I have another allowing me to wear sunglasses? He looked at me with a smile and wrote another piece of paper.

I thanked him again, put on my blue beret and tried to salute (I hadn't been told how to do that yet). I was about to leave when he called me back. 'I imagine,' he said, 'you don't really want to be a soldier, do you?' 'No, sir,' I replied. 'A bit peeved, eh, about this grade three business?' 'Yes, sir,' I said to the doctor, who came from a similar background to my own and was doing his time as a national serviceman, too. 'OK,' he said, 'I'll recommend you to the medical board for a discharge.'

I couldn't believe my luck. But it would take time. For the moment, I had to carry on as if I were in for life. Without having to wear boots, my quite genuine foot pain had disappeared, but not all the pain of military life. There were the usual shots (in this case, meaning injections, so it wasn't a word much used thereabouts for medical purposes). After one of these, I stood on the parade ground, waving my injured arm. The sergeant caught me in mid-air. 'What are you?' he screamed, looking me closely in the eye. 'Are you a fucking helicopter?' 'No, sir,' I said. 'You do not call me "sir", I am just a lowly individual called a sergeant, but to you I am God. You are a fucking helicopter. What are you?' I whispered, 'I'm a fucking helicopter.' 'Louder,' he said. 'What are you?' 'I'm a fucking helicopter,' I generously agreed.

A few of the guys in our barrack room discovered that nobody seemed to notice if you disappeared on a Saturday morning, just so long as you deigned to return on Sunday evening. So, since I seemed to live from one Saturday noon to the next, I decided to join them. Indeed, nobody complained as we walked through the barrack gates. Nobody asked for a pass. So I went to Stoke Newington to see the grandparents – and then took the train to Luton.

Then came the week when it wasn't so easy. We arrived to be greeted by a gang of gentlemen wearing stylish red caps, which, even with my limited knowledge of army procedure, I knew spelt trouble. The military police usually did. Something about them seemed to say that they didn't like National Servicemen, particularly those who didn't share their belief that army life was a gift from God to be cherished. That night, we were all put on orders to see the CO. We were marched into his office with the sort of shout that I thought totally unnecessary. I didn't dare say that I could still hear him, even if he spoke just a little quieter. I did protest that I was excused from marching. 'Are you trying to be clever, laddie?' he asked. 'I want to know the reason for this mass exodus.'

I decided not to demonstrate my superior intelligence. I even agreed to stamp my feet. The CO was not exactly the fatherly type. 'We needed a guard detail and you weren't there. But you will be now. You're all confined to barracks for a week.' Not just that. During my 'jankers' I was given almost the worst jobs to do around the place. Actually, not quite the worst. I was denied the delights of cleaning the latrines. Instead, I had to peel potatoes for the officers' mess. And what a mess it turned out to be. The potatoes had to be turned into chips. Which would have been fine, had the pail in which they were placed not developed a life of its own. It was so heavy that I dropped it. The filthy kitchen floor was smothered in newly chipped chips. I wasn't going to do them again. The answer was the obvious one – to get a broom and a dustpan and fill the pail again. I never found out how many officers went down with food poisoning or even worse. But perhaps the hot oil in which they were fried killed the salmonella. There could, however, have been a few chips that weren't exactly made from potatoes.

Not long after that, I allowed myself the chore of taking a slow country walk. Actually, the rest of the platoon were marching. But I was lingering behind, admiring the Hampshire scenery, enjoying the sunshine. It was then that a pair of sergeant majors came my way. I saluted. 'Do not salute us, lad,' said one. 'We are sergeant majors, not officers. Why aren't you marching?'

'Flat feet, sir. I've got a chit.'

'And where are your boots?'

'Excused, sir. I've got a chit.'

'And you're wearing sunglasses.'

'Hay fever, sir. I've got a chit.'

He was apoplectic. 'You're nothing but a pile of chits.'

The line was later copied and used in the movie *Carry On Sergeant*.

I continued my country stroll. On a green bank at the side of the road, a girl was playing a portable gramophone. Ann Shelton was singing 'Lay down your arms'.

Exactly ten weeks after my introduction to military service I was allowed to replace my khaki with a blue blazer and grey flannels. I had a piece of paper which said I could not be called to the colours ever again – even 'in the event of a national emergency'. I remember thinking then that the act of calling me up would be a national emergency in itself.

The following November, I was actually marching for the first time in my life – and not asking anyone for a chit. To tell the truth, on this occasion, I was in good company with a few thousand other shufflers who would have made any self-respecting sergeant major take early retirement. Freedland, 23306670, Private (Retired) was proudly trying to keep in step with the Luton contingent taking part in that same Jewish ex-Servicemen's parade at the Cenotaph. They wanted as many marchers as they could get, but I felt more than a bit of a fraud in the company of men with chests adorned with medals they deserved to wear (although there *was* one gentleman from Her Majesty's Corps of Dishonorable Deserters who went on parade every year). I never did it again, although I try to get to the Whitehall ceremony whenever I can. It is still an occasion for great pride.

# 6  Back to civvy street

I was a civilian once more, back on the *Luton News*, but no longer film critic. That was worrying, except that I still knew the cinema managers and they still gave me free seats in the balcony. I also got back to local political life.

I returned, too, to the world of 'lineage', freelance work. The stories had to be much better than those that would automatically get into the local press. In 1956, I found one that started off with a trickle of interest that, before long, turned into a flood. It didn't seem particularly propitious that wet, miserable night when I joined a group of enthusiastic intellectuals who turned up for a lecture in one of the equally dismal rooms at the local library.

The speaker was the Luton medical officer of health, not an encouraging thought for a young reporter. He was not known as one of the charismatic personalities of the town. He talked about public health, a real ho-hum of a subject. And then quite suddenly he turned to a subject that had obvious resonance for this audience, who were by now sitting in a blue haze and coughing more and more enthusiastically with every statement.

'I'd like', he said politely, 'to turn to smoking.' Now, what was it he could say about smoking? The cost of cigarettes? Children buying fags under age? The mess dog-ends were making in the town centre? No, he had an agenda that nobody else, or at least very few other medical experts, had yet touched upon. 'I am convinced', he said, 'that there is a link between smoking and lung cancer.' Gasps from the audience, most of whom were ready at that moment to shout 'Rubbish', except they were a polite lot at meetings at Luton Public Library. He then produced some rather nasty pictures – fortunately in black and white; colour photography was not at all usual. But then neither was the story he was telling. He demonstrated that the photograph he produced showed a cancer that could only have been caused by smoking. The owner of that lung smoked 50 a day. The good doctor had been doing his own surveys. Dozens of cases of lung cancer had come his way in the past couple of years – and they all concerned heavy smokers. It was not yet scientifically proved, but the story hit the nationals and, to my great surprise, the medical experts suddenly had questions landing on their desks.

I felt good that day – and so did the senior reporters who made up the lineage pool, taking half of everything I earned for them. But it wasn't always so smooth. One such story soon landed me in a pack of trouble. It also questioned the integrity of a senior Tory minister. It changed a great deal of my faith in human nature – and of the so-called governing classes. The innocence of pre-army service was gone, shattered, never to return. The young reporter who had grown to believe everything that people told him was true – particularly people who were pillars of the community – was now forced out into a real world of lies and double dealing and didn't like it. The shock was palpable – especially when it concerned figures who were nationally of some importance. It was bad enough when, in my earliest days on the paper, a certain Councillor Babister of Streatley accused me of falsifying his claims of embezzlement by local bus conductors (I was accurately reporting what he had said and my editor believed me). When it concerned a Cabinet minister, I railed.

The then 14th Earl of Home, later Sir Alec Douglas Home and prime minster, and I clashed at Luton Town Hall. Not that we actually engaged in fisticuffs. We didn't even shake hands. Frankly, he didn't know I was there – and that would be what all the trouble was about. Her Majesty's Secretary of State for Commonwealth Relations was in Luton to address the International Friendship League. He chose as his subject the then crisis in Rhodesia, now Zimbabwe. The area was complex. There were two Rhodesias, North and South, and, to their north, the colony of Nyasaland, now Malawi. Before long there would be a Federation of Rhodesia and Nyasaland, but for the moment there were three different colonies and he was busy trying to sort out the mess. The two Rhodesias, he declared, were fine, run by decent law-abiding white people who exercised their responsibilities to the poor ignorant blacks with justice and kindness. But Nyasaland – that was, he declared, 'the slum of Africa'.

I gave the story to *The Times*. They rightly regarded it as a brilliant tale, an admission by a British cabinet minister that his government and those decent white settlers had failed. Here was a whole country that was nothing less than a slum.

Before the ink on their copy of what was then called 'the top people's paper' could dry, the Nyasaland population was in ferment. The High Commission, manned by nice white people, were furious and made their telephone line to the Commonwealth Office red hot. Lord Home denied saying a word of it.

This was astonishing to me. There were no tape recorders in my arsenal, but I had a notebook and, although it was never my strong point, I had a pretty good shorthand note. I had been so astonished by the statement that I had underlined the note and then written it in longhand, just to make sure I knew what I was writing (a trick I still adopt when the occasion demands). Home kept denying it and told *The Times* so – adding, not terribly cleverly I thought, that he wasn't aware that there was a reporter present.

*The Times* sent a senior editor down for a lovely day enjoying the sights of Luton and spending some time with me. He read my note – fortunately situated between a council meeting and a church service and the acts of a local rapist – and said something like, 'Seems OK to me.' He agreed that this would not be a phrase anyone would make up. He was also prepared to accept that I was an honourable professional who wouldn't dream of putting words like that in a cabinet minister's mouth. After all, it wasn't as if I had got a word or two wrong. Calling a country 'the slum of Africa' was pretty uncompromising.

So was another phrase that received national attention – but not a single complaint, at least not one about me. In 1957, on my new gleaming red Bella scooter (bought, members of the pool were constantly reminding me, by lineage earnings – a fact drummed into an inquiry held by the National Union of Journalists into complaints by a local freelance that the *Luton News* boys were taking away his living) and I took off for a massive open-air Tory rally in Bedford. All the Bedfordshire Tory MPs were there to hear Prime Minister Harold Macmillan. It was a dull speech, saying how wonderful were the Conservatives ('Life's Better with the Conservatives' was their election slogan) how terrible were the socialists and how ungrateful were the people who had elected him and his MP colleagues to Westminster. And then came the bombshell:

'Let us be frank about it,' he said. 'Most of our people have never had it so good.' What was that? Most of them had never had it so good. Not, as historical lore had it, '*You've* never had it so good.'

My motor scooter and I rushed to the nearest telephone box. No emails, no faxes, no mobile phones in 1957. But, to the possible surprise of my children, they did have telephones in those days. Painfully and with an increasingly sore throat I dictated the same story to every national newspaper: 'Prime Minister Harold Macmillan addressing a Tory meeting in Bedfordshire today said that Britons ought to be more grateful. "Most of our people," he said, "have never had it so good."'

It was an unusual thing for Supermac, the epitome of Edwardian elegance, to say. Cadences of slang rarely came from the lips of a publisher who took Trollope to bed with him. Certainly, it wasn't very good English. But his speech writer thought it was a good phrase. I thought it a good phrase. I didn't know it would be quoted for ever afterwards. I didn't realise that all those political commentators, to say nothing of politicians themselves, would, in effect, be quoting *me*. What I didn't realise was that this was more than just a scoop. It was recording history.

Now the truth of the matter is that, despite the case of Lord Home, a disgraceful exception to the rule, I always, or at least usually, found Tory politicians, both locally and nationally, to be much more approachable and appealing than Labour's men and women. I thought it at the time, even though I had joined the Labour Party at the age of 17, once stood for the local council, and have voted for them ever since. In those days, you could put it down to the Tories' social skills being more advanced than Labour's and to their strongly held belief that they had a right to rule and if that required being nice to young reporters as a sort of *noblesse oblige*, so be it.

On the other hand, one of the kindest politicians I met was a man named Cyril Fenton, the Labour candidate who tried to unseat Charles Hill at the 1959 election. I shadowed him throughout the campaign. When it was all over and Fenton was roundly defeated, he gave a dinner at Luton Town Hall for his supporters, to which I was invited (and not just to cover it for the paper). It was the first time that Sara had accompanied me on a 'job'. In his speech, the former candidate paid tribute to my reporting and said he had enjoyed working with me and was so pleased I was there with my 'lady'. We were both chuffed. So was the *Luton News*. It was rare for the paper to hear anything but complaints from political circles.

When Charlie Hill first won the seat in 1950 he had defeated the sitting Labour MP, William Warbey, who was an extreme left-winger, educated before university at the Grocers School in Hackney, where my uncles Nat and Jack had been. Warbey wasn't Jewish, but sitting in a school with a Jewish majority might have rubbed off on him. While Ernest Bevin was fulminating against Jews 'trying to jump the queue' out of Europe and breaking the immigration rules for getting into Palestine, he spoke up for Zionism and then for Israel. He was beautifully spoken, with an Oxford accent which he used to considerable effect in the House – not least fighting his own side's Palestine policy, for which I remained grateful. For much of his time in Parliament he and I engaged in a correspondence, usually with me asking for a place in the gallery of the House of Commons and he proposing that I wait for my luck in the ballot for seats. But he also suggested that I joined the Labour League of Youth. I went to one meeting and didn't like it one bit.

I was much happier at the Luton Judean Youth Club, where I learnt there was a world out there I didn't know about – and half of it consisted of girls. It was more likely to produce those than the Social Zionist party that I continued to run on Sunday afternoons. This was supposedly a discussion group, but we liked to think we were a budding political organisation – and now met in a barber shop, owned by the local Communist Party convener. We had one non-Jewish member, David McLaren, who called himself a Christian Zionist. (The first published story I ever wrote was about David, who played the violin and was about to broadcast on the BBC Children's Hour Young Artists programme – I remember the piece word for word to this day: 'Young man with music in his blood is 17-year-old David McLaren...').

Before long, I had grown out of the 'SZ' . I think I fell in love the first time I went to the Judean club and was given a dancing lesson by a young lady whose bust prevented us otherwise getting too close. I was happy to accept the problem. Later, I edited the club magazine and then established a library which could also double up as a printing works. The real reason was that it gave me a chance to be with this girl (and her successors in my affections) on Sunday mornings without any questions being asked.

It was an education in so many ways. With my new friends I discussed the new music and the new films. One day we decided to see one that seemed to appeal. It was called *Singin' In The Rain*. Like all of us, I was captivated by the movie – as I hadn't been since seeing *The Jolson Story* and *Jolson Sings Again* (no, not yet – they're still to come in this story). In those days, the musicals were so infectious, you left the cinema singing the songs, not just whistling the icecream. After *Singin' In The Rain*, we positively danced out of the theatre – convinced we not only could recite our own dialogue but also invent the choreography. When the others left, I continued dancing – all the way to the number one bus. A girl waiting at the bus stop thought I was chasing her and called a policeman. I blamed Gene Kelly and the cop thought I was mad enough to be believable.

The club taught me to be sociable at a time when I thought I was anything but. When Daphne, a girl with whom I was more than somewhat taken, as my favourite writer Damon Runyon may have put it, told me I was a 'very popular feller', I was stunned and not a little delighted. She was the first girl I ever kissed – just before the Coronation, I seem to remember. No doubt the national euphoria about the new Elizabethan age rubbed off in ways that few anticipated or advertised.

I look upon that club, held in three dingy rooms above the new synagogue in Bury Park, with great affection and gratitude. They awarded me a silver cup for showing my appreciation at learning a number of the facts of life, both in and out of the library. I never really learned to dance, but I tried my best – to the sound of Johnny Ray, Doris Day and Frankie Laine. I have the memory still of my friend Harold jumping on a table and miming to Laine's *Jezebel*. I tried it with Al Jolson, but with less success with the dancers.

Harold and I became great friends at the club, as did Maurice Davis and Vivian Phillips, all three of whom remain my closest friends (and our wives, too) to this day. Vivian met his wife Maureen at a club function. When the four of us called on Maureen at her home in St Albans, we were greeted by the sound of her father calling out, 'The four Shmellicks from Luton are here.' We are still the Four Shmellicks (loosely translated as...no, it can't be translated), and every time one of us has a family wedding or other celebration, we are photographed together.

Joining the club was a passport to even more romance and more maturing of my political instincts. I represented the Lutonians on the Association for Jewish Youth's members' council, of which I became acting chairman. London was another eye-opener for this provincial and I wanted to get there to work as well as to enjoy the riches my metropolitan fellow members councillors enjoyed – like being able to spend half a crown (12½ pence) on a saltbeef sandwich in Blooms in the East End.

By now, I had established a good and adult relationship with Harry Ritvo. Some people thought we were too close, but I admired the single-handed work he was doing to bring an inspiring Judaism to his Luton flock. He was getting rather more religious, which upset a lot of the old-timers.

On Yom Kippur in 1957 he made his usual condemnatory speech of the lack of religion in the town. 'This is my last Yomtov [festival] in Luton,' he proclaimed. 'I'm going to live in Gateshead.' Gateshead was the home of a famous *yeshiva* or Talmudic College, a citadel of ultra-Orthodoxy, but nobody took him seriously. He had said as much before.

'I really intend to go,' he repeated. 'Gay gezuntaheit' ['go in good health'], retorted the president of the synagogue, Tony Corton. 'I'll make you sandwiches.' Neither of them knew it at the time, but it really was the last Yom Kippur for Harry Ritvo in Luton or anywhere else. By 1958, he was dead from cancer – at the age of 52. 'Here lies a toff,' said the distinguished Dayan (Judge of the Beth Din religious court) Maurice Swift, using an antiquated term that was nothing less than the truth.

I missed Ritvo a lot. We used to joke about him, particularly when I met his former deputy, Izzy Wilner, who was to become my uncle-in-law. There was always a tale to tell, always a laugh in telling it, but he was a good man and a very strong influence, even though I never adopted his strain of Orthodoxy (there were numerous others who did, several of whom – strangely, all from poor, unbelieving homes – became rabbis).

A lot of time was spent on club work and romancing new girls in the big city, to say nothing of buying half a crown's worth of saltbeef sandwiches. It occurred to me that if I spent as much time on my work, I might get out of Luton. I dearly wanted a job on a national newspaper. I wrote letters to news editors, went to interviews, got close to jobs on a few occasions, but nothing seemed about to take me out of the comfortable rut in which I was engaged.

But there were good stories in Bedfordshire. Like the dull dinner given to pay tribute to the town's civil defence workers. Nothing much to report there – until the chairman congratulated the lady in charge of the day's exercise in which imaginary fires were put out, using buckets handed from one volunteer to the other. 'I want to praise the exceptional work of Miss Jackson,' said the man. 'She has done nothing but pass water all day.'

Plainly, it was a good time for stories. Not least among them were the ones involving the large number of stately homes in the district, on which I was becoming the local expert. The notably effeminate curator of one took an instant liking to me – perhaps I thought, a little too instant and a little too much liking. We bumped into each other at St Pancras Station, where he insisted on accompanying me into the gentlemen's lavatory. Nothing happened, and I even accepted his invitation to tea and personally toasted crumpets at his flat. Later, I realised I probably shouldn't have done that, although I wasn't compromised beyond being offered a return engagement very soon. I didn't pursue the offer.

Woburn Abbey was a different matter. I was on the scene when John Russell became 13th Duke of Bedford and we instantly built up a rapport. He was not the first to go into the stately home trade – opening his house to the general public to pay off something like £4 million in death duties, following the death of his father, a near fascist, and millions still owing from his grandfather's demise, too. But he was the first to take it into show business.

The Bedfords were an eccentric family. The Duke's grandfather, Herbrand, the 11th Duke, was an autocrat who (in a way like Charles Hill) had both country and town cars. When his chauffeur reached Hendon, the Duke would dismount from his country vehicle and transfer to the other car. A new chauffeur would then salute him, open a door, dust down the leather seat and place a rug over his lap. His wife, meanwhile, was one of the first women to fly – probably because it was a chance to get away from the husband to whom she hadn't spoken in years (she was acutely deaf, but the reason for their lack of communication was that she hated him). One day, the 'Flying Duchess' disappeared in her Tiger Moth into the bright, blue yonder (actually, there was a snow storm at the time).

John, or Ian as the family knew him, didn't speak to his own father, hated his politics and resented the fact that he hadn't been allowed to go to a normal school (because the 12th Duke had hated his days at Eton so much).

Becoming the 'Showman Duke' was his own eccentricity, as far as the rest of the aristocracy were concerned. He had roundabouts and traction engine rallies and the competitors rushed first to scorn and then to copy him. What none of the others did, however, was to have a nudist camp on their grounds. The Duke of Bedford did, and when I was sent to 'cover' the event, to coin an inappropriate phrase, I learned more about the human body, particularly of the female kind, than I thought I wanted to know. But it was a great story that went round the world and from then on I was at least once weekly retailing the events of the Duke's life to the *Daily Express*'s William Hickey and most of the other diaries. Between us, we made up a whole slew of stories. They made him a national figure, constantly on the infant British television 'press conference' TV programmes and the centre of magazine articles. It was a good relationship to our mutual benefit.

Now there had to be changes in my personal as well as my professional life. A cousin had seen an advertisement in the *JC* for a dance put on by a charity committee. Would I like to go? Since my social life had now, for the first time in years, disintegrated into one that was about as active as that of an inmate at Dartmoor, I said yes. It was at the Café de Paris, once the favourite night club patronised by the former Prince of Wales and the rest of what was, appropriately, known as café society. In the late 1950s, Jewish charities took over such establishments on Saturday nights. The purpose was simply for youngsters in their early twenties to meet each other. Sometimes you met the same people every week, but occasionally there was someone new to dance with at places like my then favourite joint, the Empire Rooms in Tottenham Court Road, which was usually good for a dancing partner who might become something more (although not all that much more – as I would say years later, if only I knew then what I knew now). The

Café de Paris was a more elegant and sophisticated place, half populated that night by mainly more elegant and sophisticated ladies.

On this night, I was making little progress. But then in a corner of the large room, talking to a friend, I came across a young lady called Sara. I asked her for a dance.

# 7  Sara

You could call it love at second sight. On that first meeting, which I am sure lasted no more than ten minutes, there had to be something about her that attracted me. She said she had come from Israel, which was a good start. She knew about Luton. Her uncle Izzy Wilner had worked there. She talked. Not at all like a lot of the other girls I had met at dances, who barely uttered a word. In fact, a lot of them made me wonder if they had voices at all. The only thing I ever heard from some was a polite giggle.

Sara, though, was different. And she looked nice, too. In a green dress. I said, 'Could we do this again some time?' which apparently she thought was an unusual chat-up line. I took her phone number, although I didn't have a pen or paper on me. Had I been a Boy Scout instead of a member of Luton Judean Youth Club, I might have been more prepared. As it was, my journalistic training had given me a good memory.

I phoned BIShopsgate 3643 about three days later. From the *Luton News* office, of course. I wasn't going to spend my own money on a call. Besides, I didn't want anyone at home to know my business. Her aunt answered. Sara was having a bath, but she'd call her.

I suggested a date – to Sara, not the aunt. 'Saturday night?' 'OK.' End of conversation. I wasn't all that sure myself. Yes, she looked quite nice... but still, it was just an evening. There would be other nights and other girls.

We arranged to meet at Tottenham Court Road Underground station. She lived in the East End and I wasn't prepared to schlep there to call for her. Besides, this wasn't an evening for the trusty Bella scooter.

Tottenham Court Road wasn't the nicest spot in London. The quotient for sobriety over alcoholism was comparatively low and it was a popular haunt for transvestites. Even then, I was feeling guilty about bringing what my mother would have called 'a nice Yiddisher girl' there. As I waited, I wondered about what I was doing. Would I know her?

But then I saw Sara. And I did. Standing on the escalator, an apparition in black. Beautifully made up. Honey-blonde hair nicely styled. I knew then I was in love – at second sight.

'I didn't think I'd recognise you,' she said. It wouldn't have been necessary. I knew her at that instant and was delighted that I did. We decided to go for a coffee – in one of those coffee bars about which I once wrote a song after going to one with a girl who was, I noted, 'a coffee bar cutie with that Espresso ecstasy'. We ordered that frothy coffee, which set me back ninepence a cup, and talked, and decided to go to 'the pictures'. We saw a terrible movie called *An Eye For An Eye*, with the German star Curt Jurgens. As the lights went up, we looked at each other and laughed. If we could survive that, the omens were good.

There was another cup of coffee and, when I looked her way in the light, I was overwhelmed. For years afterwards, I insisted that she keep that black dress.

Sara Hockerman had had a difficult life, I soon learned. She and her brother and a sister who died in infancy had been born in what was then Palestine. Her father was a qualified ordained rabbi, with a brilliant brain and about as much common sense as a lamppost. He didn't want to work as a rabbi and tried his hand as a diamond cutter. As a diamond cutter, he was a pretty good rabbi. His failure to make a living forced his wife, Feige, to go home to London, where she had been born, and to take her children with her. War was about to break out.

They spent the first years of the war in digs in Wheathamstead, a little Hertfordshire village which, ironically, was just a few miles from Luton. But Feige had no money and needed to go back to London to work in a factory. Sara and her brother were evacuated, going to a religious Jewish school to which they had to walk and where all meals had to be eaten (rather than risk being contaminated by a non-kosher boiled egg at the home of a kind landlady). Then one day an uncle called to tell her that things would never be the same again. Her mother had been killed in what would prove to be the very last air raid of World War Two – a V2 rocket had slammed into the block of flats where she lived with a younger sister in the East End. It was the eve of Passover 1945.

For a few years, she and her brother stayed with her mother's elder sister, a beloved aunt, who rejoiced in a number of names. To her husband Max (a mean, difficult man who thought putting his hands in his pockets should be reserved for pulling out his handkerchief) she was Judy. To her sisters, she was Yiddis. Most of her nieces called her Yidi, although there were a few who knew her as Yetta.

She was a highly religious woman, who kept the Sabbath to the letter, read more prayers than was probably good for her and maintained the dietary laws of kashrut to the extent that she wouldn't dream of even having a cup of tea in a non-kosher restaurant. Her real religion, however, was doing good – for anyone who needed it. She also ran her husband's tiny off-licence and grocery shop – the kind that today's generation knows nothing about, but which is still remembered romantically by older people who complain as they stand at a supermarket checkout, waiting to pay for things they could never have found or afforded in the days when Yidi was in business.

It was a shop where she worked 12 or more hours a day, humping heavy boxes, climbing ladders and slicing cheese, packing butter and helping local down-and-outs who knew she was a soft touch for a sandwich (one of them, a tramp, was taken to the nearby London Hospital – and gave her name as his next of kin). Max found other things to do – like counting the money in the cash register or working for the local Liberal Party. Yes, Yidi kept the family virtually single-handed.

She wasn't a beautiful woman. She never made up. There wasn't time for it. Her hands were like those of a manual labourer. Her clothes were basic and frequently smelt of the herrings she drew out of a barrel or the smoked salmon she was expert at cutting. The smoked salmon was a luxury in those days, but people would find a few pence to pay for a few scraps for Shabbat.

There were no children of their own, which was probably a blessing since she wouldn't have allowed them out in the rain, lest they catch cold. In addition to Max, she also looked after his two

1.One of my great-great-grandfathers, Yitzhak Yakov Wexler.

2. Yehuda Yudel Mindel, my great-grandfather.

3. Nathan Micket, another great-grandfather.

4. Etta Bayler Micket, my great-grandmother.

5. Beside the seaside: my grandfather, Barnet Mindel, with my mother, just before World War One.

6. My grandmother, Annie Mindel, an Edwardian beauty transplanted from Latvia.

7. My grandfather (right) with his brother, the officer, World War One.

8. My grandparents on their wedding day, 1905.

9. My mother and Sylvia outside their father's shop. *My* father probably dressed the window.

10. My parents, Lily Mindel and David Freedland, on their wedding day, 1930.

11. Probably my first picture.

12. Me at 18 months. Signs of my future good looks ...

13. Sara – no wonder it was love (at second sight).

14. The Reverend Harry David Ritvo – before his hat was bashed in.

15. In the army now – if only for ten weeks. I never thought the uniform suited me.

16. Our wedding day, 1960.

17. Dad – always a joker. He was rarely photographed without his pipe. The hat was Jonathan's.

18. Sarala, 2003. Ellie is in the background.　　19. Sara and me, Madeira, 2003.

20. The Four Shmellicks – me (second left) with my dearest friends, Maurice Davis, Vivian Phillips and Harold Bass.

21. Sara and me with our children. Left to right: Fiona, Robin, Jonathan, Sarah, Dani, David next to her, me and Sara, 2004.

22. Relaxing with three of my grandchildren – Jamie, Beth and Ben.

23. Ellie and Beth with their then baby cousin Sam.

24. My two youngest grandchildren, Sam and Jacob.

25. My younger granddaughter, Ellie.

mentally retarded brothers, his sister in the same condition, Max's mother (who thought the sun shone out of every inch of his body and resented Yidi's presence, but took for granted that she would feed her and tend to her needs when ill), an epileptic brother of her own – and Sara and her brother. In 1949, she reluctantly agreed that the two children should be returned to their father in the Tel Aviv suburb of Petach Tikva. Her conscience never stopped pricking her for doing so.

Life for Sara in Petach Tikva was even harder than in the East End of London. The house had been built by her father's brothers, and the sloping ceilings and caved-in walls showed it. Her grandparents, her father's mother and father, dominated the place and ate all the good food. Sara was malnourished and at one time suffered from typhoid. Eventually, in 1955, she returned to London, to live with Yiddi – and to meet me two years later.

She tried at one time to play hard to get. 'I never go out with the same boy, Saturday and Sunday,' she said. Like an idiot, I believed her. I came from Luton, she was in East London and our evenings usually consisted of a trip to the cinema preceded by a 'meal' at a Lyons corner house. She had a portion of grilled mushrooms. I made do with a cup of tea and a roll and butter. 'You eat like a bird,' she said. The point was I didn't tell her about my budget for the weekend – £2, including my fares to and from the metropolis. I even stood for her going out on dates with other men – all prearranged by her uncle. When this man and I eventually met, he had the audacity to say to me: 'We hoped that she would find another beau.' So there was no love lost between us.

Frankly, I couldn't wait to take her away from that environment. I think her religious relatives thought I was simply a snob. But the house on Turner Street, on the very corner of the road where my father had been born, was unpleasant and I hated the idea of Sara living there. Her background was very different from mine and it took my mother time to get to know her. My father, on the other hand, adored her instantly and so did my brother Geoffrey. Mick Mindel, Sylvia's husband, who had himself grown up in the East End and as leader of the Jewish tailors' union did most of his work there, saw in her a soul sister. He and Sylvia were largely responsible for bridging the family gaps, and I'll always be grateful for it. In 1958, we became engaged. Eighteen months later, at Shacklewell

Lane, we were married. Her Uncle Izzy, minister of a tiny synagogue in Ruislip, Middlesex, and husband of another of Feige's sisters, officiated because the Stoke Newington rabbi had had a heart attack the night before.

Various people on both sides made speeches. My Uncle Nat, from Israel, proposed the health of the president of his country. And a telegram was read from my darling grandmother. She was in hospital, dying from cancer. Between the ceremony and the dinner, we called on her at Bart's Hospital. She wore an orchid on her nightdress.

Sara's Uncle Max revelled in the role of host – except that he refused to pay for the wedding, for which we had forked out ourselves. He even insisted that I pay for the tips for the waiters and waitresses. The old convention was that at the end of the marriage dinner, these good people would ask: 'Would you like to appreciate the service?' It was at one that the father of another of my uncles replied: 'No, I wouldn't' – which meant one tip fewer for the woman who had not long before doled out a bowl of chicken soup for his sustenance. Now those days were over and hosts were required to make up for those who no longer were expected to lay down five bob for their benefit. Max insisted on being given all the honours, but still refused to pay a penny for the privilege. Rather than upset Sara, who would have been put through hell had she insisted on my not being responsible for all the costs, I caved in. But I still resent it, 44 years later.

# 8   Fleet Street

By now, I had a new job. And a new life. I had turned down the chance offered by my editor to become a senior reporter on the group's paper in Aylesbury, Buckinghamshire, because I didn't want to leave home. But it was certainly time to leave Luton, even though I was anxious not to follow the usual route of serving time on a larger provincial paper, an evening or a daily perhaps. I wanted to get to London – and in a hurry. I had a number of interviews – several of the papers put me on a shortlist. The *Daily Express*, my real goal, made promises that were never kept. I went along to the Labour Party's organ, the *Daily Herald*, then losing money, but firmly established as one of *the* papers of the age. Yes, they said, I could have a job. I almost kissed the news editor's hand as it was proffered. My dream had materialised. There was, however, a slight catch. I would have to change my name. 'You see,' he explained, 'we have a great many Jewish writers – you know, the excellent Dennis Eisenberg, David Nathan, our theatre critic...' I said I couldn't do it. What integrity! It was a very long time before I stopped wondering whether I should have been proud of that integrity or just settled down to nursing the wounds of stupidity.

The paper that did say yes without strings was the *Daily Sketch*, the poor brother of Fleet Street – even poorer than the old *Herald*. But it *was* Fleet Street, or at least a few yards away on the Thames Embankment. In that age when people took reading the news more seriously than just watching it on a TV screen, it had a circulation nudging a million, which today would be considered highly respectable, but everybody knew it wasn't going to be enough.

It was a tabloid, but it was before the age of page three nipple counts. In fact, there was no *Sun* shining from the street of ink then.

There was no sensationalism. We covered virtually the same stories as the other papers, although we could get quite excited about cats being caught in trees and I remember a scoop (a term we never used in those days; it was reserved for all those movies about reporters with the word 'Press' sticking out from their hat bands – eventually, fact copied fiction) I hit upon when covering a strike in lovely downtown Balham (as Peter Sellers would describe it on one of his superb comedy LPs). I found a bunch of women who were about to warn their husbands that if they didn't stop playing silly buggers and end the strike, they were about to deny them their marital rights. In those days, *The Times* wouldn't have liked it, but it was a good tabloid *Sketch* story and one I wasn't going to share with other reporters on the same story.

On consideration, that was probably a little unfair, since, to my great surprise, Fleet Street ethics declared that you shared a great deal more than was traditionally believed. If you were in a pack – as I'm almost ashamed to say I was that day – you gave a note or two to a colleague who had arrived late or had been away chatting to a policeman when something happened a mile or two away.

Very often those packs came from a single newspaper. On a big story, the *Express*, the one paper I had wanted above all to work for, since it was simply the best and often the biggest (circulation more than four million) would send four or five reporters. I was the sole representative of the *Sketch*, but proud to be so.

Our principal rival was the *Daily Mirror*, which had a circulation four times as big. On my very first day working on the paper, I was assigned to a story about one married woman in three being unable to conceive a child. Sara met me from the office at the end of that day. I was able to show her the first edition. My story was the front page splash. What a triumph, I thought. The front page lead on my very first day. What an omen for the future. The following morning, I took the train from Luton and found myself sitting next to an old colleague from the *News*. I bought a *Sketch* to flourish before her. I didn't read it until we were sitting down. I was all ready to gloat. I unfolded the front page, a big smile on my face. A smile had rarely folded so quickly. My story was nowhere to be seen. Between the first edition and the last, Sir Philip Gibbs, the eminent writer, who had revealed the sad news about Britain's low fertility rate in a new book, had had second thoughts and killed my lead story stone dead. He rang the editor to say he'd got his figures all wrong.

There would be other big stories while I was on the paper. One of them was about two cadets from Britain's elite military academy, Sandhurst, going AWOL.

I flew to Jersey in search of the two men. I wore a long cream mackintosh. As I walked into the hotel into which I had been booked, I was immediately surrounded by a group of other men of my age. They were reporters from rival newspapers who thought my military appearance was a sure sign that I was an officer in waiting – of a court martial. I didn't reveal that I was Freedland, M. R., Private (Retired). They were notably disappointed when they did discover my identity. 'I'm from the *Sketch*,' said I, above their groans.

They were not the only people who groaned at me in 1960. Loud, very loud, noises of discontent came my way from Sir Laurence Olivier, the first superstar celebrity I ever met on business. Our paths crossed, as it were, when he was in the midst of his celebrated divorce from the lovely Vivien Leigh, who was having mental problems and no longer providing the world's greatest actor with the solace he needed in bed or anywhere else.

I joined the pack at London's St James's Theatre where he was appearing on stage, but not in the vestibule. Eventually, I braved him as he got out of his car, his face as contorted in anger as if he were grumbling about the winter of discontent. This was spring, but not the way he saw it. 'Sir Laurence . . . ' I began. He growled. 'I DO NOT give interviews,' he spat.

My news editor, a tough old bird called Herbert (Bert) Pack, who I am sure had the proverbial heart of gold and called everyone 'Love', wasn't satisfied. 'He lives at Eaton Square,' he ordered. 'Go and find him there. He's got no show tonight. Ring his doorbell and don't go away until you've spoken to him.' He probably knew that this was a difficult task, but good reporters revel in difficult tasks. I had to decide for myself that I was a good reporter. It wasn't the *Luton News* and I had to prove that I knew it.

That night, I rode my Bella scooter down to Eaton Square and rang the doorbell at the Olivier residence. No answer. I didn't expect one. After half an hour, I tried again. Still no reply. But then I hit on a solution to my little problem. If I positioned myself on my fairly long, cream-coloured saddle, I could lean back quite comfortably –

and ring the doorbell simultaneously. That prank started at 8.30. The bell was rung continuously and still no reaction. At midnight, I was relieved by another reporter. At 12.05, he had a bucket of water thrown over him.

It was hard to do, but I was beginning to admit that a bucket of water was also being thrown over my Fleet Street career. I liked the idea of writing important stories about important people (and without mentioning 'Luton' once in the copy), but after an ambition to work there which had been with me for more than 15 years, at 25 I was beginning to doubt my love for the place. I still wanted to be a national journalist. There was no doubt about that. But was the *Sketch* where I wanted to do it? I wasn't sure. Things were complicated by the early days of married life. Sara and I were blissfully happy. We had a new home of our own in the north-west London suburb of Kenton, a cosy Tudor-faced semi with a tiny garden that we both used to gaze upon with pride.

But the hours in Fleet Street were not made for a happy marriage. Because I was new and because I was young, I had the worst shifts of the week. I would have to get in at 7 p.m. and not arrive home till 2.30 a.m. Day after day, Sara and I would wave to each other – she from the platform of a red London Transport bus and I from the Bella. I worked on Sundays, too, although we always had Shabbat together. When I did have a day shift, I hurried home – instead of going to the pub and networking, which could have done me some good, I later realised.

When possible, Sarala, as I now called her, came with me on stories. One Sunday, we went to Wickford in Essex, where a man was tormenting his wife by keeping a real full-size lion in their garden. A brilliant story. Especially when the man's wife revealed to Sara that she was pregnant. 'He complains about me having a baby, but doesn't do anything to stop it happening,' she said, woman-to-woman. Having a lion in the back garden was, he reckoned, the ideal way to bring on a miscarriage. As it turned out, he was wrong – and, as a result of my story, the lion was taken off to the nearest zoo, the man protesting, the wife thinking about divorce.

The biggest story in Fleet Street at that time of 1960 came from itself. The *News Chronicle*, now virtually forgotten but in its time a bastion of liberal (with a small 'l') journalism, folded. It didn't affect the *Daily Sketch*, at least not directly. But Sara and I talked about the state of national journalism and my own contribution to it. Was the writing on the wall? As was to be proved before long, it looked that way. She had a very good job with a City company, there were no children yet and I had always fancied being my own boss.

# 9  Freelancing

I was starting up a business. It's hard enough for anyone to do. For a journalist who could barely add up a set of figures, it at first seemed impossible. Yes, I got despondent – before I started. I thought I'd never make it and contemplated looking for another job. I even registered for unemployment benefit – but found the task of lining up for the dole too humiliating. After all, I was just going on 26 and had no business taking the state's money when it was due to more deserving people.

So how did I start? By writing features for the *JC*, which were instantly rejected. By going to the local courthouses, sitting in the public gallery (I didn't want to upset the area's own journalists, who would quite rightly – and, before long, did – take exception to someone poaching on their territory, by sitting at the press table). I did it twice a week, which I considered kept me out of mischief, but it made me no more than a few shillings for my efforts. What turned out to be a real breakthrough, however, was something I had remembered from my Luton days. It was known in the trade as 'overnights' – the London evening papers (by now just the *Standard* and the *News*) had to fill their early editions with dateless material that was set in type, literally, overnight. A great deal of the stories came out of the local papers from my corner of London – followed up, I have to say, not just pinched, which would have been thoroughly unethical. I also became an adept reader of council minutes – including the one from the London borough of Camden, which administered Karl Marx's final resting place, Highgate Cemetery. One entry said that new workers had to be taken on. Until then, they would have to operate with a skeleton staff. Such grave decisions could not be kept away from the general public, and news editors everywhere were suitably grateful.

It didn't take long before these good people and I would get to know each other fairly well. One became a dear friend. Joe Dray of the *Standard* was a warm man who did his best to try to hide the fact. He stood no nonsense, did Joe. If someone was attacking the way an official behaved, he expected you to get the other side of the story. The only annoying thing about that was that sub-editors placing the story in the paper discovered it was too long and constantly cut out the last couple of paragraphs – inevitably the ones beginning, 'Mr X denied doing any such thing. He said: "They don't know what they are talking about..."' I felt Joe shrug his shoulders as he told me such behaviour still didn't absolve my journalistic duty to be fair to all sides. What the subs did was not my problem. I had to do the right thing. It was a good lesson and as a freelance I was still learning lessons.

For a short time, we had a great scam going. Nothing illegal, but, as far as I was concerned, a licence to print a handful of ten-shilling notes. The paper's editor was angry at the loss of that wonderful British institution, the corner shop. Joe happened to mention that it might be a good idea if I did some investigating and found a few 'Small Shopkeepers'. I found them everywhere (Sara's Aunt Yiddi and Uncle Max among them). I'd go in search of a corner shop, interview the owner and, before long, snap him with my camera as he sold a can of soup, climbed a ladder in search of a jar of sweets or cut a side of smoked salmon. I had small shopkeepers who fitted suits, sold antique silver, and handed skeins of knitting wool.

Before long, I had made enough to buy a better camera. I paid for it in one night – when a local MP took the head of London Transport for a ride on the horrendous Northern Line tube to show just how bad things were. I wrote the story and took the pictures. It made a whole page. And a page in the *Standard* was worth having.

Day after day, I sent off, rushing to the last post, half a dozen overnights – about a council sacking its chief officer, about a school that was threatened with closure, about a new civic centre. I became highly proficient with these. On one memorable day, I wrote 90 overnights (many of them merely news-in-brief items, like 'Joe Bloggs is to be the new Harrow borough librarian'). I established new contacts, always the most fundamental job of a reporter. One of them, Harrow alderman (an office soon to be abolished) Horace Cutler, fed me stories for two decades – especially when he became leader of the old Greater London Council. We first got together when he sued a local newspaper for libel. I was a little worried about talking to him. I discovered then that people in trouble want to give their angle on a story.

As a businessman, earning the munificent minimum of 12s 3d (just over 60 pence) an item, I was beginning to make a reasonable living. It was, after all, the early sixties and in my second month I had equalled the salary I was getting on Fleet Street. In a few months I was making £40 a week, and that really seemed good money. I know my mother was impressed. Sara and I could, I reckoned, afford to start a family.

In 1963 our first child, Fiona, was born. It was before the days when fathers were expected to be in on the birth of their children. Thank God. The sister at Kingsbury Maternity Hospital told me to go home, but said I could be present for the first stages of labour. When I phoned the next morning, she said all was going well, and Sara was now in the third stage. 'Good,' I said. 'When she gets to the first stage, let me know...'

An hour or so later, I was taken into the nursery. There, lined up for inspection, were a dozen or so grey metal cots, each with either a blue or a pink card attached above the head of the baby. I didn't need to be told which of the ones bearing a pink card was mine. I recognised Fiona without a formal introduction. She looked just like me. Fortunately, that didn't last long. In a month or so she had become the most beautiful baby I had ever seen.

Just 13 months later came Dani, baby number two. Joe Dray rang about an overnight. He was about to complain. I knew that voice. 'But,' I stammered, 'I can't do anything about that. My wife's just had a baby.' 'Oh, my dear chap,' he said, 'forget about the overnight. Run along. If you want any help babysitting...' The last was a joke. But I knew I had breached his tough exterior. I never thought I'd be unhappy again. Ever. Two lovely daughters. Dare I ask for anything more? I didn't think I'd want to.

There were other papers and other relationships. In 1965, after a run of very good stories for their paper (paying me something like £25 a time – really very good money) the *Sunday Express* offered me a job. 'Where were you five years ago?' I asked the news editor.

'I would have kissed your feet.' Not just a Fleet Street paper, but the *Express*. Now I couldn't afford to accept their offer. But by then, I had stopped being just a jobbing reporter, although I knew how much I owed to people like Joe Dray and the gentleman from the *Express* who had kept me in business. I still sent off my overnights and still answered the occasional call to 'Freedland of Kenton' to cover stories they thought might be potentially interesting. It was amazing how few of them really were. But I wasn't going to be too superior to do such work. It was an honourable profession and I was proud of it. One Saturday evening, a mass protest at the United States Air Force base at Ruislip led to scores of arrests. I covered it for the then infant *Sunday Telegraph*. They were delighted, and I was delighted that they were delighted. I think they paid me £15 to show just how much I was appreciated.

I also appreciated the fact that I got together with an agency called Exclusive Press Features. I sold them the idea of a series of interviews – in which I asked a group of celebrities 20 questions for a Q and A feature that the firm thought it could sell all over the country. It did. Evening newspapers throughout Britain bought the interviews and so did a great many in the Commonwealth and in America. Every one of them had my name at the top. A byline was almost as valuable as a cheque. Since the cheque was no more than £5 a time, they were lucky just how much I valued that byline; they had never had such success with a series.

The American papers particularly liked the chat I had with the writer James Thurber, one of my idols for his stories like *The Secret Life of Walter Mitty*, which became one of my all-time favourite movies with one of my all-time favourite stars, Danny Kaye – who was another one of my chosen celebrities.

I liked Thurber, too – even though we never met. He was old, blind and not well when he came to London to discuss business matters. I spoke to his wife on the phone, day after day. Eventually, she said, 'Well, send my husband a list of questions and he'll do his best to answer them.'

I did and he replied. He said, however, 'I can't answer a questionnaire. See if you can get your answers from this letter.' 'This letter' was a Thurber short essay written exclusively for me. I had asked him about the effect of modern science on the world. 'If a man ever goes into space,' he responded (this was 1962), 'we should remember that a monkey did it first.' And to a poser about the amount of time he spent writing, 'My greatest problem is convincing my wife that when I'm looking out of the window, I'm working.'

I knew what he meant. Danny Kaye was asked about his success as a performer, twisting his tongue incredibly as he sang lyrics by Mrs Kaye, Sylvia Fine. 'I'm a wife-made man,' he said. 'She has a great head on my shoulders.'

One of the questions I asked every respondent was: 'Who would you like to be if you were not you?' Harold Wilson, then shadow foreign secretary and not yet in the running to be Labour leader, said: 'Freddie Trueman'. I asked him the secret of public speaking: 'Try to be funny. For most of my career, my speeches have been very turgid.' They wouldn't be so for long. When he fought the election that made him prime minister for the first time, he chided the then PM, Alec Douglas Home (to my delight, naturally) on saying that he liked to have a box of matches to help him counting. As he discounted all the Tory party's financial plans, Wilson said: 'Prime Minister, have you got your matches handy?'

I spoke to the man who would be Wilson's deputy (and very unhappy with the role, too), George Brown. 'Want a drink?' he asked. 'No thank you,' I replied. 'Well, *I*'m having one.' Throughout the chat, Brown (about whom the phrase 'tired and emotional' had been devised, to explain his behaviour on a TV programme about the death of John F. Kennedy) got more and more drunk, and more and more phrases were masked by the sound of bottles and glasses being clinked.

I later met Brown in Brussels when I went to the Belgian capital on a press trip, aimed at encouraging young journalists to preach the European gospel. It was 1964 and an election was in the offing. Brown had been saying every time Labour won a by-election: 'We're on the way, brothers.' We sat at an open-air Brussels café. 'Are you really on the way?' I asked. 'All I know', he said, 'is that I'm on the way to a f . . . king drink.'

Lord Hailsham saw me at his home in Putney. He was soon to become Quintin Hogg again (he had succeeded his father to the title and then given it up in a vain attempt to become Tory leader; when Margaret Thatcher entered Downing Street, he was Lord Hailsham once more – and Lord Chancellor). He was kind and warm, and gave the impression of living in genteel poverty, which I am sure could not have been true. But the furniture in the huge house was distinctly the worst for wear. 'Dogs, you know,' said his wife, looking at the somewhat filthy chair on which the good lord had sat at the last coronation.

Among my other 20-questions victims were Yves Montand and his wife Simone Signoret, who talked about being France's first show business couple. Then there was Georges Simenon, creator of Maigret, who talked about his books and the earlier potboilers, but I only wish I had got on to the subject of his prodigious activities with women. Edward G. Robinson was staying at Claridges. For me, he was a natural. We talked about his paintings, about *Little Caesar* ('I always thought that if I could get into films with a face like mine, I hadn't done too badly'). But why didn't I talk about his being victimised during the McCarthy era? And no mention of the Hollywood moguls? Certainly, nothing about his Jewish background. Why did I stay off course when it came to discussing the origins of the guy born Emmanuel Goldenberg? I would eventually learn.

One of Edward G.'s fellow Warner Bros. gangster stars, George Raft, came to work in London as the front man for a gambling casino. I saw him at his West End flat, which could have come out of a scene from one of his films. And so could he. I am not sure that he was wearing spats over his beautifully shined black shoes, but his silk dressing gown was wonderfully evocative. What, I asked him, did people think of his image? 'They loved me,' he said, 'but they used to ask – "why did you have to die?"'

Safer would be Coco the Clown and Larry Adler, who would become a dear friend for the rest of his life. We didn't talk then about McCarthy either – although it was because he was about to be drummed out of Hollywood that he came to England in the first place. (It was not a subject I avoided with Paul Robeson.) Fortunately, over the years I more than made up for it. We talked about his favourite entertainer. 'Al Jolson,' he said. Well, after that, we had to be friends for life. Larry was an interviewer's gift. Actually, he admitted he liked being interviewed. Certainly, as I discovered during 40 years of friendship, he just liked talking. Since he was to become the last living contact with people like the Gershwins, the Astaires and all the other greats of Broadway, to say nothing of Jolson himself and Eddie Cantor, he was to be good value as well as a good friend.

Then there was Peter Ustinov. I suggested that he was one of the twentieth century's most prized conversationalists. 'Oh no,' he said. 'That's a dangerous reputation. People think that about Dr Johnson. But all he had to say was, "Sir," and all conversation stopped.'

There were about 40 of those interviews. It was a superb training ground for what would eventually become a staple of my work: talking to well-known people about themselves and about other celebrities – even though in my immaturity I left out so much.

But what you get to know about celebrities talking about celebrities is a recognition that they think nobody is more celebrated than they are themselves.

What I had learned, however, was that to keep going one needed to have regular work. I went back to my journalistic roots and the gamekeeper suddenly became a poacher – working in verdant rural Bedfordshire and in swinging London, with a trip over to Wales on the side, at the feet of one of the great philosophers of the twentieth century.

# 10   A duke, an earl and a few naked ladies

It's when some new career move comes along that I realise how much I owe to my days on the *Luton News.* It taught me not just the elements of journalism and how to sell that journalism, but how to maintain good contacts. It's not just what you know, but who you know in the newspaper business. It's both who you know and what you know about establishing a relationship to your mutual advantage.

People talk about journalists failing to honour agreements, telling lies, never seeking the truth and driving people mad, demanding interviews. You can't sustain *all* those arguments. To do so is to talk in oxymorons. You can't complain about a disregard for truth and at the same time be angry about a journalist's interference while trying to get at that very truth. Answer 'no comment' and you have to be prepared for certain assumptions to be drawn – and they're not usually the ones you want to hear.

'You cannot hope', said a poem pinned on to the wall of the reporters' room at the old *LN,* 'to bribe or twist. Thank God, the British journalist. Considering what unbribed he'll do, there's very little reason to.'

Most important of all is the simplest injunction to a reporter: tell the truth and be fair. If for no other reason than that you might want to talk to people a second time, that's something that should be engraved on every journalist's heart. Another good reason is that being fair is what one's life should be about.

Very early on in my freelancing career, the idea came to mind that before I made new contacts, I ought to foster the ones I already had – not least the ones I had made in Luton, among the hat factories and motor works. It was a dreadfully ugly place, but my parents and my closest friends still lived there. And it was still what an American Air Force officer had told me, 'a thriving metropolis'.

I sold a story about Bill Gowland to the *Guardian*. And I decided to call on the Duke of Bedford at his stately home, Woburn Abbey. I had spoken to him on the phone while on the *Sketch*. I had his personal number, so it wasn't difficult getting to him when he was in the midst of a celebrated divorce action. Those were the days when to end a marriage, you had to provide grounds. There was cruelty, either physical or mental. And there was adultery. You had to prove them all. And in court. The Duke was 'found' in bed with a so-called actress, with the improbable name of 'Annabelle Lee'.

The lady was no actress and he wasn't just 'found' in bed in that small hotel in Brighton. The whole thing was a put-up job to give his second wife, the Duchess, a good excuse to sue him for divorce. I rang him from the *Sketch* office. 'The Duke's not here,' said an easily recognisable voice. 'Who are you?' I asked. 'The night watchman,' said the voice. It was as much a deception as his moment in bed in Brighton, but probably a lot less fun.

He was more willing to identify himself when I arranged the appointment to see him at Woburn. We talked about the divorce action. He wasn't happy that he had had to go through the Brighton charade, and I said I thought there could be worse ways of getting into trouble. 'I don't mind the blame if I've enjoyed the game,' he said. I thought that was reasonable, but I got the impression that he and the actress did little more than get into bed at the required moment and pour themselves a couple of drinks.

He gave me a story or two – or rather we talked over a couple of ideas. And that led to a more exciting idea. How about employing me to look after his press interests? To be, in fact, his PR man? It was a rare breed in the 1960s, and the notion intrigued us both. I was offering him a different idea from one that would come from a conventional PR agency. I am not sure I knew just what a marvellous 'account' I was proposing I should take over, but then I was careful to point out that I wouldn't be operating out of a posh office in the West End, with a big desk, thick carpet on the floor and a team of beautiful secretaries at my beck and call. The more I emphasised that I wouldn't need those things, the more I thought how nice it would be to have that desk, that carpet and the beautiful secretaries attending to my every whim. He said he was interested,

but didn't want to spend any money at this stage. I felt very sorry
for a man who owed £4 million, but wondered if the couple of
thousand I was suggesting would really make any difference.
Nevertheless, the time might come.

Before long, the Duke was divorced and had remarried – a
woman I had first met when he was in the midst of one of the early
publicity stunts at Woburn Abbey. She was Nicole Milinaire, a
television producer about to film a new series called *Dick and the
Duchess*. She was sexy and she was French. And when she heard
about my idea, she said she liked it.

Nicole said, 'Come to our London flat.' I went. It was a tiny
mews residence round the corner from Claridges Hotel (before long,
they would spend £30,000 on a house in Regents Park, which gives
you some idea about how long ago the sixties were). The Duchess
was there alone. Her new husband was away, but coming home
soon. Perhaps he'd be along before I finished my cup of tea, served
in Nicole's beautiful china set. When we got talking about my
knowledge of Woburn, my journalistic experience and the fact that
I was a charming, intelligent young man (at least, I think that was
what she said) I felt that she was a lady with whom I could do
business. She thought that, too. As I got up to go, there was the
sound of a key in the door. The Duke was home. Totally ignoring
me, she and the man whom, in our conversation,she had called
'Yan' (her pronunciation of 'Ian') were in a clinch, the kind of
embrace that the Hollywood morals czar Will H. Hays banned from
the screen.

As I left, she said, 'Write me a letter with your ideas.' I did. I
wasn't sure at the time if she just wanted to get rid of me, so that
things between her and Ian could take their course. Apparently,
however, she was talking business. 'I knew I was right,' she said in
reply to my lengthy list of ideas for Woburn promotions. 'You have
some very good ideas.'

So I entered the world of PR. 'Stunts are what we want,' I said.
'Stunts are good,' said the Duke. 'What have you got in mind?' It
turned out to be an idea – and a moment to savour, one that
couldn't possibly come again, which is what all the good ideas are
about. 'You said,' I pondered, sitting in a not terribly comfortable
and slightly worn chair, looking out at the spreading acres of
Woburn Park in front of the house, an area that was strictly

forbidden to the general public, no matter how many half crowns they paid, 'you said that your father lost his coronet?'

'That's right, he lent it to somebody who never returned it. I've no idea who it was.' Since the 12th Duke wasn't exactly on intimate conversational terms with his son, the then Marquis of Tavistock, they never talked about it.

The Duke was intrigued and was peering over his spectacles at me now. He was still a young man, in his mid-forties, but the glasses gave him an air of sagacity. Certainly, he didn't look like the 'Showman Duke' that he was now being billed as. He wore exquisite Savile Row suits, and when he lifted his trouser legs you couldn't avoid noticing that he kept up his socks with black suspenders, the kind that my father used to wear, but no longer did. He made a point of telling the media not to call him 'Your Grace', which in those days most journalists would. Tugging at the forelock would have been too much, but we were brought up to show deference to titles. The image he was creating for himself was that of a modern man, but just so far as it was good for Woburn – and that was why the idea of a duke without a coronet was so tempting.

'What have you got in your devious mind?' he asked.

'Well,' I said, 'if you haven't got the coronet and don't know who has, let's advertise for its return.'

'Advertise?'

'In the personal column of *The Times*,' I suggested. 'I doubt if you'd get an answer. People who borrow coronets are notorious for never returning them. But if you do, it would make a wonderful story. Just advertising would be enough to get the papers and everyone else humming.'

I was, of course, right. No one did come forward and admit that next time there was a coronation, he would be wearing the Duke of Bedford's coronet. But the advertisement when it appeared ('Wanted. Return of coronet, borrowed by an unknown duke after the Queen's Coronation. Please contact the Duke of Bedford, Woburn Abbey, Woburn, Bedfordshire. Tel: Woburn 666') had precisely the affect I had anticipated. *The Times*, naturally enough, carried not just the advertisement, but a story on its main news page – and so did every other newspaper in the country and most of those in every other country that knew what a) a Duke and b) a coronet were. The Americans went crazy about it. And so did the BBC. The

*Today* programme, fronted by the genial Jack De Manio, interviewed my client, who couldn't have been more happy. Actually, he
could have been – and he was when the turnstiles at Woburn
became almost literally hot with the use to which they were being
put the following day. (I had planned it so: the story went out on
Thursday for publication in Friday's papers, in time for seemingly
half the country to decide they were going to go to the Abbey that
weekend.)

For three years that sort of thing was repeated, almost weekly. We
arranged for celebrities to go to Woburn for house parties – and not
just the huntin', shootin' and fishin' lot. Twiggy and Mary Quant
went. When my hat manufacturer chum Maurice Davis (one of the
Four Shmellicks from Luton) told me they were planning the town's
annual Easter Bonnet Parade, I suggested that they hold it at
Woburn. They did. The papers and the TV news programmes were
full of the hats on show at the Duke of Bedford's stately home and
the curvy models wearing them – and of celebs like Lionel Bart and
his girlfriend, the singer with a tickle in her voice, Alma Cogan.

It was good to get commercial interests on side. So we set up joint
ventures, like having the Miss Pears winner (a pretty little girl who
could pose for the famous 'Bubbles' soap ads) coming to Woburn.
Miss Pears 1963 behaved impeccably, I'm pleased to report.

The best ideas are the ones about which the people proposing
them feel most passionately. I thought it would be great for the
Bedfords to go to the Soviet Union – no British aristo had done that
since the Revolution, almost half a century before. We said they
were going and they intended to go, but the idea had to be shelved
for the Duke's own personal reasons.

Not so, however, their trip to Israel, which I organised via the
Israel Government Tourist Office, who couldn't have been more
delighted. This was where my personal interests came into play.
They loved the Israeli wine – which was a real boost to a country
whose viniculture was best known for the sweet red liquid it sold for
Sabbath and holiday (particularly Passover) sacramental use. I
suggested that the Duke be offered some trees – the traditional
welcoming gift for VIPs. That was all arranged before he and the
Duchess left England, and there was an ornamental certificate to
prove it. It then struck me that it wouldn't be a bad idea to show
them where *their* trees actually were. What I didn't know was that

trees are ... well, trees. No one knows whose trees are where. But, at my behest, they did a little fibbing – had a plate made up and stuck it on a post near where the trees they would visit were planted. The Israelis thought that was such a good idea that it was later featured in a film about rich Americans wanting to visit the results of their munificence.

To go with the visit, I got Sara to translate the Woburn guide book into Hebrew. That was a big hit in Jerusalem.

Woburn was close to Luton, at least now that the first motorway, the M1, was in use. So it was a chance to go to my parents' home for lunch and to visit old haunts. I'd occasionally pop into the *Luton News* offices. On one of the first of these, the then editor Tommy Yarrow came out of his eerie. 'Ah,' he said, 'the Duke's man.'

Not many former congregants at the Luton Synagogue had been called that. I venture to say, even fewer than had entered journalism.

It was a time when the cinema newsreel was dying out, but was being replaced by 'interest' movies. The ABC chain had *Pathé Pictorial*. The Odeons, *Look At Life*. I suggested that they looked at life in a stately home (guess which one?). They did, and I went round cinemas in the London area pinning up pictures of Woburn. Sara had just come out of hospital with our firstborn at the time, and neither of us had been into a cinema for months. I will never forget the joy at experiencing that special (at the time) warm, smoky movie theatre smell. It's with me still, every time I think about it.

There was even a Woburn film festival – which went up like a lead balloon. Well, you can't be right all the time. We promised a holiday in Jamaica to the winner of the best amateur film competition. One of the outside sponsors said they couldn't, after all, manage that and, instead, we gave the man who had made a splendid 16 mm. film a new cine camera. He asked what had happened to his Jamaican holiday and said that, in any case, the camera he already had was better than the one he was now getting. Somehow we managed to placate the man, who made a lot less fuss than I thought he was entitled to make.

But what brought my relationship with Woburn to a less than glorious end was when I suggested that the Miss World contestants should be entertained at the house. 'Let's do it differently,' I put to the Duke's comptroller, Jack Barton (who had produced *that* show, *Dick and The Duchess* and was later to be producer of the ITV

*Crossroads* soap opera). 'Let's make it an Elizbethan evening – with serving-wenches and all that stuff.' It was such a good idea that the Duchess sold the rights to the evening to *Life* magazine. I pointed out that that sort of thing (now quite common, as proved by the 2003 battle between *Hello* and *OK!* magazines over the Michael Douglas–Catherine Zeta Jones nuptials pictures) wouldn't go down well with the rest of the media, particularly the ones we depended on most, the British papers. We would, I suggested, alienate all of them. I was right. Woburn was unofficially blacklisted for years. Nothing was heard of the place in any newspaper or in any broadcasting medium for a very long time. Nor was much heard of me in connection with the house or the Bedford family. Our relationship came to an end. But I still held it, and the Duke in particular, in great affection.

About 10 years later, I did an extensive interview with the then Marchioness of Tavistock. I had liked both her and her husband, Robin the Marquis, who was heir to the dukedom – a man as charming as his father, but much less extrovert. He was almost shy, and neither he nor his beautiful wife, a former deb of the year, Henrietta Tiarks, had ever wanted to live at Woburn. At least, not until it was absolutely necessary. It was predictable that the Duke would be there for years to come. He was still only in his mid-fifties, in good health, and his whole life seemed to revolve around Woburn, the house and parkland he had saved from the bailiffs and turned into his own. But then quite suddenly in the mid-seventies, he had decided to call it a day – or perhaps 'un jour' – and go off to live in France. The stately home of the Duke of Bedford was now that of the Marquis of Tavistock.

We had a wonderful chat that day with the Marchioness. Sara came with me and we had lunch in the sculpture gallery in front of the famous statue 'The Three Graces' by Canova. 'We had some Americans here last week,' she told us. 'And one of the women asked, "Which one is the Duchess?"' They didn't get on terribly well, it was clear to see. As she said, 'When we go to bed, I'm always frightened the Duchess is going to walk out of the wardrobe.'

In 1978, I went to Paris to interview both the Duke and the Duchess. They were perfectly charming. Her Grace asked for certain things to be removed from the piece – but she had said them, and the editor of *Woman's Own*, for whom I wrote the feature, refused. I don't think she disliked me for that. She was, and probably still is, very pragmatic: what has gone has gone. Or, to quote the Bedford (Russell) family motto made famous by Doris Day, 'Che Sera Sera'.

One of the suggestions I made when working at Woburn was that the sculpture gallery ought to be let out for Jewish weddings. I had my own children's marriages in mind, I have to say. The Duke thought it was a good idea. Nearly 30 years later, both Fiona and Dani were married there. In my speeches, I pointed out that it was very nice of the ducal family to put the name of the mother of the bride on their coat of arms.

As a sad footnote to the Woburn story, the Duke died in 2003, to be succeeded by Robin – who died just eight months later. The present Duke, whom I met shortly before his succession, is a very pleasant young man.

My professional relationship with the Russell family continued in a way I couldn't have anticipated. On one of the occasions that I had travelled to Woburn, I was introduced to a distant cousin of the Duke who was, in his way, by far the most distinguished member of the clan. He was a mere Earl. But this Earl was one of the great thinkers of the twentieth century, one of its most eminent mathematicians – Bertrand Russell, by then a very old man.

He was also a very left-wing old man, a lifelong pacifist leading member of the Ban the Bomb organisation, the Committee of 100, which he had founded. He had taken part in – and been carted off from by policemen – countless demonstrations. Now, though, he was spreading the word with a new organisation, run on his behalf by an American named Ralph Schoenman. Schoenman spotted me at Woburn and asked if I would work with 'Bertie' and the foundation. With Woburn at an end, I thought I might as well. It gave me a chance to meet and chat with the great man. It really was an experience to treasure.

Russell lived in a house called Plas Penrhyn at Penrhyndeudraeth, one of the most beautiful spots in the heart of the North Welsh countryside, with a view of Mount Snowdon. Penrhyndeudraeth could not have been more spectacular and nor could 'Bertie', a man with a high-pitched, almost squeaky voice as instantly recognisable and distinctive as the mane of white hair and the sharp Russell nose, not unlike that of his kinsman, the 13th Duke of Bedford. He and the Duke could not have been less alike, however. The Duke wanted to keep the lands that he believed were rightly due to the aristocracy. The Earl equally wanted the aristocracy to keep in its place – and not take too much advantage of the House of Lords to proclaim their dangerous right-wing policies.

We talked about that when we met, and we talked about his love of young women, which had got him into serious trouble more than once. And we also discussed his anti-bomb campaign, to say nothing of the other passion which was then even more important to him – to get America out of Vietnam, where they were, he said, 'eviscerating' pregnant women as well as setting light to their homes.

The interview was broadcast on the BBC's *Woman's Hour* programme, for which I was doing quite a lot of work in those days (long before the show decided to concentrate on pregnancy, diets, bathing suits and other fashion and females in the workplace). The BBC and its listeners seem to have found the interview of some interest – but not the corporation's archives department. I could never forget the anger and the embarrassment of the producer, a lovely Welsh woman called Anne Howells, when she told me the tape had been wiped. 'It's history,' she almost wept. And so was the fact that the tape had gone. Neither could be changed.

The Bertrand Russell Peace Foundation didn't last long in my life, but I was always glad I had that relationship with 'Bertie', even if I didn't entirely share all his philosophies.

There was another somewhat oddball character who briefly entered my life, an extrovert gentleman who liked to be thought of as a rough diamond. David Kaye ran a greetings card company, and used the sort of words in his everyday conversation that, had they appeared on birthday cards, would have got him thrown out of every stationery shop in the country and landed him in court. I produced a quarterly magazine for the firm. It wasn't my cup of tea but it opened my eyes to an industry I only really knew anything about on 18 December.

One of the stories that Kaye never stopped talking about was the time he met the American comedian Jack Benny, a man who was best known for a) his alleged meanness – his most famous sketch was the one in which he is held up by an armed burglar who says,'Your money or your life', to which Benny replied, after much deliberation, 'I'm thinking it over' and b) the fact that, even in his seventies, he was claiming to be 39. Kaye went up to him at a Hollywood party to which he had been invited, banged him on the back and said: 'I *really am* 39.' He was not amused by that, but Kaye was.

Just a few months after that, I bumped into Jack Benny in the lobby of the Plaza Hotel, New York. He was carrying his violin case and I dared myself to say, 'Are you who I think you are?' He smiled. 'That's a better line', he said, 'than the one used by someone last week. The man said, "Do you know, Mr Benny, you're my number-one fan?"' He didn't smile at the David Kaye story, but did when we met more formally and, much more importantly for me, about five years later.

That occasion at the Plaza Hotel was in itself, however, of a certain significance – if changing your life could be considered significant.

My life changed because it was my first trip to America. I immediately fell in love with the country – as I knew I would. To see the skyscrapers for the first time, to beathe in the heavy, typical New York air was not an event to be lost from the memory bank. To see stars and politicians who were in the news sipping an icecream soda was something to write home about – and fired my ambition to meet more of them, to write about them.

For the moment, however, I was in New York as part of my PR business. Just a couple of months earlier, a photographer called Owen Barnes, a man I had vaguely known in Luton, had approached me to do some work with him. We were moderately successful in selling stories with pictures, but nothing very spectacular came out of our relationship – until he mentioned meeting two men, one named Henry Moss, the other Harry Fox. They ran a boutique in Carnaby Street and he thought they wanted some PR. Was I interested?

Was I interested? Well, of course I was interested. As 1959 turned into 1960, the *Daily Express*, that paper I so wanted to join, had asked a simple question: what would the new decade be known as? They had the feeling that, like the Naughty Nineties of the previous century or the Roaring Twenties of that then present one, it was crying out for an adjective.

By 1966 the name had been established. These were the Swinging Sixties. And, as never before, London was at its centre. *Time* magazine had its famous cover story about 'Swinging London' and everybody was talking about Carnaby Street, the tiny thoroughfare off Regent Street, where the new kind of fashion was born.

I didn't know much about that kind of fashion – miniskirts, fur collars on 'Afghan' coats, short haircuts and the whole panoply of a town that suddenly was swinging its heart out. Barnes and I met the two men at a London club, and I said that I was sure that if I could get Woburn on the map, I could do the same for Carnaby Street. That had an air of extreme chutzpah about it. Carnaby Street was already well known. So finding something new to say wasn't going to be easy. But I had one great weapon at my disposal. Carnaby Street was known as a centre for men's fashions – Lord John and John Stephen and Irvine Sellers had introduced the world to the Nehru jacket, to velvet trousers and to suits that I wouldn't have wanted hanging in my wardrobe, let alone to have on my back. But Moss and Fox ran Lady Jane, which was going to do the same for women's clothes – if only people knew of their existence.

If they were going to get people to know about them, there had to be publicity. Did I really think I could help? I wasn't going to say no, and nor was Owen, who was ready to take the pictures. My first idea wasn't exactly inspired. If we were writing about women and fashion, let's have women in the pictures. I thought it would be fun to have a girl running round the street in her underwear. Forget it, said the world's press. There was nothing interesting in that. And nor was there – apart from the interest it had for the lucky prurient few who were in Carnaby Street that morning. It was my second idea that did have a little interest. Ok, rather a lot of interest. No, I'll admit it. Modestly, I'll reluctantly say, it was one of the best stories I ever had anything to do with.

It came about the night I was walking along that street and noticed a window dresser, pinning a garment on to one of those plaster mannequins that every clothes shop had. Every clothes shop had men or women who pinned garments, suits, dresses, coats on to those lifeless figures. But what if we had *live* window models? The answer could be seen in double-page spreads all week in the *Daily Mirror*, the *Express* and every newspaper you could think of. TV cameras swung into the swinging street and fought for room with the crowds who blocked the pavement and prevented cars from driving on the road. *Time* magazine rejoiced in the fact that its prophecy about Swinging London getting even more exciting was proving true. Its rival *Newsweek* wasn't too proud to acknowledge it, too.

At one time, it was impossible for any customers to get into the shop for reporters and cameramen blocking their way. Henry Moss and Harry Fox were arrested and fined for obstruction. Even building up a criminal record was worth the fame and the business I had brought them.

The pictures went into the archives – and every time someone now does a film about the London of 40 years ago, shots of Lady Jane and Carnaby Street are included.

That was why I went to New York. Owen Barnes and I tossed up as to who would go there with our clients – and I won. As soon as I landed at the newly renamed JFK airport, I had set up a press conference for Fox and Moss. They had a splash in the Brooklyn *Star Ledger*, which satisfied them enormously. In Brooklyn, we found a shop not unlike Lady Jane and organised a live-models display for them, too. The New York dailies loved it and so did the proprietors, who for reasons I could never understand (well, yes, I suppose I can), had a notice outside, announcing the appearance of 'Paris models'.

Fox and Moss took it as an opportunity to sell to the big stores in Manhattan. They got the idea right of doing it at the Plaza. At least, that part of it was my idea. They had booked into a place called the *Belmont* Plaza. I told them they had the wrong Plaza in mind, and so, on my advice, changed to the most prestigious hotel in town. The big buyers came to the suite, which they probably wouldn't have done in the other place. Drinks were laid on – and so were the girls, which I thought was incongruous when trying to sell to establishments like Saks Fifth Avenue. Not nearly as incongruous, however, as Henry Moss happily eating an orange while the Saks buyer consulted the merchandise.

Back in London, the next three or four years (by which time I was acting alone) were replete with other stunts, other window models – this time girls posing nude in the window of Fox's new shop, Lady Jane Again – girls posing in large-scale bird cages (we'd never get away with that today – and, I suppose, neither should we try).

One day, I arranged for the busty star Jayne Mansfield, better known for her body than any acting ability, to come to Lady Jane and pose in an intricately made lace dress. She said it suited her perfectly because she never wore any underwear. She also insisted that she be allowed to keep the dress. Since pictures of her in the gown appeared in all the national newspapers (and, incredibly for the time, not just the tabloids), it was a good investment for the pair.

I had Fox stand for Parliament – as an 'Independent Carnaby' candidate in a by-election. He and I did things that were totally illegal at the time – like having an American-style girls' band playing, complete with cheerleaders. He lost his deposit, but decided that, like their fines for obstruction, it was worth it. He and his partner contemplated buying a race-horse, called Lady Jane, of course, but this idea proved rather more expensive.

When Henry Moss left the enterprise, Harry Fox ran it alone, together with a series of male managers who usually found an opportunity to go into the dressing room while young ladies were changing. Part of the Carnaby Street culture was that these women didn't seem to mind. They were part of the scene – to the extent that they came into Lady Jane with full purses. Some of them didn't dip into those purses to actually buy clothes. A roll of labels with the words 'Lady Jane of Carnaby Street' on them was enough. Fox was kind enough to say that it wouldn't have happened without my publicity ideas. I'm rather pleased to agree with him.

There was another group of Carnaby Street boutiques who took me on, too – this time purveyors of men's clothes. In fact, I got to know the Carnaby crowd quite well. They were a fascinating bunch, a mixture of (as they used to say in those days 'with it' entrepreneurs who hit the fashion nail on the head in one swoop, and elderly Jewish and Greek businessmen who spied a new opportunity and grabbed it to considerable advantage. I heard one of these gentlemen talking to his accountant, who had been at a charity dinner the night before, attended by Sir Keith Joseph, later to be Margaret Thatcher's guru-in-chief. 'What was he like?' his friend asked. 'You'd be amazed,' he said, 'double-breasted lapels on his dinner jacket.' I am not sure if it was that which decided me to say I had had enough. I decided, however, that I had had enough. The poacher wanted to be a gamekeeper again. And there were new things on the horizon. One of them was a third child, a baby we called Jonathan. There was another baby called Al Jolson and a third named *You Don't Have To Be Jewish*.

# LIFE TWO

# 11   *You Don't Have To Be Jewish*

I didn't want the job. The offer came in the early months of 1971 – at roughly the same time as the commission for my first book. And *that* I wanted to do more than almost anything I had ever done. So could I do that, continue with my freelance journalism and all those overnights? To produce and present a Jewish programme – was that the way I saw my career going? Frankly, I didn't think so.

For one thing, the offer was to work on BBC Radio London. Yes, it was the BBC and it *was* their flagship local station, but... it was local radio, and the connotation of being back on the *Luton News* was perhaps more obvious to me than it was to anyone else. Yes, London was the capital, one of the biggest cities in the world, but it was just a local station. More than that, in those days it broadcast only on VHF, the then name of FM, and the BBC was still at the stage when it was running advertising campaigns trying to persuade people to buy a new radio set – just as, 30 years later, they are trying to spread the digital message.

Radio London sounded great – if you lived in Paris, Moscow or anywhere else where the sound of a capital attached to the word 'Radio' bespoke influence, importance and ability to press all the switches. If you were part of the BBC establishment, on the other hand, it had little influence. But it was trying, which was why it wanted to add a Jewish programme to its list.

Indeed, the Jewish community had for years been aiming at a programme devoted to them and to the things that interested them. The BBC, at that time the only player in the broadcasting game, wasn't interested. As a sop to British Jews, it offered compliments, mainly on the lines that the community was so integrated into life in the UK that it didn't need a radio or TV programme, certainly not the way that the West Indian and the growing Asian groups, who had little command of English, did.

But Radio London, covering an area with by far the biggest Jewish conurbations in Britain, was different. It wanted a Jewish programme and had already had approaches. The *Jewish Chronicle*, for one, wanted to run a radio show and had already bought an antiquated tape machine to show their eagerness. Peter Redhouse, the ebullient station manager of Radio London, wasn't keen. The *Chronicle* already had a monopoly on Jewish communications and he wasn't about to let that increase.

Redhouse and I got on well – which was perhaps surprising considering the fact that he had not long before rejected a piece I had been commissioned to do for the Radio Four *Today* programme, which he was then editing. He had to come to our home 'town' of Elstree (geographically in Hertfordshire, although virtually a north-west London suburb) to give a talk and I filled him in on its being a good place to bring up children, close to a home for horses and only half an hour from the centre of London. I didn't tell him about Hartfield Avenue, where we lived in a newly built house (we bought it as a plot of land for what today would just about pay for a greenhouse) on an estate full of professionals who knew everyone else's business better than their own – which accounted for the amount of illicit sex being practised by a number of the residents.

We ourselves walked out of more than one party at which keys were exchanged for purposes unconnected with baby-sitting arrangements. It was also a place for rows (when the name of the then current TV series *Peyton Place* was invoked, most people in Elstree talked of Hartfield). I clearly recall the fight between my next-door neighbour and a man living down the road who complained about the woman's au pair hitting his child. 'I will decide who gives my children capital punishment,' he declared. It was a time when colour TV was becoming the fad. One woman knocked on our door to show that she had caught up. 'I'm watching BBC One,' she said. 'Can you tell me if it's in colour? I can't seem to get it.' But I got it all right. She was just letting us know she had bought a colour set.

What she also got was another au pair. Her little boy stopped Sara in our garden while her husband was blissfully mowing his lawn a few yards away. 'Auntie Sara,' said the 3-year-old, 'we've got a new au pair. Daddy went into her room last night and Mummy smacked him.'

We wouldn't talk about that on the radio, although the temptation would be tremendous. That was, if I decided to do the show.

Other Jewish broadcasters had got into the loop, but for various reasons had been rejected. I had made my first broadcast in October 1962 and had already done quite a lot of radio – mainly for the old south-east slots on Radio Four, in which I told stories like the tale of Bill Gowland and his industrial mission, about Gypsies and about the flooding of farm land, and on the BBC's *Woman's Hour* programme – on Carnaby Street and on Christmas cards (see, I was making full use of my contacts), on the care of the homeless, even on helping recidivist ex-prisoners (that was putting the Freedland imagination to extremes, although I did have friends who weren't so sure). But there were more important broadcasting milestones. I had done my first music documentary on Al Jolson – inevitably – on Radio Two. It could have been better, but I wanted more, and round about the time that all this came up I was working on a series on songwriters for the network. That was what I wanted to do – to write books and do radio shows about big stars and music makers.

That was the root of it. And then came a visit to the house in Elstree from the station's deputy editor. 'We want to do a Jewish programme,' he said. 'That's nice,' said I, thinking that there might be the odd contribution I'd like to make. I didn't think in terms of taking over the programme myself. I had never done anything like that. Of course, I knew I *could* do it, but there was that thing about *local* radio. And there was also something else: did I want to be known as a professional Jew? Absolutely not.

And yet there was another something tugging and nagging and almost persuading. I had a call from the Board of Deputies. 'Do you think you could come and talk to us about a Jewish programme?' No harm in talking, I thought. Peter Redhouse, an impressive man who had clearly been brought in from the *Today* programme to add gravitas to the London station, had already told me that he was hoping the Board would advise on the Jewish show. More than that, he hoped they would pay for it.

Going to the Board's headquarters at Woburn House, an office building that, inside, looked like a cross (if that isn't an infelicitous word to use in this context) between an Edwardian hospital and a condemned tenement building, was the first eye-opener. It was the first introduction I had to the people who believed they were running the Anglo-Jewish community – which, I would eventually realise, was not quite as true as they hoped.

The call came in the person of the chairman of the Board's Radio and TV Committee, a somewhat inhibiting man who would later become not just a member of the House of Lords, but also head of the firm of solicitors representing a galaxy of class-one (which means, not usually showbiz) celebrities ranging from poor Princess Diana to the disgraced peer Jeffrey Archer.

'Mr Freedland,' he said, 'would you kindly come to Woburn House at five o'clock on Tuesday evening?' Victor Mishcon, a former chairman of the old London County Council, was not a man you said 'No', to – as I quickly realised. But since I didn't want to do the job, I gave it very little advance thought.

So I presented myself at the boardroom of the Board, a repetition of words that struck me as funny at the time. The assembled dignitaries did not seem the sort of people I had come across very much in my life. For all my interest in Jewish affairs, I didn't know the people who ran the community. I had very recently become a deputy – a sort of MP in the Jewish parliament, which of course was nothing of the kind, but the synagogue had elected me as their representative and that was a reason to go to a plenary session. The first advantage, I realised, of running a Board programme would be that I wouldn't be required to go to another one.

The assemblage that Tuesday night were gathered around a big boardroom table, covered with green baize, which was probably exactly how it had been when the Victorian figures whose portraits hung behind the table were in power – men like the august Sir Moses Montefiore or the more recent Neville Laski QC (he had been there at the start of World War Two) and Barnett Janner MP, president in the sixties.

In the chair – and *what* a chair; more like a throne – was a man for whom I immediately developed considerable affection: Sir Samuel Fisher, former mayor of both Stoke Newington and Camden, chairman of the London Mayors Association, head of the Metropolitan Water Board, secretary of the London Diamond Bourse and one of those people who would take on a new job at the drop of his diary (in which he listed his appointments in tiny

handwriting that could have fitted on the back of a postage stamp).
Why, I wondered, didn't he do the Jewish programme himself?

He was so down-to-earth, so normal that he almost convinced me
that I *did* want to do the show after all. He assumed that I did and,
for once, I wasn't about to disabuse him of the notion. I was asked
all sorts of questions by him, by Mishcon, by a lovely old maiden
lady schoolmarm who rejoiced in the name of Trixie – Trixie
Barwell – and I got carried away. If I really did want this job, I knew
I had struck lucky. We were talking about tape-recording. I got
talking about actuality, the sounds behind the interviews that made
a piece seem lively and interesting. And then I said the words that
made these Jewish bigwigs lean forward and take note. 'You know,'
I said, 'even silence sounds different when you are in different
places.' I could feel the radiated satisfaction, the nods in my
direction and in the direction of their colleagues. It was like a bench
of magistrates considering a case and deciding on a guilty verdict. I
was about to be pronounced guilty of knowing my job and
sentenced to run a Jewish programme.

Victor Mischon rang me the following day. 'We'd like you to do
this,' he said. 'As a service to the community.' I said I wasn't sure.
'Well,' he replied in the considered tones of one who knew the way
the world spun, 'we wanted to get you before you were asked to do
a programme on Radio New York.' I was flattered and said 'Yes'.
Well, almost yes. I agreed to go to the offices of Victor Mishcon and
Co. in London's High Holborn and talk it over.

He sat in a big chair in a big office and I felt like one of the
minions of Benito Mussolini, who felt so intimidated by the time
they reached his desk at the end of dozens of feet of carpet that they
forgot what they were asking for in the first place. I, on the other
hand, still hadn't said yes. I wondered if Mr Mishcon felt
intimidated. It was not a thought that lasted long. We discussed the
programme and he liked what I said.

To me, a Jewish programme had to be...well, Jewish. But that
didn't mean it had to be parochial. This might be Radio London,
but I was convinced that Jews in the capital were more interested in
Jewish issues in South Africa than they were in those in Southend. I
think I said that Jews in Ilford weren't in the least concerned with
what was happening in Hendon and vice versa. I thought it had to
avoid the one factor that seemed to keep Jewish radio alive in

America – a hefty dose of schmaltz. As far as I was concerned, schmaltz had its place on the top of a saucepan of chicken soup and not on the air – besides which, in our household it had to come off the chicken soup, too.

I thought we ought to play Jewish music – a lot of it. But I'd only feature 'My Yiddisher Mama' when it was absolutely necessary. There was plenty of other very good, very Jewish music. I wanted to keep up with Jewish culture as well as Jewish news. But the programme would not aim to get news. I thought our job, to be realistic, would be to provide a background to that news. I said I believed that our programme should be a cross between the BBC Radio Four prime news slot, *The World At One*, and the then Radio One *Jimmy Young Show*, which was much more lighthearted at the time. Before long, it turned out that Jimmy Young would be more like us than we were like him.

'I like it, Mr Freedland,' said Mishcon, who then proceeded to tell me how much a candidate for the job (which I most certainly was not) wanted to be paid. I said it wouldn't be enough for me. 'Well,' said the worthy solicitor, who might have fitted very well into the seat of Mr Jaggers in *Great Expectations*, 'I think that perhaps, as I already said, you ought to regard it as a service to the community.' 'Fine,' said I, 'but if I do it, I'm not going to be able to afford such a donation.' We settled for £500 more – that is, if I finally did agree to do the programme.

He then asked me for lunch at the fairly swanky Europa Hotel, near the American Embassy in Grosvenor Square. 'So nice to see you again, Mr Freedland,' he said. 'Call me Michael, please,' I said. 'If you don't mind,' he answered, 'I'd rather call you "Mr Freedland."' It took me a little time before I realised the thinking behind the formality. If he called me 'Michael', I might be expected to call him 'Victor'.

'I hear you're doing the Jewish programme,' said Peter Redhouse when I next walked into the studios in a converted mansion in London's Hanover Square – a very good address. 'Very pleased. What are you going to call it?'

There were other Jews working at Radio London at the time and I called a meeting. Yes, I was going to take on the show. Yes, I would be very interested in any ideas anyone had. Nobody came up with anything worth considering. I remember 'Jews Is News' was one of the names suggested. 'Shouts a bit, doesn't it?' said Redhouse. Screamed, more likely, I thought.

It was then that I remembered a comedy record someone had given me a few months before – and a poster that was on all the hoardings in New York when I had last been there. It showed, on one, a Red Indian (sorry, Native American – we weren't quite so politically correct in 1971) or a Chinese gentleman placed in the middle of a slogan: 'You Don't Have To Be Jewish...to enjoy Levy's Rye Bread.'

'What about "You don't Have To Be Jewish?"' I said to Redhouse. 'Very good,' he replied. 'I like it. It means that the programme could be listened to with equal interest by non-Jews.' I thought that might be stretching things a bit, but it was my general idea. Convincing Mishcon, however, might be somewhat more difficult. This was a man, I figured, who lived in an ivory tower and would want something far more conventional.

We had another lunch at the Europa. 'Pleased to see you again, *Mr Freedland.*' 'Pleased to see you again, *Mr Mishcon.*' We ordered Dover sole, which usually can be certain to put me in a good frame of mind. It plainly had the same effect on him. It was a very affable lunch and Victor (sorry, *Mister*) Mishcon was turning out to be a very affable man.

I explained that I never ate meat when in a non-kosher restaurant. He said it was a rule that he (the son of a rabbi) used to follow... well, until his army service. Eating meat was much more usual then than now, when every restaurant has a large fish selection and, usually, a vegetarian dish of sorts. 'I never have,' I said. 'Well, I am afraid *I* have', he replied – and then, in an aside, added: 'Anyone overhearing our conversation will probably think we are talking about adultery.' We were on the same wavelength (highly appropriate when talking about radio) at last. And, yes, he liked the idea of *You Don't Have To Be Jewish.*

There now had to be very firm ground rules that I was prepared to lay out myself. The first were the thoughts I had already presented to Mishcon – yes to background to the news, to talks to cultural and political figures, yes to exciting Jewish music. But no to schmaltz (remember the scene in the political film *Primary Colours* in which the presidential candidate modelled on Bill Clinton goes on a Jewish show in Florida? Every time he wants to talk about international politics, the presenter asks: 'And tell me, who's your favourite actor?'). I also said no to parochial matters. To that, I added another: I wasn't going to talk to people just because they were Jewish. The *Jewish Chronicle* at the time used to go into paroxysms of ecstasy every time they discovered that a cameraman's great aunt had a Jewish grandfather (that, thanks be, doesn't happen any more). Someone suggested an interview with a Jewish policeman. Fine, I thought, providing he could tell a Jewish story – was he useful for the Met when it came to dealing with Jews? Did he suffer anti-Semitism? The answer was no to both. In fact, the only connection was that he was born Jewish himself and sometimes was known to go to synagogue.

Note that word 'synagogue'. Because we were aiming at a not exclusively Jewish audience or, indeed, even at Jews who didn't know much about Jewish life and culture, there would be no 'in' words. We wouldn't talk about 'shul'. When Pesach came around, it would be 'Passover'. I think I took that a little too far when it came to the test, but on the whole it would be right.

Peter Redhouse seemed to approve most of my plans. But, although, he didn't insist on it, he wanted as many London stories as possible. I delighted him fairly soon after starting operations by doing a piece about the old Mazek Hadas synagogue in London's Brick Lane, which had started out as a Huguenot church, and was now being converted into a mosque. That was a perfect Jewish and a perfect London story. But London didn't mean Edgware – unless, that is, there was a very good Edgware story. On the other hand, there was no reason why, when it came to it, we couldn't talk to an Edgware rabbi. When the Board of Deputies heard about my plans, they wanted assurances that I would talk to only Orthodox rabbis. No, I said. Not while I am doing the show. I might belong to an Orthodox synagogue myself, but I wasn't going to let it influence what I did on *You Don't Have To Be Jewish*. The programme had to be representative. There were more Orthodox Jews in London than any other kind and this might be reflected, but I wasn't going to exclude the thought that the Reform and Liberal communities might have interesting stories to tell.

There was only one stipulation that came from Redhouse – and this did give me pause. 'Please don't discuss Israel,' he said. He wasn't being anti-Zionist. He just thought it might bring a few problems. At the time, I didn't have the courage to fight him on this. The Anglo-Jewish community were pleased at the idea of having their first regular radio programme. The *JC* put it on its front page. 'Kol London,' the story was headed – 'Kol' being 'Voice', as in Kol Yisrael, the Voice of Israel. When it was all confirmed, the deputy editor, Joseph Finklestone (whom I had known since my early Luton days – we had once both attended a journalism weekend seminar at Cambridge) asked me: 'Are you going to call it "Kol London"?' I'm afraid I was pleased to tell him he had got it wrong.

The letters flooded in and, it appeared, they indicated a great deal of community support – and a great many people offering their services, most of them saying they would make very good presenters. I tried, delicately, to emphasise that that job was not available.

The support that I got was gratifying – not least of all from the Chief Rabbi, the then Dr Immanuel Jakobovits. Jakobovits was a brilliant man. You only had to stand next to him to realise that he was more than just a cut above every other rabbi in the community. None of them came close to him, not one had his bearing – or, probably, his brain power. His knowledge and the rabbinical authority that he represented were unparalleled.

We had known each other for about four years. Coincidentally, I had been in the congregation at the Fifth Avenue Synagogue in New York on my first visit to America, the congregation that he himself had established in 1958. On that Sabbath in June 1966, Sir Isaac Wolfson, the industrial and chainstore magnate who was president of Britain's principal Orthodox organisation, the United Synagogue, was there, too. It very soon became clear that he was at Fifth Avenue to offer Jakobovits the job of Chief Rabbi. Israel Brodie, the former Chief Rabbi, had recently retired and the United Synagogue had offered the job to Jacob Herzog, an Israeli diplomat, son of a former Chief Rabbi of the Jewish state and younger brother of Chaim Herzog, later the country's president. Herzog had become seriously ill (he died soon afterwards) and had resigned before taking office. Jakobovits, who had been one of the candidates before his appointment, was approached again.

Now he was playing hard to get – or so it seemed to those in the know. On that Sabbath, he took as his theme the notion that Moses did not believe it right for one man to set himself up above any other. I saw the then young (still in his forties) Rabbi Jakobovits at the synagogue two days later. He said he had no ambition to be Chief Rabbi.

It was at that point that a complicated courtship dance began. There was one other man in view, the former South African Chief Rabbi, Dr Louis Rabinowitz, an eminent, eloquent spiritual leader, born in Edinburgh, who had, nevertheless, blotted his copybook at the time of the struggle to establish a Jewish state. A man more than ten years Jakobovits's senior, he had served as a chaplain in World War Two and had an impeccable military record. But when the British started executing Jews in reprisal for the killing of their soldiers, Rabinowitz not only condemned the action, he tore off his medals and threw them to the floor. It might not have cost him the Chief Rabbinate – things had cooled down considerably by 1966 – but it put him in second place if Jakobovits was willing to leave his comfortable life in New York.

Eventually, Jakobovits said yes and Rabinowitz wrote him a letter declaring: 'The best man did not win.' The new Chief Rabbi, bristling with enthusiasm and energy, came to London to take up residence at Hamilton Terrace, St John's Wood. The day after his arrival, I called on him for an interview for the *World At One* programme. The house – 'I have had official residences for most of my adult life, but nothing as grand as this' – was still being decorated. His youngest daughter (there were six children) was still crawling, and the first bit of reorganisation had been to put guards on both ends of the stairs. We talked about his plans. He was going to put the unification of his community first. Brodie, a man plainly out of his depth, had for two years been at the centre of a religious-political storm which had developed into something close to a schism. He had outlawed the immensely respected and knowledgeable Rabbi Dr Louis Jacobs by preventing him from taking office as head of Anglo-Jewry's principal religious seminary, Jews' College. His aim was clearly to stop him becoming Chief Rabbi on Brodie's retirement. It was an event that caused pain, derision and a great deal of publicity both in the *JC*, which ran a concerted campaign on Jacobs's behalf, and in the national press.

Brodie was a man labouring under an inferiority complex, and it showed in his attitude to Jacobs. He spoke beautifully with an exquisite Oxford accent, was educated at Balliol, had been a rabbi in Australia and, as senior chaplain to the Forces, had also had a brilliant war record. When a new Chief Rabbi was appointed in 1948, those qualifications were considered more important than being a 'Talmud Chacham', a man so learned in the Talmud and other Jewish writings that he would be consulted by rabbis and laymen alike for religious judgments. And that was what rankled with him. When what became known as 'the Jacobs Affair' blew up in 1964, he considered this as his opportunity to show his mettle. He took the side of his ultra-Orthodox colleagues on the Chief Rabbi's court, the Beth Din, and condemned Jacobs, the man they considered to be a heretic. No longer could they doubt his religious knowledge and capabilities. Unfortunately, that was the step that tore Anglo-Jewry asunder and created the atmosphere in which Immanuel Jakobovits took office in 1967.

On the day that I called, he had already received visits from his lay leaders, pressing him to try to bring order back to the community. In fact, when I got there at about 10.30 in the morning, he told me he hadn't yet had time to 'daven', to say his morning prayers.

His own background was very impressive. Chief Rabbi of Ireland while still in his twenties, he had gone to America determined to preach all over the country, convincing lecture audiences that one could be both Orthodox and part of the twentieth century. He had written a number of books and had, at the age of 47, already become recognised as one of the leading authorities on Jewish medical ethics.

But he also had a reputation as something of an ultra-Orthodox obscurantist figure. In that interview with me, he said that Orthodoxy was totally compatible with everyday living. He also said that, while he would not be compromising his Orthodoxy, he wanted to meet people in all sections of the community, and he wanted to know the leaders of other faiths. Before long, he and the Archbishop of Canterbury, Michael Ramsey, were close friends – and he had invited Louis Jacobs to the house in Hamilton Terrace.

When *You Don't Have To Be Jewish* was announced, I interviewed him again. What struck me was the warmth of his enthusiasm and welcome for the programme. The *JC* didn't like what he said. For too long, he said, there had been a monopoly in Jewish communications: it was important for there to be competition. More important, though, was the fact that he had already begun to heal wounds. The obscurantist was so sure in his own faith that he had no worry about letting other rabbinic thinkers have their say – and their place in the community.

It was the beginning of a long friendship – one that had its difficulties, but which I always treasured. It was also the beginning of a close association between Sara and I and his wife, the attractive and effervescent Amélie. Born in Germany but raised in France, she loved most of all to be recognised as a good wife and mother – and for her *joie de vivre*. She scored highly on all three.

When Jakobovits took office, he said the first thing he was going to do was appoint a public relations adviser. What no one knew at the time was that he was already married to her – the rabbi's daughter to whom he had proposed at the top of the Eiffel Tower and who pulled him out of his rabbinical shell, as if using a pair of velvet-covered pincers. She became his hostess, but above all his conscience and his adviser.

Jakobovits always knew her value to him in his public life as in his private existence. He spoke in that first interview about the importance of family, which you only expected him to do, yet there was an air of sincerity that couldn't have been manufactured. He related that to a specifically private problem which he knew was at the bottom of a considerable communal difficulty. 'Unfortunately, I have had to leave my two sons behind in New York.' Was that what a loving family man would do?

As far as he was concerned, it was – because by doing so he was underlining an intense crisis. There was no Jewish school in London to which he would want to send a couple of intelligent teenagers, one that would not only give them a religious education of the standard that he demanded, but would also offer the kind of secular education that would fit them for the modern world.

His priority, pre-dating Tony Blair almost 30 years later, was going to be education – and then education and finally education. With that, he was setting in train the network of Jewish schools that is now the pride of the community – with an ever-expanding number of the places being founded in the early twenty-first century by men and women who themselves benefited from the Jakobovits education revolution and legacy.

# 12  Bored with the Board

Anglo-Jewry was in a strange time warp in the early 1970s. It was passionately in love with Israel. But it was a love affair that centred around the JIA, the Joint Israel Appeal, which on the eve of every Yom Kippur conducted appeals to raise money for the Jewish state. People gave generously. At the time of the Six Day War in 1967, they gave till it hurt. Men were known to sell their businesses and send their proceeds to Israel. Synagogues which had been painfully collecting for years to improve their buildings or put up complete new structures sent the whole lot to Tel Aviv. But once British Jews had put their hands in their pockets, that was it. They asked few questions about their faith or about the organisations that were promoting it.

There were no cultural organisations to speak of. Indeed, in one of the first editions of what we began to call *YDHTBJ*, I dared to say that the People of the Book bought so few books that the saying ought to be abandoned. I particularly wanted to bring the People of the Book to book.

There were still grandparents around who spoke with foreign accents – let alone rabbis – and that had a deep resonance for the community as a whole. It meant it had old ways. When it welcomed the arrival of Jewish radio, it did so in the old way. People wanted control, censorship. They weren't going to get it with me, and they certainly weren't going to get it with the BBC.

All this became apparent with that dinosaur, the Board of Deputies. Helping make *You Don't Have To Be Jewish* happen was perhaps the most constructive thing it had done in generations. When I was running the programme the most difficult question to ask was what the Board actually did. Answering the question was even harder. The truth of the matter was that the people who had money were the ones being courted, and they therefore regarded themselves as leaders of Anglo-Jewry. If there were representations to be made about Israel, it was they who went to the Foreign Office or to Downing Street. Certainly, there were occasions when the Board was received or was invited, but the idea that it was Anglo-Jewry's parliament was laughable.

I remember once asking one of the more intelligent Board members, June Jacobs, if she could foresee a time when a woman would become president of the organisation. Her answer was direct: 'I can't think of a reason why a woman would want to be president.' It took a quarter of a century before the impressive Jo Wagerman would find that reason, only to have her term of office cruelly curtailed by illness.

On the whole, the Board was run by self-serving nonentities who considered themselves more important than did anyone else. There were, of course, exceptions. Mishcon was one. Sammy Fisher was among the first men in years who added not just dignity to the office of president, but had a streak of common sense running through him that was all too often absent from the organisation's principal deliberations – deliberations which could more correctly be called petty squabbles inflamed by insane jealousies. Fisher ought to have been president earlier – and for longer. By the time he handed over the keys of office to his successor, he was already a sick man.

Yet even *he* had ideas that didn't fit in with the age in which men had already gone to the moon. Woburn House was nothing less than a disgrace. I was not the only one who begged for a move. The Board, despite its impotence, still managed to invite dignitaries to its meetings or to the special lunches that it held with increasing frequency. But, to Sammy Fisher, that was one very good reason to stay where they were. 'It's not good for the goyim to think Yiddin have so much money that they can afford luxurious premises,' he declared.

It was a view that went back to an all too obvious immigrant mentality. Those lunches, incidentally, were calculated to make or break friendships. Distinguished guests who survived the occasions were friends indeed. Diners (or rather lunchers) sat down at uncomfortable tables to a feast of a piece of lettuce, a slice of smoked salmon and an indifferently cooked sample of cold gefilte fish. I happened to be close to the door as the former Prime Minister Harold Macmillan was being escorted to his car after speaking about the value of the Jewish community to the nation. He did not look like a man who had never had it so good – and said so. 'Worst lunch I've ever had in my life,' he muttered as he was driven off to his club – where he probably sated his thirst, if not his appetite.

The attitude of the Board to *YDHTBJ* was better than I thought I had a right to expect. They thought it added prestige to the community – and hoped it might do the same for themselves. Members were convinced that I wouldn't be able to say 'no' when they offered their services as broadcasters. And so they didn't like it when 'no' I did say. They didn't like it either when I interviewed them and they were so bad that the results were unbroadcastable. That was something they couldn't understand – and more than one disappointed worthy wrote to the *JC* to complain about my cavalier attitude.

It could have been worse had Victor Mishcon not been around. I think he truly believed in what the Americans would have called the First Amendment to the Constitution – guaranteeing freedom of speech. It didn't figure in the Board of Deputies constitution, but Mishcon was not the sort of man you could easily argue with . His stentorian tones from the platform where he sat as a vice-president were enough to quell debates and arguments with which he didn't agree (which was why he constantly failed to be elected to the presidency; he would have made a distinguished representative of Anglo-Jewry). But he, too, wanted his pound of journalistic flesh.

He insisted on hearing the programmes before transmission. It was not a regimen that lasted for very long, and it didn't amount to censorship. When Mishcon made his regular trip to Hanover Square (and, bless him, it was quite a chore), he convinced me that he was just there to help, in case anything slipped in that I might not have realised was legally dangerous. Since newspapers employed their tame lawyers (although none was so distinguished) for much the same purpose, it was difficult to argue about it. Peter Redhouse saw the sense in that, or so he said. On the other hand, I was prepared to argue my corner and I don't ever remember being forced out of that little piece of Freedland territory.

At first, members of Mishcon's Radio and TV Committee – in truth, the Mishcon Committee, since no one ever quarrelled with him – were invited to join him on these expeditions. Fortunately, none of them ever did. There was the time, however, when the nonagenarian Reverend Isaac Livingstone, the former minister of the Golders Green Synagogue (in the days before Golders Green meant very, very Orthodox), one of only two Jewish clergy who still wore a dog collar, offered his services. It would have been nice to greet him with the words, 'Reverend Livingstone, I presume?' but Mishcon was able to spike his guns. 'Oh, Reverend Livingstone, I would so love to ask you to do this, but do you not think it would be very tiring for you?' That was the end of that.

Before long, Victor Mischon himself decided it was too much for him, too – or else he trusted me. 'Would you be so kind, Mr Freedland, to give my secretary a ring and tell her what you are planning this week?'

I was so kind and agreed. Occasionally, I let my sense of humour get the better of me. 'This week,' I told her once, 'I'm discussing Jewish property dealers.' I could feel her face growing red across the phone line. 'Oh, I don't think Mr Mishcon would like that very much,' she said. She was just about to go to tell him the terrible news when I told her not to worry – I wasn't going into the business of dragging the Jewish community into disrepute. Anyway, it was against the policy I had instigated of only covering distinct Jewish stories, not stories about people who happened to be Jews. (There might have been exceptions. Had a Jew become prime minister, I think I might have done something about it – except that I would have talked about the problems of a Jew having to choose bishops and asked questions like, 'Will there be a mezuzah [the metal box installed on the doorposts of Jewish houses containing the *Shemah*, the injunction recited thrice daily, "Hear O Israel, the Lord Our God, the Lord is One"] on the door of Ten Downing Street? Will the PM be having a seder there?').

By then I had come to realise what an asset Victor Mishcon (who still called me Mr Freedland) was to Anglo-Jewry, and how much I owed him.

Redhouse and his deputy, John Murray, were equally happy to leave me to my own devices, which I took as being as much a compliment as a gesture of trust. But there was still one instruction that continued to be handed down from above: you must not get involved in the Israel conflict. That amounted to ignoring Israel. It was a pity, but I didn't rail against that – at first. There was much else to talk about. I later realised that the relationship between diaspora Jews and the Jewish state was totally underestimated by the BBC management. Was it any different from the one that which existed between our other fellow countrymen and, say, Australia and New Zealand? The phrase 'kith and kin', which came into common usage at the time of the Falklands conflict, wouldn't be much heard of for the next decade.

The first programme we broadcast was, I now realise, quite a historic event. It was on 23 May 1971 that I introduced the show, in tones I would now like to expunge from human memory. (The BBC still liked clipped Oxford English, and I wanted to show that Jews could speak like that, too. My father used to tell of the fellow who got into an argument with a man who couldn't understand what he was saying. 'Don't you know the King's English?' he asked indignantly. The reply was a joy to students of the language's various interpretations. 'Of course I know the King's English.')

Tones apart, I can now concede that it wasn't at all bad. It was a time when *Fiddler on the Roof* was still running in the West End and was about to become a film. I chose its theme as our signature tune. As the first bars of Isaac Stern's opening violin tour de force faded (I became very good at fading) I announced: 'You don't have to be Jewish to recognise that as the music from the most successful musical of all time to have a Jewish flavour. Nor do you have to be Jewish to listen to and I hope enjoy the next 20 minutes, the first programme on BBC radio to be aimed at the Jewish community.'

That's all it was, 20 minutes, once a fortnight (before long, it would be broadcast weekly and for a half-hour, which later turned into an hour), but it was on a Sunday afternoon, then a great time to listen to the radio. When it was switched to a Sunday morning, things really started jumping.

We began with a 'vox pop' of London Jews, who answered the question, 'What do you want to hear on a Jewish radio programme?' The responses ranged from 'plenty of choral music' to 'I don't know why you want a Jewish programme at all. There are enough segregated programmes. But if you do have one, it'll have to last for about four hours every day because they'll never stop talking.'

In a way that young man – who I suspect was the son of the woman asking the question, Sylvia Margolis, and if it was, he became a senior BBC man himself – was right. There would never be a shortage of people who were willing to talk. Actually, I had got some idea of that fact just a few weeks before, when we had a kind of dry run for the programme. We went on the air one evening at about 8 p.m. and stayed talking – and listening – to people who rang up our Radio London number until well after midnight. On that occasion, we did talk about Israel and I'll always remember Rabbi Raymond Apple, then minister of the Hampstead Synagogue but shortly to return to his native Sidney, Australia, desperately trying to explain what would happen if and when the Messiah came. No, he said, He wouldn't have to ride a white horse.

We tried not to be so esoteric on the programme itself. That first Sunday in May – I liked the sound of that – I renewed my acquaintanceship with the comedian Jack Benny, who said that he loved Jewish jokes, but hated it when they were told by non-Jews. And then there was Leo Rosten, the writer of that evergreen manual, *The Joys of Yiddish*. 'A rich man stands in the synagogue and says, "I'm a nothing."' Next to him is a beggar. He, too, says, "I'm a nothing." The rich man looks his way and says, "Look who says he's a nothing!" And then there are the stories about shlemeils and shlemazels. 'A shlemazel is a man who buys a suit with two pairs of trousers and promptly burns a hole in his jacket.' Or, 'My father used to say, "Sleep quickly, we need the pillows."'

There were inevitably greetings from Victor Mishcon himself, who hoped it might bring the Jewish community in touch with their non-Jewish neighbours and that they might learn more about each other. He sounded good and I imagined that the community gave a sigh of pride as they heard him.

But how much did we know about ourselves? That was the theme of my talk with the Chief Rabbi once he had got over his welcome. What was his principal task? 'It is to bring the Chief Rabbinate into the twentieth century.' There were not a few who would have hoped it could be dragged into the nineteenth on the way.

He said he knew his office had to cope with 'a much wider diversity in Anglo-Jewry as against the situation of a hundred years ago, when this was a much more homogeneous community. To that extent, I think greater freedom of diversity of opinion will have to be provided for.'

That was good news for the community – and good news for *YDHTBJ*.

Spiritual leadership had to come by persuasion rather than authority. 'I intend to use persuasion rather than power and authority.' It was not easy to change things in this 'traditional, almost hidebound country'. There was good news for Anglo-Jewry – since taking office four years earlier, 'we have for the first time children chasing schools, rather than the other way around. All our schools have long waiting lists.' But school hours were longer, and his congregants didn't like what came next – 'People just don't work hard enough here.'

We would hear that again and again in the years to come, and very often on *You Don't Have To Be Jewish*. There were not enough rabbis – 'This is going to be a problem of alarming proportions. We may have to close down congregations in ten years simply because there aren't enough spiritual leaders.' (Years later, he said on the programme: 'We have to pay them more, if rabbis could assert themselves as "leaders".' In later editions, he would say: 'We don't pay them enough. If you pay peanuts, you'll only get monkeys.'

My reporter Marilyn Allen spoke to children about being Jewish – 'When a friend asks me if I like pork I have to say I don't know because I've never eaten pork,' lamented one 10-year-old.

Then there was the question of old people. We gave coverage to that marvellous organisation, the League of Jewish Women, who were constantly dealing with tragedies among old people. One of its leaders was willing to do what many of us thought of as the unthinkable – to say that the community didn't always look after its own and that, occasionally, they tolerated the same sort of neglect that constantly filled the nation's newspapers. She had just experienced finding an old lady literally frozen to death in her armchair ('She was so stiff, her bottom wasn't actually touching the chair. Nobody had been to see her.') That was a story that should have made a bigger impact. But we were inexperienced. In a later edition, we wouldn't be so choosy.

It was necessary, I made clear, to see both sides of the Jewish story. We were not going to act as a PR exercise for Anglo-Jewry. Nor, though, were we going to ignore the fun.

Jack Benny finished the programme by telling what he said was a true Jewish/black joke. 'Sammy Davis was staying in London at the Playboy Club when I was here last time. I rang him there and they said he had left word that he could be found at the White Elephant.

When I phoned him there, I said, "Sammy, there must be a hundred restaurants in London called the Black Elephant. You have to be at the *White* Elephant."'

Not long afterwards, Sammy Davis himself came on the air on *YDHTBJ*. He was Jewish, he said, because he loved Judaism. Israel? 'Next subject, please.'

Victor Mishcon rang up the day after transmission and said just one word. 'Congratulations.'

If Sammy Davis could say, 'Next subject, please', in truth it was always how I looked at things on the programme. Always thinking about what we were going to do next. In our second programme, we marked the festival of Shavuot – we played music by the London Jewish Male Choir and spoke to a Reform rabbi who was going to Eastern Europe. That business of Jews behind what was still the Iron Curtain would recur again and again to the point of it being a *YDHTBJ* campaign. But what was truly memorable in that second edition was the interview with Elie Wiesel, the philosopher-writer who had been snatched from death in Auschwitz and who had coined a word to describe what had happened to Jews in Europe between 1933 and 1945 – Holocaust. Words were what we talked about. Not just *that* word. 'One of the worst things about the Nazis was that they corrupted language,' he told me. 'When I think of "night", I think of night in the camps. When I think of "fog", I think of fog there.' He then joined another survivor, a London psychologist named Eugene Heimler. They compared notes, providing, as they did so, alternative attitudes to forgiveness. 'Elie,' he said, 'you have written a book called *Fog*. I wrote *Night of Fog*. You keep talking about it. I say it is necessary to stop.' 'I can't,' said Weisel. Few people were then talking about feeling guilty at surviving. What did he feel? 'Guilty,' he said. 'If I hadn't have survived, someone who died would have done in my place.'

I wouldn't have admitted it at the time, but, despite the plethora of volunteers to appear on the show, there was the worry of being able to fill up the time every programme. So much planning had gone into preparing the first edition, how could we keep it up? After all, there weren't many of us doing it. I did the interviewing, although there were occasional other contributors. The truth was I *wanted* to do the interviewing. I wanted it to be *my* programme. But it was hard work. I got to be quite a dab hand with the razor blade and white sticky tape – although occasionally people spoke without finishing words and sometimes without beginning them either. These days, it's much easier. Radio interviews are recorded on computers. If, in the course of editing, you chop off part of a word or part of a piece of music, you can get it back again. I wouldn't like to guess at the number of times I searched for a half inch of tape that had got sliced on to the floor, looking for half a word or a bit of chorus.

Anglo-Jewry was a strange, insular country in those final days of the twentieth century. It sent delegations to meet the great and the good, particularly those in Israel. It held conferences in the Jewish state, principally with the hope of being told how wonderful and important they themselves were.

I was in several of these delegations myself. I went to the home of the British ambassador in Tel Aviv with members of the Board of Deputies, an incongruous gathering of Jews who had been telling their Israeli friends that they were all the same people, but pretending for once on this visit to be as English as was the envoy. They wore blazers with regimental badges on the pockets and discussed cricket scores. The ambassador was host, but the 'guests' were trying to make him feel at home by, for once on the visit, feeling as foreign as he was.

It was an attitude that spilled over to the Israelis. Sometimes, they didn't say how much the Anglo-Jewish efforts and money were appreciated. In 1981 Teddy Kollick, mayor of Jerusalem, was quite rude when he told them that the only thing they had to offer Israel was themselves – or at least their children. 'Who do you think is going to save you if you have problems,' said Kollick in one spirited exchange, 'Mrs Thatcher?'

I was glad that he mentioned the children of those 1981 delegates. This was a group led by the magnificent Arieh Handler, one of the unsung heroes of the community – and one of its best brains, a banker who had escaped from his native Germany in the nick of time. For years in the late 1930s, he had been going backwards and forwards between Berlin and London as an emissary for B'nai Akiva, the religious Zionist youth movement. How he had managed to do that under the wide-open eyes of the Nazis was always a mystery, but it was an established fact that every time he came back to Britain he had a dozen or so children with him. After the war he was active in Zionist politics, and he became one of the few surviving witnesses of the creation of the state by David Ben Gurion in 1948.

He was someone to look up to on that visit. But there were few others you could say that about. One kippah-wearing 'leader' – not usually regarded as Orthodox and so dubbed by a member of the party as 'nouveau frum' – argued forcibly with Kolleck, using what he believed was his best elegant English, 'I don't wish to contravene your ears,' he declared solemnly. It is easy to be snobbish about such things, but the fact is he was not at all unusual and probably should not have been part of an official delegation, whose purpose was as much to impress as to be informed.

Fortunately, Chaim Herzog came round to the ambassador's residence and was in his best create-a-good-impression mood. He also wore a blazer.

Back home, British Jews tried to traverse what was sometimes a pretty shaky tightrope. But its very shakiness was rarely of their own making. In the late 1980s it was clear that Britain's black population, by now for long having beaten the Jews into second place in the numerical positions of the country's ethnic groups (and very soon to be heavily displaced by the Muslims, who had hardly figured at all 20 years earlier when the idea of a neighbourhood mosque was something out of a fantasy) were bearing the brunt of anti-immigrant prejudice.

The National Front, in those pre-British National Party days, was virtually ignoring the Jews – although its leader at the time, Geoffrey Tindall, in an interview with me for an *Evening Standard* piece, did ask the pointed question: 'Did you know that the Jews even have their own radio programme?'

It struck me that the black, originally West Indian, population were precisely where Jews had been 80 or 90 years before. Jews stood up for other minorities and were willing, indeed happy, to advise and, more importantly, to help.

I thought it was something that we should broadcast, indeed shout from the rooftops. And I thought I knew just the way to do it. Radio London at the time was broadcasting a very successful series called 'Black Londoners'. We used to follow each other around the Thursday evening schedules. Its presenter, Alex Pascall, was a charming, intelligent friend who ran the famous Notting Hill carnivals in August, a wonderful demonstration of ethnic pride. He also invited me to his Rotary Club.

I suggested that he come on *YDHTBJ* to discuss similarities between our two communities. Within five minutes it became clear – there weren't any. Pascall tried to be kind. 'We both had the immigrant experience,' I remember his saying. 'But unfortunately we have little in common. You are organised differently and much more successfully. You are better educated than most of our people are.' And then he said the words I had hoped he would not say: 'You are much better off than we are.'

He didn't say all Jews are rich, but I am afraid that was what I believed he was saying. He didn't make things any easier for my proposed dialogue (which I believed then and still believe would be useful) when he said, 'You see, Michael, it is all a question of class.' Perhaps it was an indication of how established Jews were. That moment apart, I don't believe the issue of class cropped up in a single programme during the 23 years of our existence.

Sometimes I floundered looking for a reason to do a broadcast or to record a particular subject, but not often. More than once there were programmes that caused a degree of embarrassment – not because I didn't think we did them well (there *were* those, of course) but because we got into tussles that had no place in that sort of programme at that time of day. There were Jews who didn't like to be called Jews and got us into knots that were difficult to unravel, simply because a single item in a 20-minute programme wasn't enough to get to grips with an issue. Later, I devised the single-subject show and that provided a lot more scope. Sometimes, though, we discussed intimate matters that I was glad we had the guts to deal with, although I'm sure they made my mother blush. For instance, the time that agony aunt Claire Rayner came and talked about the role of women in the community. Fine. Great idea, I thought. Except that she and another contributor, a lady who rejoiced in the name of Regina Dollar, got close to scratching each other's eyes out – over sex.

Now, as virtually everyone in Britain still knows, Mrs Rayner is a doughty woman who is not easily upset. But on this occasion, Mrs Dollar struck a chord, and the tough Claire took it over and played every minim and crochet like a concert pianist who discovers his stool on fire in the middle of a concerto.

Somehow, Regina had got on to the subject of menstruation and said something like, 'Of course, no Jewish woman would indulge in sex during this time.'

Claire thought that this was the most obscene thing she had ever heard, and proceeded to demolish the argument to the point of providing Radio London with the most lively debate it had yet heard (there would be others, courtesy of *YDHTBJ*). 'What a lot of rot,' said this ex-nurse who now spent most of the time she wasn't answering pleas from the lovelorn in *Woman* magazine, writing romantic novels ('except Fridays when I'm chopping liver like everyone else'). 'You are crazy. It's ridiculous. Does no harm at all.'

What I do regret is taking aboard certain suggestions that I wasn't keen about in the first place. Sylvia Margolis had suggested a series called 'Some of my best friends'. Since that sentence usually went on '...are Jewish' it gave a totally wrong impression of what we wanted to do. I kept emphasising that the programme was not to be regarded as a PR exercise for the community, but that was not, either, the sort of connotation I wanted on *YDHTBJ*.

Nevertheless, some of those items revealed absolute gems – not least the time it featured the then extremely well-known (and now forgotten, which gives some idea how long ago the 1970s were) Lord Greenwood, the former Labour minister Anthony Greenwood, scion of a deeply committed socialist Christian family and son of Arthur Greenwood, one of the first men to sit in a Labour cabinet. Greenwood had been an MP for Leeds, the city which at the time had the biggest proportion of Jews in its population in Britain. As their MP he once accompanied a party of constituents on a mission to Israel. One lady, he told me, asked: 'Tell me, Mr Greenwood, what was your name before you changed it?'

I liked to think that no Jewish celebrity (who had a Jewish story to tell, that is) who visited London from abroad escaped my clutches. Two of the most memorable were a pair of opera-singing brothers-in-law who hated each other, Richard Tucker and Jan Peerce. They studiously avoided mentioning each other, but gave a marvellous insight into the changing worlds of cantorial singing, since they were both part-time cantors. It also gave us a marvellous opportunity to play their music. Tucker said he wouldn't dream of combining the two kinds of music, either on the stage or at the synagogue. Peerce said he thought they could aid each other. Years later, David (Dudu) Fisher, who was a cantor and who would star in both the Broadway and London productions of *Les Misérables* (wearing his *kippar* at the Royal Variety Performance), told me that he very much combined the two.

Israel, as a party in the Middle East dispute, might be beyond our terms of reference, but occasionally it had to come up in discussions. There could be no gainsaying that fact, although it took time to become a regular part of the menu. In 1972, there could be no doubt that we just *had* to discuss the country. The Olympic Games in Munich had been the scene of the murder of 11 Israeli athletes by members of Yasser Arafat's PLO. To the disgust of probably every listener to *You Don't Have To Be Jewish* and to Jews everywhere, the organisers suspended the games, arranged for all the participants to stand in silent tribute – and then continued as if nothing had happened. This was a matter that had to be covered – simply because it was an intensely Jewish issue, not just an Israeli (or even an Arab) one.

I struck lucky with this, if anything could be held to be lucky when innocent people are murdered. I discovered the existence of a remarkable 80-year-old man named Herbert Saltzbach. He was a German-born Jew, living in London, who was still a German – more than that, a German diplomat, working at what was then the West German Embassy in Belgravia. As cultural attaché at the embassy, his principal task, as he saw it himself, was reconciliation. I asked him how he felt. 'Horrified,' said this man who had been a Prussian officer in World War One and a British army captain in World War Two. 'I feel discouraged, hardly able to express my personal feelings. It is absolute despair. It happened in Munich, happened in Germany. Once again, people will blame Germany.'

Robert Rietti, an actor who has devoted much of his professional and personal life to Jewish causes, used to end most editions of *YDHTBJ* with a quotation from the Talmud. The Munich massacre happened a few days before Yom Kippur, the most sacred day in the Jewish year. 'What will be my thoughts on this holy day?' he asked. 'That my people gave the world its greatest law and that just a few days ago, 11 of my people were gunned down.' It was one of the most moving renditions I had heard before or have heard since, and I would love for someone to include it in a High Festivals anthology. That a man with such thoughts and such talent to express them could do so on the programme, I liked to think, said a great deal for the standing it was developing. The whole sequence incidentally ended with the singing of Kol Nidre, the declaration at the start of the fast, by Simon Hass, a regular on the show whom I dubbed 'the prince of cantors'. It was no more than the truth.

Anglo-Jewry was, naturally, horrified and unified in their hatred for the perpetrators of that heinous crime in Munich. But there was another side to the whole matter, and I was glad to provide the opportunity for that other side to be given some kind of expression. Once again, the Chief Rabbi pulled no punches. Yes, of course, he mourned the victims and wanted the murderers brought to justice, but another question had to be asked: what were the Israelis doing there in the first place?

It was partly a question of what were they doing in Munich, but much more a question of whether Jews should be participating in an event that celebrated Helennistic ideals, so contrary to those of Judaism. Jews had given their lives rather than be sucked into such an alien tradition. 'Did you not feel a sense of pride at seeing the Magen David [the Star or Shield of David] flying among the banners and flags of the world?' I asked. 'No, I did not,' he said.

No one had raised that issue before. It was not my view, but I was glad that I had the opportunity to present it. Immanuel Jakobovits was once more proving that he had deeply held views, opinions to which he would stick like some kind of superglue, and it was my duty to give him an opportunity to express them.

Likewise, it was our duty to demonstrate all strands of Jewish opinion. The people who wanted to make sure that only Orthodox rabbis got a hearing on *YDHTBJ* were to be bitterly disappointed. Right from the beginning, the Reform and Liberal movements told me of their plans and developments and, if it was merited, those plans and developments would be discussed. There were frequent rabbinical 'spots' talking about ideas or events from a religious standpoint, and it is probably fair to say that they got their representations commensurate with their size in the community, as did the ultra-Orthodox Lubavich group, whom I found amazingly resilient and wanting to grab at every modern means of communicating their message – to wherever there were Jews. It is no coincidence that tiny communities in Britain as well as in virtually every other country have Lubavich rabbis looking after their needs.

(Jakobovits wasn't so pleased about that. He once told me, 'the ultra-Orthodox sects are the ones who really care, who provide rabbis and could end up the largest section of the community. But who will administer our administrations? Who will govern Israel?)

From the beginning Rabbi Feivish Vogel invited me to his headquarters at Stamford Hill in the heart of Orthodox North London and offered all the help and co-operation he could give. We had many a fascinating talk both on air and in private.

Similarly, there was an invitation to the Reform movement's 'cathedral synagogue' at Upper Berkeley Street near Marble Arch. Assistant Rabbi Michael Goulston wanted to put forward some ideas and I was glad to give him an opportunity to talk about Reform Judaism and its attitudes to contemporary issues. It could have been the beginning of a long friendship, except that very soon afterwards he phoned me at home from a hospital bed. He was ill, but neither he nor any of his doctors knew what was wrong. Before long, he was dead.

They were a remarkable, articulate bunch, those Reform rabbis. Some of them were a little too intellectual for the tastes of a Sunday morning radio audience, but it didn't take long to identify the ones who were the brilliant broadcasters. Dow Marmur of the synagogue in Golders Green was a Polish-born Danish citizen who eventually would go to Canada, but while here he was a regular on the air. So was his successor at Alyth Gardens, Charles Emanuel, a chatty American whom I still like enormously. But the gift that the Reform community had to offer to the rest of Anglo-Jewry and to my audiences was the man everyone knew simply as Hugo.

# 13   Hugo – and others

Rabbi Hugo Gryn was to become one of my dearest friends. As the senior rabbi at Upper Berkeley Street, he had a reputation as a preacher of sincerity and great talent. As a friend he was a man who carried love in his coat pocket, ready for whenever it was needed. He didn't give love, he showered it. As a broadcaster, he was a brilliant find that others would later discover.

Quite early on, he would come on the air at the time of a Jewish holyday and speak on the significance of the occasion – colouring the interview with music, sometimes cantorial, sometimes Chassidic, sometimes Israeli. He was always meticulously prepared, with a set of cards to help him along a trail that he had begun for himself. Never, though, did he really need those notes. Despite what may have been said in later years (a story that will develop as this tale proceeds) he knew his Judaism with every fibre of his body. Even the then Dr Jakobovits told me that he only wished Hugo had not chosen to be a Reform Jew, as he would have made a great Chief Rabbi once he himself retired.

When he spoke about the festivals, he talked not as a Reform Jew, but as a Jew. What not enough listeners recognised was that he never took a Progressive approach to Judaism. No one could quarrel with anything he said about his faith. He may have preached Reform, but he broadcast traditional. Yet he gave unusual slants on those traditions. For him, the Day of Atonement was the occasion of Jewish unity – 'the Day of At-One-Ment'. He also needed to explain the drowning of the Egyptians as recalled on the Passover seder. The salt water into which we dip bitter herbs at the seder didn't represent the sea in which the Egyptians perished. More, it signified – as stated in the mishnah – the tears of God that his own children were dying.

There was another point about him: as Sara has often said, when you met him, he made you yourself feel wise. That was a marvellous gift. He was an intellectual who, unlike most of his colleagues who liked to boast of their intellects, tried to hide the fact. He spoke as a human being to other human beings.

I will always remember the time I went to his office at Upper Berkeley Street, waiting for him to come into the room while he spoke to his secretary outside. There was a certificate hanging on the wall, the one that showed he had achieved a doctorate of divinity. 'Hugo,' I said when he came into the room and ordered us each a cup of coffee before deciding where we should go for lunch, 'I didn't know you had a doctorate.' Unlike colleagues who could call themselves 'Rabbi Dr', Hugo never did.

He smiled. 'Actually,' he said, 'I've got three. But I'll tell you a story. I had just been granted my first doctorate at the Hebrew Union College in Cincinnati, sat at my desk and waited for the phone to ring. Eventually, it did. 'Dr Gryn here,' I said. "Oh yes," said the voice, "this is Rabbi X." That man had five or six doctorates, but the title 'rabbi' was more important. That was the one and only time I ever used that title.'

But he could always claim the title of good broadcaster, as could numerous other rabbis. Perhaps the best of the Orthodox bunch were two Scots, both of whom had served not just their congregations, but one congregant in particular – me. Rabbi Alan Plancey at the Elstree and Boreham Wood Synagogue had the gift of switching from a serious subject to his own brand of humour at just the right moment and almost seamlessly. He could also play the bagpipes – and had learned how to address a radio audience as though he were speaking to his wife (since I knew his wife, I think that was a reasonable comparison). It was something that Rabbi Cyril Harris picked up easily, too. Cyril was the very young 'Reverend' in the pulpit of the Kenton Synagogue on the first Shabbat of our married life. I know I came home that day to my chicken soup revealing my certainty that I had just witnessed the next Chief Rabbi but one. He was the most beguiling preacher I had heard. I stuck by my forecast for about 30 years – and was almost proved right. He was for a time candidate to succeed Immanuel Jakobovits but settled for the job of Chief Rabbi of South Africa, where he was to be an immense success, not just in his own community, but with Nelson Mandela and his ministers, too. Listening to him on *You Don't Have To Be Jewish* was always one of the joys of tuning in. (He was kind enough to say in his own memoirs that he learned his broadcasting skills on *YDHTBJ*).

There were other gentlemen of the Jewish cloth (gabardine?) who were, shall we say, not quite so good. Like the rabbi who couldn't get used to the idea that he was sitting in a small room in front of a microphone. He wanted to preach and he was used to standing in a marble pulpit – and throwing his arms around, which wasn't as bad as the way he threw his body around. The mike picked up, on a rough estimate, only one word in three, but since the other two words weren't terribly interesting, I kindly said thank you and allowed him to take his bowler hat and walk out with a smile on his face.

I was pleased to say that I took to most of the ministers of religion who came on the air. There was one, however, whom I could have done without. This was a newly appointed rabbi to a London congregation who had come from America to begin a new life (I always wondered what could be better for a rabbi in London than in America, but let that pass – or rather he let it pass when I asked him). 'You know,' I said, 'I have a very good relationship with most of the rabbis I know and we like to use first names with each other. 'OK,' he said, 'that's very good. My first name is "Rabbi".' It was the last time he appeared on the show.

Hugo (Rabbi Dr Hugo Gryn, that is) would have told him where to get off. He knew how to deal with people. On both sides of the Jewish–Christian divide. I always hoped that he listened to an interview I did with the Reverend Lord Soper, probably the most eminent Methodist in Britain, a brilliant broadcaster, a leading socialist and a man whom I had met before and admired for his stand on so many of the issues of the day. He had known my old pal Bill Gowland, which was a good starting point.

The last time he appeared on *YDHTBJ* was in the mid-1990s, when the big issue of the day in Anglo-Jewry was the question of the eruv (the notional fence around an area which allowed Orthodox Jews to carry on Shabbat or to wheel pushchairs) that was still just being talked about in north-west London. Soper, one of those Socialists who lived in plush Hampstead Garden Suburb, was one of the eruv's most vociferous opponents. Why? I asked him. Simply, he told me, because it was divisive. Jews should not try to inflict their religion on other citizens living near them. They should do their worshipping in their synagogues.

For the sake of fairness, quite apart from my own religious sensitivities, I railed at this. 'How can you say that, Lord Soper?' I asked. 'You're a man who made your reputation preaching from a soap box in Tower Hill. Why should you be allowed to do this in the open air and Orthodox Jews not allowed similar rights – except that they are not asking to be able to preach in the open air, just to put a few yards of wire on poles which almost no one will see?'

He wasn't expecting this, and floundered. 'It's very different,' he mumbled, but probably for the first time in his life had no real answer. That was when I brought in my heavy artillery. 'The founder of your faith, John Wesley,' I reminded him, 'established his ministry by preaching in the open air all over the country. He wanted to convert people. Are you suggesting that people looking at that wire will suddenly decide to stop being Methodists and instead become Jewish?' That was the point at which our conversation ended. I don't think he expected that on a programme called *You Don't Have To Be Jewish*.

It did remind me, however, of one of the several visits to *YDHTBJ* of one of my favourite comedians, George Burns. 'There was a Presbyterian church near where we lived,' he told me. 'How a Presbyterian church got into our New York neighbourhood, I'll never know. But I heard that they were giving Ingersol watches to boys who sang in their choir, so my pals in the Pee Wee Quartet and I decided to give it a try. Next day, my mother was hanging out the wash. I told her I didn't want to be a Jew any more. "I've been a Jew for eight years and got nothing. I was a Presbyterian for one night and got an Ingersol watch." My mother said nothing but "Help me hang out the wash." As I did, water got into the Ingersol watch, the watch stopped – and I became a Jew again.'

That was an exercise in how not to handle inter-faith relations if ever I heard one. Hugo Gryn had better ideas. Indeed, much of Hugo's work was in that field. But what about meetings of Jews and Jews? That would linger for years. Eventually, as we shall see, Hugo himself became part of a huge row centred around that issue and one that was initiated, unwittingly, by *YDHTBJ*. But it was a long time coming. In an early meeting with Chief Rabbi Jakobovits, I suggested that he have a discussion with a Reform or Liberal rabbi.

It had never happened and, I had to concede, would be unlikely ever to take place. 'That would be very difficult,' he said. 'There is the question of status.' He said that the United Synagogue, which was his principal employer, would be unlikely to sanction it. Actually, I think that he himself didn't want to give a sense of equality to any other rabbi. There was also, of course, the fact that the Orthodox community were very jealous of any suggestion that Reform or Liberal Judaism were in any way equally acceptable.

'So,' I suggested, 'what about a Christian clergyman? The Archbishop of Canterbury, for instance?' I saw his face brighten. He stroked his beard. 'Yes,' he said, 'that might be easier.'

Easier it was indeed. Thus on 27 February 1972, the Right Reverend Michael Ramsey came to the Radio London building to discuss the differences between Christianity and Judaism. 'I am well aware of the common heritage that we have,' said Ramsey. 'We share the Old Testament and the Prophets. Where we differ is that we have Jesus Christ, and I am well aware that Jews do not share our belief.' He and the Chief Rabbi hit it off like a couple of diplomats in an amazingly friendly session of the UN. Jakobovits told the Archbishop that Jews and Christians had a very different approach to their beliefs. 'Ours is not so much a faith as a way of life. We are governed by a series of dos and don'ts, of commandments that control all our lives.'

Very interesting. But what was really exciting about that meeting was the part not heard by the audience. I waited for the two eminent gentlemen at the Radio London entrance. Standing to attention next to me by the huge glass doors was a BBC commissionaire wearing what I took to be his ceremonial uniform. The Chief Rabbi arrived first in a spanking new Rover (it still was a prestigious marque). The Archbishop, with a shock of white hair and eyebrows so long I wondered if they affected his sight, came next – in a rather battered blue Morris Minor.

As he entered, seemingly dispensing blessings on the way, the commissionaire opened the door for him and gave a Boy Scout salute. He hesitated as he closed the door behind him and then said: 'Good afternoon... Your... er... er... Your Arch.'

Of course, *I* got it right. I knew to call him 'Your Grace', although it became 'Archbishop' as the programme proceeded. I was pleased that we were able to initiate that example of inter-faith relations –

an exercise I repeated three years later with Ramsey's successor as Archbishop, Dr Donald Coggan. Coggan, I pointed out, was well known for his evangelism within his own faith. But what about efforts to convert Jews?

'I sometimes hold my head in shame as I think of what Christians did to convert Jews,' he said. What was nice about this man, who looked much more of this world than his delightful predecessor, was that he had learned Hebrew and was able to say a few words to Jakobovits. I asked him for a message to our listeners. 'Well,' he said, 'I think the best word would be "shalom".'

It was, of course, a word used a great deal in our programmes. Not least when Archbishop Robert Runcie came to talk about the Lambeth medal he was presenting to the then Sir Immanuel Jakobovits or when his successor George Carey, ten years later, discussed the world with the next Chief Rabbi, Jonathan Sacks. He liked it so much that he said he wanted to repeat the experience. He, too, used the word 'shalom'.

# 14  *Who* is *a Jew, anyway?*

It wouldn't be true to say that the question 'Who is a Jew?' dominated the Anglo–Jewish scene, but it was one that cropped up from time to time – especially when the community's religious establishment battled on the matter, Reform and Liberal rabbis saying that conversion should be made more accessible, if not easier. Hugo Gryn maintained that Jews, of all people, should be in a position to welcome newcomers and so add to their numbers, rather than turn people away. 'It is not exactly kind,' he said. On the other hand, he wouldn't allow the suggestion that his synagogues should be a 'wastebasket' for those prospective proselytes who had been rejected by an Orthodox Beth Din. The Reformers – and the Liberals – still demanded periods of instruction for converts, and in some cases could be pretty rigorous.

One of the most moving experiences during all the time that the programme ran was an interview with Geoffrey Wigoder, the Orthodox editor of the *Enclyclopaedia Judaica*, and his wife Devorah. She had been converted from Catholicism by the first Chief Rabbi of modern Palestine, Rav Kook, and was later married to Geoffrey by him. She had a brother who was a priest and a sister who was a nun. Later she wrote a moving book about her experiences – which she dedicated to 'One of the Six Million whom I have tried to replace'.

I found that a lot more heartening than the stories I broadcast and wrote about the very rich people – including members of the Rothschild clan – who went to Israel for a 'quickie conversion' and subsequent wedding conducted by a rabbi whose price might have been a little more than a mere guarantee that the converted spouse would lead a 'Jewish life'.

The problem with that requirement was that very few Jews accepted as 'hallachically sound' were themselves living that sort of 'Jewish life', eating only kosher food and keeping the Sabbath and festivals, and yet converts were expected to live in strictly, if not ultra-Orthodox, homes for months (and sometimes) years on end. Nevertheless, I met some of those people who did go through the arduous process and, one by one, declared themselves to have 'finally come home'. One is now a synagogue warden.

Jewish tradition does declare that, once accepted, a convert should be treated just as any other member of the faith. Yet it is sometimes hard to accept that adults with no Jewish adherence whatever who discover that there was an unbroken female line since the time of a Jewish great-great-grandmother can be accepted and allowed to marry in an Orthodox synagogue, while one who always considered him or herself Jewish, but whose parents had a suspect marriage certificate, can be banned from standing under the chuppah marriage canopy.

I remember a real cat being thrust among the pigeons when the daughter of Holocaust survivors was at first unable to have an Orthodox wedding because her parents were unable to produce that very certificate, or *katubah*. I made a vituperative comment on the programme about the only documentation that they could offer being the number tattooed on the bride's parents' arms. Chief Rabbi Jakobovits rang me angrily, asking if I knew the efforts his office made, travelling from one end of the world to the other, to help establish a bride's or bridegroom's bona fides. I said that of course I did. Within two days, he had granted his approval for the wedding.

Sometimes, whole communities needed that kind of sanction. None more so than the Jews of Ethiopia, who in the early years of the twentieth century did, in fact, get recognition, even though until recently they were known as 'Falashahs', roughly translated as 'exiles' – in other words, with no real home until they were allowed to emigrate to Israel. They remain one of Jewry's exotic communities, now fully accepted as Jews, even though they have no more DNA similarities with me or my family than do a tribe of Gypsies who might have strayed into Outer Mongolia. They totally demonstrate my objections to the use of the phrase 'Jewish race'. We are, however, all part of the Jewish people.

Because of their exotic status in the world Jewish community, they have become the subject of numerous books – one of the best by the late *Jewish Chronicle* proprietor, David Kessler. Kessler came into the Radio London studio to publicise the book and unwittingly created one of those incidents that are not easily forgotten.

'Michael,' announced the cockney sparrow receptionist at the Marylebone High Street front office desk, 'there's a geezer here who wants to talk to you about the book he's just written and I don't think it's very nice [which she pronounced 'noice']. It's all about flashers. I don't suppose you want to talk to him.'

Actually, I did want to talk to him and it turned out to be a memorable chat about a people who have mostly gone to live in Israel, taking their culture with them – and, alas, bringing out the sort of prejudices one would have hoped a Jewish state would never have known.

There were other newcomers whom Jews in Britain were more pleased to welcome.

By the early 1950s the McCarthy era in Hollywood had reached its nadir. Careers were destroyed and lives lost as a result of the relentless probings of the junior senator from Wisconsin. It was described as a fight – when it was not dubbed a battle or a crusade – by McCarthy's henchman Martin Dies.

What became very clear to me for the first time, and to most of our listeners, too, was that it was as much an anti-Semitic fight as an anti-communist one. We got to hear from Carl Foreman, the writer of that classic World War Two epic *Bridge On The River Kwai*, how the Oscar for that movie went not to him, but to a mysterious man named Michael Wilson, who plainly didn't exist. He told us about the tragedy and how Britain had offered him a home.

Larry Adler became the fount of all wisdom on the issue. We talked about his arguments with Isaac Stern about playing his mouth organ in Germany. 'I believe that music should be a way of getting people together, not driving them apart,' he said. And then he remembered playing for a group of survivors of the Belsen concentration camp – and of the tears running down his cheek as he played a selection of Yiddish melodies. 'Play "Belz",' said one emaciated inmate of the camp, overwhelmed by the first opportunity in five years to hear a tune from his *shtetl*.

Adler had never been a party member, but knew he was about to be blacklisted. He came to England, wrote the theme for *Genevieve*, one of Britain's most delightful post-war movies, and heard that the music had been nominated for that coveted Academy Award. Except that the nomination certificate had gone not to him but to the musical director, Miles Mallison. 'I was delighted when I heard that it hadn't won,' he told me on the air. Subsequent programmes revealed details of the anti-Semitic demons in the whole process of clearing Hollywood of its supposed reds.

It was a time when Jews in Britain were still feeling sensitive about suggestions that they themselves had communist links. Quite amazing to think that, now when anything goes. I remember doing a programme about the old Jewish East End. My uncle, Mick Mindel, who had been head of the old Jewish ladies tailors' union, came on with a group of other veterans of the area around Aldgate Pump to discuss those days and inevitably we talked about his time as a member of the Communist Party. The number of protests amazed me. Later, when the former Jewish communist MP Phil Piratin came on, the postbag was huge.

In a later series for BBC Radio Two, I was able to go into much more detail about the McCarthy era. The case of David Raksin was one example. Unlike Adler, Raksin, the composer of the theme music for *Laura*, the only example of a film score being more famous than the picture itself, *was* a member of the party. 'I didn't work for two years and had a family to bring up – with no money left. I had to borrow what I could. Then one day a producer asked me to write the music for a new film. I was delighted and worked on it for a week. Then I had a phone call from that producer. He told me that his boss, Howard Hughes, had heard of my appointment and said that if he didn't fire me, the producer himself would lose his job.'

I talked to several Hollywood Jews about the whole issue. The writer Sidney Sheldon burst into tears when he spoke of the friends whose lives were destroyed by the Dies committee. The last survivor of the Big Band era, Artie Shaw, talked about how he was barred from his radio programme because he had been accused of being a fellow traveller. 'They asked me if I had joined a peace committee, which they said was a communist organisation. I said that if they could find me a Republican peace committee, I'd join that.'

As usual when face to face with a Hollywood personality – Shaw had put down the clarinet, which he had played so beautifully, in

1954, and had not picked it up since, although he did show me the instrument in its worn red-lined case – I talked about himself as a Jew and about Jews in music. He was not happy about that. 'What the hell difference does it make whether a man is a Jew or not? And what is Jewish music? No such thing.'

I wasn't about to argue with him, since there had been so many others in his profession to challenge that assumption. So we talked about that other great Jewish clarinet player, Benny Goodman. 'Benny once got me involved in a deep conversation about our clarinets and who could get most out of the instrument. I told him, "Benny, don't you ever want to talk about music?"'

It was fairly obvious that Mr Goodman was not the favourite of many others in his business. André Previn played with him once. He and a group of other musicians were taken to a cellar in Goodman's house. 'It was very cold there, and I told Goodman that. "Yes, I suppose it is cold," he said, and went away, we hoped to do something about the heating. No, he came back wearing a sweater.' Which might, I suppose, go under the heading of Jewish humour. I'd already had plenty of that – and so had the programme.

There were always the funny moments – like the matchmaker Heidi Fischer promising me a special deal for my children after I had given her a few minutes on the programme. I told her that was not why she was given time and that, fortunately, my children weren't in need of her services. But it gave us a great opportunity to play 'Matchmaker, Matchmaker' from my favourite show, *Fiddler on the Roof*.

Perhaps I should have taken advantage of Bernice Weston's offer of free membership of Weightwatchers. Sara undoubtedly thought so, but the integrity of my position as a broadcaster wouldn't have allowed it. (An offer from the man in charge of Rolls-Royce or Rolex watches would have received similar short shrift – well, I like to think so.) But Bernice, a New Yorker through and through, was great value. She is a natural comedienne and offered a score of stand-up jokes that would have won her an engagement in the Catskill Mountains Borscht Belt whenever she wanted one. Her topic: Jews and food.

There was, for instance, the story of the Jew who, bearing all the signs of being a victim of Mob violence of the kind that should never happen to a nice Jewish boy, falls into his mother's front hallway after the old lady opens her door to the blood-saturated figure. He has barely mouthed the word, 'Mama' before she tells him: 'First you eat, then you talk.'

Or the Brooklyn-born soldier newly enrolled in the US army who for the first time experiences gentile food. 'Mama,' he writes, 'I don't know what to do – the fire has gone out.'

I liked almost as much the author who came to the studio dressed in cowboy boots, chaps and a stetson. Kinky Friedman, when he isn't writing detective stories, goes round country and western clubs in America singing songs about Jews in the Wild West – with a lot less bitter irony than Sasha Baron Cohen (otherwise known as Ali G) does on TV. I found Kinky just as funny.

We seemed to specialise in finding offbeat entertainers (as I suppose we did offbeat politicians and writers). Few were quite as unusual as Dr Murray Banks, who was a psychiatrist when he wasn't telling jokes. He told quite a few for our listeners. Like the Jewish man suspected of possessing pornography. 'I don't even have a pornograph,' he replies. Or the *shnorrah* (beggar) who calls on a Jewish housewife. 'Will you have yesterday's soup?' she asks. 'Yes,' he replies. 'Then', she answers, 'come back tomorrow.'

I was no less delighted with my father's favourite comedian, Alfred Marks, who told a string of stories, mainly about the old Jewish East End, that were just the kind I have always enjoyed every bit as did my dad. But at first he wasn't so happy about doing so. 'I know your kind,' he said, not altogether sympathetically. 'You just want me to work for *gornisht*.' If he hadn't used that word, I might have decided it was a very anti-Semitic remark. Except that he did relent – for the benefit of everyone listening that Sunday morning.

There was the story of the bearded Chasid who sits alone in a railway compartment, until the guard approaches him. 'I'm sorry, Sir,' he says, 'but this carriage is reserved for the Archbishop of Canterbury.' 'So how', asks the man in his typical Yiddish singsong, 'do you know I'm *not* the Archbishop of Canterbury?'

(I've always liked the story of the bearded man in his *streimel* and *kapota*, who gets off the train at a station in South Carolina, only to be greeted by a crowd of jeering small boys. 'Vat's the matter,' the man asks, 'you never seen a Yankee before?')

Marks also recalled the funeral procession in the East End. Car after car blocks the Whitechapel Road for seemingly miles.

Eventually, an exasperated driver gets out of his car and knocks on the window of one of the funeral vehicles. 'Who died?' he asked. 'The gentleman in the front car,' replies the mourner nonchalantly. Or the man who can't find his father's tombstone. 'The trouble is,' he says, 'he put everything in his wife's name.'

The East End remained a topic of conversation, stories and memories throughout the run of *YDHTBJ*. Wolf Mankowitz, the writer of that iconic story *A Kid For Two Farthings*, took me round his own birthplace and recalled the *seder* evenings in his grandfather's house. There was the cup for Elijah, which forms the centrepiece of the table at that wonderful family evening, a cup of wine poured out in the none-too-likely event of the prophet paying a visit in the course of the night. 'By the time of the second *seder* night, the wine had begun to evaporate, so I assumed that Elijah had come to our home. My grandfather said we were very privileged. "Just imagine", he said, "if the prophet Elijah came and drank in *every* house. He'd be *shicker* (drunk)."'

We ended that day at Blooms, the Whitechapel restaurant that is now but a memory (its Golders Green incarnation is a weak replica of the place where saltbeef and latkes never tasted better). We got talking to a waiter, one of those men who manage to keep their thumbs out of the overflowing plates of chicken soup or borsht (or at least they do when they reach the public room) and who always look as though their feet hurt. They are men who have a joke as ready as the bill, although I haven't yet met one who could emulate the waiter at New York's Lindy's restaurant who, when asked what the fly was doing in his soup, instantly replied, 'At first glance, I'd say the backstroke.' This man proudly boasted to us of his sons, the surgeon and the barrister. 'Just think,' said Mankowitz, 'he has dedicated his life, shlepping round this restaurant, to send his sons to medical and law school.' It was a profound comment and was, in many ways, also the Jewish story.

# 15  Russia – a tale of refuseniks

That word 'shalom' was never more frequently used than when we were in the midst of the long campaign on behalf of the then Soviet Jewish refuseniks. The government of Leonid Brezhnev was banning the exit of Jews from the Soviet Union and making it difficult for them to practise their religion – and had inadvertently made them the focus of the movement for free speech and free dissent in the country.

In Britain, it was also the focus for one of those intra-communal rows which, in retrospect (and sometimes at the time) are such fun. There was a beautiful ex-*Daily Express* model called Barbara Oberman, a delicious woman who was as intelligent as she was attractive – and as politically savvy. She was extraordinarily right-wing, a supporter of Menachem Begin's Herut party, and active in the Soviet Jewry campaign. Barbara believed in direct action – like letting out a collection of mice in the Royal Opera House, Covent Garden, during a performance by the Kirov Ballet. She was once a member of the women's organisation set up to help families in the Soviet Union, called 'The 35s' – a name chosen because that was roughly the age of its founders (they would now be close to being the 75s). She split up from the 35s and thus began one of the great Anglo-Jewish rivalries.

Every time the lovely Barbara appeared on the show, Doreen Gainsford from the 35s wanted equal time. If for no other reason than that I was keen to support the campaign, I had no objection to that. They usually had a good story to tell – like bringing to Britain Avital, the wife of the refusnik Anatoly Scharansky. Time after time, Avital told how her husband, now Natan Sharansky, a prominent member of Ariel Sharon's Likud government, had been arrested on trumped-up charges of hijacking an aeroplane, how he was languishing in a Soviet jail, how he was trying desperately to get out, to live in Israel, how she was trying to smooth the way for him, how she had become Orthodox. All wonderful stories. There would be others – like the fight for a woman known as Sylva Zalmondson, who dreamed of being able to live a Jewish life in a Jewish state.

The 35s knew the value of publicity and how to use it. Their answer to the problem of making people aware of the cause and of Sylva Zalmondson was to use star power. And what a star – Ingrid Bergman came to London to attend a lunch where she could talk about Ms Zalmondson.

It was close to the end of Bergman's life, but she was still one of those names to cherish. She joined the 35s, whom she said she admired greatly, for lunch – a bowl of thin cabbage soup, a chunk of brittle black bread and some very salty herring. It was what they had been told was a typical prison meal, the kind that Sylva Zalmondson was having to experience.

She came on to *YDHTBJ* to talk about how she as a woman felt for this prisoner of Zion, the name given to the jailed refuseniks. Interviewing her, as my reporter Ann Kaye agreed when she met her on another occasion for the programme, was one for the memory book. I was tempted to say something on the lines of 'of all the gin joints in all the world . . . ' but this wasn't Rick's, it was London, and she wasn't quite the beauty of her *Casablanca* days, yet the star appeal rubbed off and before long Sylva Zalmondson was free. Meanwhile we had a great scoop, and I was proving that this wasn't the usual sort of stuff you got on local radio.

The cause of Soviet Jewry was something I felt passionately about, and it fitted very well into the sort of campaigning I believed we should do on the programme. Week after week, we found reason to say something about our brothers and sisters in what we generically called 'Russia'. In 1976 I made my first trip to the Soviet Union, to see the campaign and the problem at first hand.

I went with a group from my adopted home of Bournemouth, who did what Jews usually did when they went to Russia – taking prayer books, Jewish Bibles and dried food like vursht salami and chicken bouillon cubes, which the prisoners of Zion could make into soup in their cells. All of this was, of course, illegal, but you hoped that at least some of it would find its way to the people who needed it.

You were allowed to take a certain amount of material in with you for your own use, but the customs authorities were getting tough. One of our group had his sacred books confiscated – but the rest of us got away with it. My trouble seemed to be the copy of *Playboy* magazine I had brought with me. 'This is not allowed,' said the man in the khaki uniform. I tried to convince him that I had purchased the publication simply for the intellectual content of its articles, particularly one on the role of women in Soviet society. I said that it was notably praising of the way women occupied so many of the most important jobs in Russia and the other republics – more doctors, farm workers, all vital cogs in the Soviet world. 'Not allowed,' he repeated and drew a white line on my suitcase. When I got to my hotel room, the *Playboy* was nestling between my white shirt and my underpants. The customs man was kinder – and plainly had a better sense of humour – than we had imagined.

It was a cold, crisp April in 1976 when we flew into what was then Leningrad. Certainly, we were glad to get to the hotel, even to meet the dumpy women on the landings of each floor, the ones handing out keys and informing the KGB when we arrived and when we went out. Even that couldn't blunt the feeling of relief we felt when we went into the two rooms that the four of us shared.

We had brought some food for ourselves, which was a clever move considering the stuff available at the hotel – none of which we could eat, mostly because of the kosher dietary laws, but also because one look had a strictly negative effect on our tastebuds. Borsht, a staple of Jewish diets, seemed fine – until we saw the sausages floating on the top. There was also herring, the salty kind. I am not sure that the Russians realised it was known as 'schmaltz' herring in our community (I was never sure why; schmaltz is chicken fat). Either way, I didn't like it. Now, pickled herring would have been a different matter, but they didn't have pickled herring in Leningrad. So the vursht would be useful. But we had to remember not to do what my dear friend Harry Wayne had done on a similar visit a few months earlier. Like ours, his hotel room was overheated. Not a good place to store food, so he had his vursht on a string, hanging out of the hotel room window – nine storeys above the street below. A few minutes later, his brother-in-law came into the room. 'It's so hot in here,' he said. 'For God's sake open that window.' He did – and the vursht was probably enjoyed by some

Russian family who couldn't believe their luck as it fell to their feet like manna from heaven. They probably also assumed it was the food eaten by every Englishman.

We went out looking for a restaurant. But this was Soviet Russia, and it was 1976. The nearest to one that we saw was a grim, dank place that sold drinking chocolate. Nothing more – just drinking chocolate. It was all part of the Soviet experience, like the queues outside virtually every food shop – a queue outside the store selling bread, a queue outside the one offering strictly rationed meat, another outside the shop selling cheese, one outside the fish shop, too. A woman doing her household shopping in Leningrad had to reckon on its being a day's experience. We, though, were having a week's experience, calling on just a few people we had heard about – refuseniks who maintained something of a Jewish life and couldn't wait to come out.

The four of us needed to talk about our plans. But we couldn't do it in the drinking-chocolate shop. We couldn't do it in a hotel room either. Who knew where the bugs were? We assumed that there were bugs – just as, allegedly, the Labour Party leaders Michael Foot and Denis Healey assumed when they went on an official parliamentary deputation to Moscow. They hunted for a hidden microphone. They searched the room and then decided they had found it, a heavy-looking knob under the carpet near Foot's bed. It looked as if it needed to be unscrewed. With great effort, they finally managed it – and the chandelier in the room below crashed to the floor. We were more careful. We didn't talk about anything more than what we were going to eat. We certainly didn't mention the people we were going to see, not their names anyway. And we didn't talk about how we were going to get to them. Like other people who had taken the Thompson holiday excursion we had officially gone by, we planned our trip to the Hermitage museum, which had been the Czars' winter palace. I had a collection of tapes in my case (amazingly, neither the tapes nor the recorder had been confiscated or even, apparently, seen by the customs man) which I was duplicating on the spot and which I now decided to call bars of chocolate. Fiendishly clever we were in our efforts to thwart the KGB.

Not that we didn't think we were being watched. There was one officer in a crisp blue uniform, with numerous forms of gold ornamentation on his cap and his coat pocket, who seemed to be taking an inordinate interest in us. Wherever we went, he went too, until we caught our first taxi. At that point, he walked away. It is amazing how self-important you can feel when you are doing something that might be considered illegal in foreign parts.

There were refuseniks to see, Jewish institutions, such as there were, to visit. That was the easy part. There were no Jewish institutions, apart from the synagogue. It was a big building reminiscent of Orthodox shuls anywhere else in the world. It had the smell that I recognised from the very few occasions I had gone to houses of prayer in London's East End. But this was different. To the smell of mustiness was added the odour of decay. This was old and falling to pieces. It was dusty. The pews were well worn, which, in a way, was an encouraging thought. It meant that they were well used – except that you couldn't help thinking that the days when they *were* well used had long gone.

On Shabbat I went to a service there. Perhaps 50 people, strangely of a wide age range, were sitting with heads down in their prayer books, in the hope that nobody would recognise them. There was a cantor and a rabbi, both reputedly KGB appointees. We had been advised not to tell anybody at the synagogue about the purpose of our visit, certainly not to divulge the names of any of the people we were to see.

But, later in the week, we did meet the president. I gave him a plaque with the Israeli crest engraved on it. The crest showed the ancient Temple menorah, Israel's official state symbol. 'Ah,' said the man, 'Chanucah!' A menorah, although with eight branches rather than six, is lit on every night of that winter holiday. Was the man deliberately pretending that he didn't know of its Israeli or Zionist associations? Or was he just ignorant? Perhaps it seemed I was baiting him. I wasn't trying to do that, certainly. Somehow, there is always a feeling of blood relationship with co-religionists in other countries and there is great comfort in that. I wanted to feel that in the huge but shabby synagogue in Leningrad. I hoped it would feel like another example of the very small Jewish world I felt in almost every other country that I visited. In that place it didn't. In people's homes, it surely did.

We called on several people in their humble flats, all of whom seemed to have a gleaming samovar as the centrepiece of their living rooms. There wasn't much else – but a number of them showed us their Shabbat candlesticks, hidden in cupboards as we had learned that the Maranos of post-Inquisition Spain had done. The amazing thing was that these people weren't themselves in hiding. None of them was reluctant to talk or to give their names. I wasn't so sure. The 'chocolate bars' I had recorded were distributed equally among the four of us.

Our group was told about the nearest thing to a Jewish youth club – perhaps Zionist cell would be a better description – and asked if we wanted to go to see it. Of course. We all – including my tape recorders – took a taxi to an address a block away in which we actually had no interest, pretended to go through the doorway, waited for the cab to disappear, looked around us in four directions for someone in uniform or who looked like a KGB man (or woman) and then made our way to our real destination.

This turned out to be the scene of one of the most remarkable events of the week, one of the most exciting and one of the most emotionally draining. There were 30 or so teenagers and 20-somethings discussing their own lives, their country (which they hoped wouldn't be their country for long) and talking about what little they knew about Israel. They wanted to know what we knew. Would Israel welcome them? Would they be able to study there? Would the girls find husbands there? Then they had a dancing lesson – doing Israeli dances, singing Israeli songs that I hadn't heard before, but would again and again in the years that followed. It's strange that the first time I heard numbers like 'Shalom' [that word again] and 'Chaverim' [Peace, brothers] was in the Soviet Union.

We had our fun moments, like the time Ilia Shostakovsky took us round the Hermitage for the first serious look. He was a clever fellow, but was always ready to learn more, particularly about the English language. I had got a little too excited at seeing the Hermitage's superb collection of Rembrandts and had split up from the rest of the party. When we did all get together again, Ilia told me: 'I have just learned new English phrase – "Where hell is Michael?"'

It was a moment to laugh, but there were plenty of the other sort and a number when the emotions became little less than overwhelming. One of those was when I went to the house of Zeina Rayniss, an elderly grandmother and retired schoolteacher. She wanted above all else to be able to go to Israel. 'I want to go to this country,' she told me. 'I want to go to *my* country. I want to be able to breathe the air of Israel, to be with *my* people. I do not want to be just a line in my passport. You see, all our lives we were "*they*". I want to be able to be "*we*".' Every phrase was thought out, deeply. Every word, every sentence, every full stop had a meaning and an emphasis. Her mind covered the whole spectrum of the refuseniks' life and the way they hoped they would be refuseniks no more. 'All my life,' she went on, 'we heard that Jews were not soldiers. Now we are told that they are the best soldiers in the world.'

From that moment until the time that the now Natan Sharansky crossed the bridge to freedom, the story of Soviet Jewry became a vital part of the programme's makeup. When the Iron Curtain finally came tumbling down, we were in the vanguard of those cheering – and telling the story of how it meant a new life for the refuseniks. We went to Israel to meet those who had found those new lives – including Zeina Reiniss and her children and granddaughter, nicely settled now near Jerusalem.

It was an invigorating experience and I remember it now as if it were last week, not almost 30 years ago. Above all, it was a valuable way of passing on the message. The programme was re-broadcast on BBC World Service and on Radio Four.

# 16   Israel

Suddenly there was a change of Radio London policy. In October 1973, it became obvious that ignoring the Middle East political situation was unrealistic. To his enormous credit, Peter Redhouse accepted my point that this was more than the average Briton's relationship with Australia or New Zealand. Kith and kin had a special meaning for Jews. It wasn't a question of dual loyalties, more the point that the American comedian Alan King had once made to me: 'America is my wife. Israel is my mother.' Unless one had a very possessive mother, that could very easily have been translated in British terms.

The catalyst for this change, this realisation, was provided by the events of Yom Kippur that year. It was a day that, as always at that time of year, I spent in the synagogue. At Boreham Wood, two things happened: suddenly the lights went out and the candle that burned all day was blown out. And then disturbing news began filtering through the congregation: someone, somewhere (we weren't supposed to do that on this holiest of holy days) had switched on a radio. The buzz was that Egyptian forces had crossed the Suez Canal and the Syrians were pouring tanks down the Golan Heights. 'The Six Day War has broken out again,' said one of my fellow worshippers. If so, this was the Seventh Day and no one was now resting.

These were Chinese whispers (to coin a phrase) from Jews who had been reading Hebrew, and no one really knew what was happening. No one was going to admit that they had actually turned on a radio. We didn't know the details – particularly the one about men with rifles in their hands going into Israeli synagogues telling all of military age or with army, navy or air force responsibilities to report urgently.

We hadn't yet heard that tanks were rolling in both directions. Nor did we know that for the first time, Israelis were being pushed back. Strangely, our rabbi at the time, the unworldly but scholarly Abraham Unterman, didn't find cause to mount his pulpit. More rumours circulated around the building, but it wasn't until we all rushed home to break the fast – and the famine of news developments – that the radios and televisions were switched on.

It was a Saturday night. With a morsel of *chalah* in my mouth, I rang Radio London and managed to worm out from someone in the newsroom Peter Redhouse's phone number. This was something we had to do the following morning, I was certain. But we had an agreement. To break it might have meant the end of *You Don't Have To Be Jewish*. Not to do so would have ensured that we would be consigned to total irrelevance. There was nothing that was more on the minds of Jews at that moment – and London Jews no less than those anywhere else in the world.

Redhouse was at home. But, amazingly, he had not heard the news. 'War has broken out again,' I said. 'We *have* to cover it.' 'I agree,' he said. 'Of course you must. How are you going to do it?' I told him I had no idea at that point. 'OK.' He added, 'Good luck.'

How that programme was put together on the night after Yom Kippur, of all times, didn't bear thinking about. But it happened. We were, after all, a news programme and, as I said all the time, if we didn't cover the one event that was more important to our listeners than anything else, there was little point in us being there. So I went for it and, live on the Sunday morning, we had one of the most exciting as well as depressing programmes in 23½ years. People wanted to listen, and – from my point of view, even more importantly – people wanted to take part.

Barbara Oberman came back to the Radio London studio – not talking about Soviet Jews this time, but as the mother of a soldier in the Israeli army. How did she feel? 'This is the moment for solidarity,' she said. 'Dear God, our people are fighting for their lives.'

Then there was the rabbi – or, rather, the reverend, the effervescent Saul Amias, minister of the Edgware Synagogue in London from the time when he was virtually the first Jew in what was to become one of the capital's principal Jewish communities. What were the ethics of fighting a war on the holiest day of the year? 'There can be no question about it,' he answered. 'The saving of life takes precedence over anything and, here, Jews are fighting for their lives. The Arabs want to drive us into the sea. If you are attacked on Yom Kippur, you carry your guns, you get into your tanks and your planes and you have enough food to keep you going.'

Others came and went on the programme. People phoned in to find out how they could help. We had the Israeli ambassador, Michael Comay, telling British Jews to stay calm but to stand by in case they were needed. There was the taxi driver who, free of charge, was offering his services to transport people to and from the Israeli Embassy or to Rex House, then the West End centre of the British Zionist movement, where he had heard a blood donor scheme was in force.

It was one occasion when it seemed that *YDHTBJ* was not only providing news to the Jewish community, but offering them a service that they dearly needed.

This became obvious when the reactions to the programme materialised. There were letters and letters and still more letters. No broadcaster could fail to appreciate that.

The one that I'd never forget came from a lady with the delightful name of Mrs Bellringer, but it wasn't her name that made me for ever after remember her. It was her very simple message. She didn't know much about religion or even what faith, if any, she had, but she did know that her grandmother, her mother's mother, born in Holland, had been Jewish. And it was listening to that Sunday morning's *YDHTBJ* that made her think of her Jewish roots. She was a state-registered nurse and wanted to find a way of getting to Israel to help with wounded soldiers or civilians. If she managed to do that, would she be allowed to take her two daughters with her? Could I possibly help?

I have to confess that I'm not the most brilliant correspondent (of the letter-writing kind). Not that I don't always reply, but I do sometimes take my time in removing letters from the pile and getting down to answering them. But this one was different. It spoke to me – I know it's a cliché, but it really did. And there was a ready reply. If it really was her maternal grandmother who was Jewish, that meant that her mother was, too – and it went without saying that she was as well. Not only that, it would also apply to her girls. They were Jewish as well.

Usually, when I do get round to that job of replying, it is the end of the correspondence. But Mrs Bellringer wrote back. She had read my letter over and over again. It had given her something to live for – as well as helping her fellow Jews. It seems that she did have to be Jewish. Now, every time I get letters that lay the writer's heart on their sleeve, I think of that occasion in 1973. You could say that it rings a bell.

The week after that ground-breaking broadcast, Redhouse suggested that we even the stakes a little. We had a discussion between a Dr Masawi, a prominent Palestinian-born London lawyer who frequently appeared on British TV, and a non-Jewish supporter of Israel, the writer Terence Prittie. I wasn't keen on giving the Palestinian a platform, but Masawi was courteous, a brilliant broadcaster, and Prittie gave as much as he took. We had a lot of letters about that, mail complaining that I was broadcasting for the enemy. I replied to each – pointing out that good journalism required airing both sides of the story (*pace* Joe Dray) and that by doing so, we were laying the ground for more pro-Israel broadcasts. Integrity was still important and, fighting battles like those on behalf of the state of Israel, it was needed more than ever.

Letters are a very good test of a programme's popularity, as is the response to phone-in broadcasts. If nobody rings up, you know that there can't be as many people out there as you would like to think. But we had a lot of listeners – 100,000 at one stage, which for local radio and for a niche spot like ours was fairly remarkable. I remember when I reported that figure to the Radio and TV Committee, they burst into applause. But the Jewish establishment kept an eye (or, rather, an ear) out for us. They bombarded us with letters – either we didn't get right the name of some obscure seventeenth-century rabbi or we were giving too much publicity to a certain MP named Greville Janner, who will be cropping up in the story as we go on.

Then there were the letters from people who did not have to be Jewish – we really did justify that title. A certain gentleman who under no circumstances could ever be likely to want to convert to Judaism was one of our most regular listeners. But he heard our Monday afternoon repeats – which then were dropped. This man was a Catholic priest and he was distraught about not being able to hear our show. 'Please bring back the Monday repeats,' he begged. 'As you may know, I have other things to do on a Sunday morning.'

It meant that we lost at least one regular listener. (Years later, when I referred to this reverend gentleman on the air, he wrote again reminding me of his name; I appreciated that). We lost a few others, too – the folks who for some unaccountable reason preferred listening to *The Archers*. Mind you, there was one woman who was convinced she had the answer to that problem. 'I would like to write you a Jewish version of *The Archers*,' she declared in an accent that was distinctly not from Ambridge. I said thank you, but no thank you. For years afterwards, I quite regretted that cavalier 'no', but it wouldn't have fitted in with the hard news stories that dominated the post-Yom Kippur War scene.

We had correspondents in Israel now. We spoke in London to people who had been to the country and seen the reaction of the Israelis. One of the most notable was the violin virtuoso Isaac Stern, who talked of playing to wounded soldiers in their hospital wards.

Soon after that war, the one that Israel nearly lost, Israel's prime minister, the much-loved Golda Meir, came to London to address a meeting of Jewish solidarity at the Royal Albert Hall. I met her at a press conference, got out my tape recorder and asked her for an interview.

'Darling,' she said, 'where do I have the time?' 'Right now,' I said. 'Darling, I haven't got the time. It isn't possible.'

I told her: 'You know how much we love you ... '

'Yes, I do, but I haven't got a moment.'

'You will be talking to 5,000 people at the Albert Hall. I can give you 100,000. Just five minutes, please.'

Golda proceeded to take ten minutes to explain why she didn't have five minutes for an interview. I said that this was a marvellous opportunity – particularly since there was a very hostile press in Britain – to reverse the usual media image. 'We can wait for their obituaries,' she said. In the end I got a very few moments in which she said how much she appreciated the support she was getting from Jews everywhere – particularly the young people. There were more letters after that.

This was an astonishing time both for Jews and for Judaism. It was a test of faith and of ritual. One London Orthodox synagogue minister kept his telephone free on the festival of Succot a few days after the war began. He thought it was more important to help a wider flock and to keep in touch with the news than to obey the prohibition on using the phone on a holy day. Another rabbi confessed that after the events of Yom Kippur that year, his faith was not just tested, but lost. I've often wondered since if he ever regained it. I always hoped so. His contributions to the programme were always enjoyed and considered uplifting by our audiences. Their letters confirmed this.

There was, on the whole, very little hate mail, which surprises me still. I had had some in the past – notably when I wrote a feature for the *Evening Standard* on the bussing of schoolchildren. It was all a 'bloody Jewish conspiracy' and a few other choice, even more unpleasant, words. His letter was addressed to the '*Jew Standard*'.

But I did get regular correspondence in the form of a postcard with a Dublin postmark. It was directed to 'Jewish Broadcasting, Portland Place, London'. I never bothered to read much of it, although it became apparent that it wasn't intended for me in particular. This was simply an anti-Semite convinced that the BBC was part of that same Jewish conspiracy. The post office at Broadcasting House simply redirected the postcards to me as a matter of course. Clearly, I was the obvious address.

We were also, I like to think, always a good address for people looking for news of the Jewish world – and all over that world. We were indeed blessed by our foreign correspondents. Few were more eminent than another of the people we could call upon in Israel than Michael Elkins, who had served his time as the BBC's man in Jerusalem and had represented the CBS network and *Newsweek* magazine.

He was the man who first told the world that Israel had won the Six Day War in 1967. Almost every news organisation had accepted the wishful thinking of Gamal Abdul Nasser that Egypt had stopped the Israelis in their tracks. But Elkins went on the BBC *Panorama* programme that first day and said that all that had been accomplished by the Jewish state in five days during the 1956 Suez campaign, they had achieved in a matter of hours. The BBC didn't believe him and he was for most of that week *persona non grata* with the Beeb. He was that way, he told us in one memorable programme, with much of the world Zionist organisation.

He wrote a fascinating book called *Forged In Fury*, in which he described efforts by Zionist avengers to add poison to the water supply of the city of Nuremberg after World War Two. That alone was interesting and history-making. But it was what he added to that story which astonished and agonised and angered Zionist groups all over the world. He said that the poison to be used – until the plot was foiled by the British – had been specially developed by Israel's leading scientist, who also happened to be the country's first president. Chaim Weizmann, he suggested, had been guilty of attempted mass murder. The American women's Zionist group, Hadassah, had, as a result cancelled a bulk order of about 200,000 copies, a blow in itself to any author.

It was, apparently, all true. In 1999 I went to Israel to spend time with the man behind the plot, Joseph Harmatz, whom I had known years before when he was head of World ORT, one of the organisations that brings most credit to Jews by its activities in vocational training, not just in Israel, but in South America, Russia, Africa and China. Once the Nuremberg scheme had been abandoned, he told me – partly engineered by the Holocaust poet Abba Kovner – he was one of the people who broke into a former Nazi barracks near that city, by then housing German SS prisoners. He and his fellow conspirators had managed to kill a few of the Nazis and made a few hundred more sick, by breaking into the barracks bakery and painting loaves of bread with poison. Alas, the story came to me five years too late for *YDHTBJ*, but made a double-page spread and the front page splash in the broadsheet *Observer* newspaper. In terms of space in a national paper, it was one of the biggest stories of my life.

The Israelis were beginning to think of my associations with the higher echelons of the British Broadcasting Corporation. What these were, I still don't know, but there was one diplomat at the embassy in Kensington who thought I could be a useful source of information for them. 'Just keep us informed,' said the attaché. 'We don't know everything that is going on, but you probably do.' He then revealed, not too subtly, that he headed the local Mossad chapter and I would be doing a service to his country. I told him as I had told others that, yes, I was a passionate Zionist, but I had to maintain both my integrity as a journalist and my position as a British citizen who owed so much to the country of my birth. If they were looking for spies, there were other more suitable candidates whom I wouldn't dream of naming.

Now that it had been established that Israel was part of our remit,

I had to go there – to meet Israelis in the streets and to talk to government people. I called at the Israeli Embassy – not offering my services to Mossad, it has to be said, but to ask them to fix an interview or two. 'Certainly,' said the press attaché, 'whom do you want to see?' I listed a dozen or so names, any one of whom would have satisfied me. 'Sure,' he said.

Week by week, I rang to find out about progress. 'Don't worry,' I was told, 'it will happen.' The day before I left for Tel Aviv, I rang again. 'Listen,' said the diplomat, who should have known better, 'you'll get what you want. But when you get to Israel, ring the government press office. They'll fix it for you.' So I did that. And what did they say? 'Why didn't you tell us you were coming? We could have arranged so much for you.'

That same situation recurred perhaps a dozen times during the life of *YDHTBJ*.

I got my interviews – by sitting in the lobby of the Knesset. It was such a short-sighted view from people who were constantly complaining about the BBC's anti-Israel stance. But then PR has never been one of the country's high spots. 'Twas always thus. When the Arab states put articulate statesmen on to news programmes, the Israelis either didn't provide anyone at all or offered a man who had had his first English lesson that very day. More than once, it was up to the *Jewish Chronicle* to field someone. But always in a separate studio. The Arabs wouldn't recognise Israel, and sitting in the same broadcasting studio with an Israeli was tantamount to high treason. Had any done so, they would probably never have been heard of again.

Unfortunately, that happened within our community, too. The Board of Deputies had few presidents as active or as concerned about the fate of Anglo-Jewry, and certainly Israel, as Greville Janner, who took over as president in 1979. He was a QC whom I had first come across when he represented a reprobate or two at Luton Magistrates Court (I think he lost). I remember taking the opportunity then to remind him that he had agreed to let me have a copy of the 78 made by his youth group, the Brady Ramblers, in the late 1950s – of Joshua fighting the battle of Jericho. It might have taken a Joshua to fight my battle to get the record. Subsequently, he became Labour MP for Leicester West (which he used as the pen-name for his never-ending supply of books advising professions, trades and industries on their legal rights). His father was the eminent patriarch of the community, Barnett Janner, who became Lord Janner of Leicester. Greville followed his footsteps all the way – as an MP, as president of the Board and as a member of the House of Lords.

Greville was cocky, which was perhaps his most useful characteristic. In my very early days in journalism I had been asked by the *JC* to cover, as a freelance, a meeting the very young barrister was addressing. I had been briefed just an hour or so before the meeting and arrived after he had started talking. 'Just like the *JC* to come late,' he said before the crowded meeting. I still wished I had given as good as I got. It was rude and it was untimely. His father would never have done that.

On the other hand, he magnificently used his couldn't-care-less-for-the-consequences attitude for the benefit of both the community and the State of Israel. He was full of ideas, most of which undoubtedly enhanced the role of Anglo-Jewry in the national psyche. As an MP, he had influence, which he thought he could extend to helping fellow Labour members. He would say he 'earn(ed) my living' by heading a firm specialising in training business people in presentation skills. One day in the late 1980s, he asked me to assist with some media training for Labour MPs. I thought it wasn't too difficult. All I would do was interview them as if on a radio programme. One of them, as I said when I did my programme 'menu' (literally, as if on the air) was the shadow foreign secretary, Gerald Kaufman, now *Sir* Gerald, a Manchester MP who had at one time written a book about Israel, a country he said he loved. Later, he turned out to be one of Israel's staunchest critics.

The other MP for whom I was providing that media training I introduced as 'a back bencher' (no, I was corrected, he was a junior shadow minister). He was very young, very willing to learn how to deal with interviewers 'like you.' I didn't know the name, so it was handed to me on a piece of paper. It was, now see if I can remember it, oh yes . . . Tony Blair.

Afterwards, he sent me a very nice handwritten note, thanking me for my help, which he was sure would be of great use to him. And if he could do anything to help me at any time, I only had to ask. Gerald Kaufman sent a similar note. Greville said how grateful he was for my help in his business – and gave me *half* a bottle of whisky.

As for Mr Blair, he came on to *YDHTBJ* to talk about the contribution made by Jews to the fabric of the country. He had had promotion since our last meeting. Now, he was shadow home secretary. But he couldn't yet have been making too much money. He wore a white shirt with a distinctly frayed collar.

Looking back now, after all those years in power, it is difficult to think of Tony Blair attacking a sitting government. But in 1992, seven months after John Major's election triumph (with a working majority to be whittled down by Black Wednesday and all that followed) that was precisely what he did.

He wanted stronger legislation against anti-Semitism, more control over the rise in the publication of anti-Jewish literature. Interesting, in 1992, there was no question of Islamaphobia. There was, he said, however, 'a greater awareness of the Public Order Act', which he wished the then government would use more frequently.

Greville's work for Jews, however, cannot be minimised. In the late 1990s and as the century and millennium changed, he worked as no one else for the truth of the Holocaust to remain in the public knowledge. He fought more than anyone else to get Nazi war criminals prosecuted and their names published – this turned out to be less successful than most of us would have wished; the few who were brought before the courts managed to escape retribution for one reason or other. But Janner was there to go on TV and speak to the press about his views and those of his supporters. As head of the Holocaust Educational Trust, he was superb. He had also succeeded in making friends in various parts of the Commonwealth. As MP for a constituency with a large Asian population he had made numerous trips to India, where he met presidents and prime ministers. One of his proudest possessions was the photograph he had taken with Mrs Nehru. It was probably on one of these trips that he had the idea for the Commonwealth Jewish Council – on which were represented the comparatively big Jewish communities in places like Australia and Canada and the tiny ones in, say, Jersey or Burma.

His influence resulted in the council being received by governments all over the world. He was on more than one occasion responsible for the Queen being guest of honour at receptions – held in one of her own homes, usually St James's Palace. I went to one of those and found my knees knocking. I am becoming less and less a royalist, but, yes, my knees knocked. (There was another of those receptions at which Sara and I stood with the then *JC* editor, Geoffrey Paul. He was introduced to Her Majesty, who said something Geoffrey didn't catch before she walked away to shake someone else's hand. 'What was that she said?' he asked me. 'Didn't you hear, Geoffrey?' I answered. 'She said, 'Oh yes, the *JC*. Fridays wouldn't be the same without it.'

But good though he was, Greville had bees in his bonnet. During one studio discussion about Soviet Jewry, I asked him to come to debate the issue of who was doing what. He came – and then saw Barbara Oberman there to oppose him. He walked out. 'Greville,' I said, 'that's exactly what the Arabs do when confronted by an Israeli. Shouldn't we do better than that?' He agreed to take part.

He was indeed one of the best presidents the Board had. As an MP, he had access to the powers that were and he didn't stand for other organisations usurping what he considered to be the Deputies' purview. However, he, too, would accept intolerable conditions to financial arrangements that, it has to be confessed, aided a body that was constantly in debt.

In 1985, the Board celebrated its 225th anniversary – one that no other organisation would consider important enough to mark. But, ever the PR man, Janner decided it was a good enough event to merit flying the flags. He asked me for ideas. I came up with a dozen or so – a Board competitor in that year's London Marathon, a special stamp. None of it happened (although, after discussing them with him, they were all claimed by the official he had brought in to run the events as his own ideas). But what did happen was a huge reception at Hampton Court Palace at which the Prince and then Princess of Wales were guests of honour.

They were presented with a leather-bound copy of the works of some obscure rabbi and Charles wittily noted that it was going to be his bedtime reading for some time to come. Considering his relations with his wife at the time, he might have thought he needed some diversions in bed.

The Princess worked the crowd and offered her gorgeous hand for me to shake. You don't forget in a hurry the world's most beautiful woman seeking you out. Her husband then asked me if I had had enough to eat. 'Actually,' I said, 'I'm feeling a little hungry.' He laughed like the proverbial drain, for he had just dined at a veritable banquet. But a few hundred other people had not. In fact, the communal scribe Chaim Bermant noted in his *JC* column five years later that he was convinced some people were still lining up at the self-service buffet. The banquet was for people who had paid a considerable sum for the privilege. Worse was that the so-called host, who greeted the Prince and Princess, was not the president, nor a member of the executive, nor even a member of the Board, but a communal worthy with plenty of money.

Even the vice-presidents, Martin Savitt and Victor Lucas, the former president of the United Synagogue, both hard-working men who were devoted to the Jewish community, were excluded from that august company because they had not wanted to fork out the cash demanded. It's an attitude that Anglo-Jewry has found difficult to shake off. The belief that money equals communal prestige takes a long time to disappear, and all it does is bring shame.

Greville, though, still thinks the whole affair was very funny, and I can see why. As he wrote to me, many years later, about the 'sad fact that we ran out of food': 'However long they had to queue up, they wouldn't have got any because our staff catered for too few. It was the most wonderful cocked-up great evening that I have ever had to apologise for!' Yes, I suppose it was funny on reflection, but the way that reflection reflected was not very good for the community either then or in memory now.

Hand in hand with that is a permanent sense of snobbery. When Greville Janner laid down his badges of office, it was widely believed that that same Martin Savitt would succeed him. Savitt, a small-businessman, had been groomed as Janner's heir. He went with him on his various overseas and community visits, sat with him on committees and was very much his right-hand man. He worked harder for Anglo-Jewry than any man I know. But he had two drawbacks. He was just a small-businessman, neither a tycoon nor a professional man, and spoke in less cultured terms than the worthy Board member who opposed him at the elections following Janner's retirement– a Newcastle doctor called Lionel Kopelowitz. Kopelowitz had been canvassing for votes for months. Savitt had been too busy looking after the Board's affairs and the community in general to do enough. But he believed he had two advantages – one, that people knew how hard he worked, people who had sat with him, who had experienced his pleadings for Soviet Jewry, for *schechita*, the Jewish form of animal slaughter, for Israel and for

Holocaust education; two, he had the support of the Association of Jewish Ex-Servicemen, an organisation of which he had served as national chairman. It was a huge group with an exceptionally large representation on the Board – not only their own deputies but other men and women, representing synagogues that were AJEX (as the association is popularly known) members. He knew that the vast majority of them would vote for him. What Savitt didn't realise was that on the day of the election, AJEX was organising an outing for needy children. Hundreds went along to help rather than attend the Board meeting. Savitt lost by six votes.

I will not suggest that Kopelowitz's vote was not made up of people who thought he would do a good job, but there were an awful lot of deputies who liked the idea of being led, if not by an MP, then at least by a doctor.

It was very much the community's loss. Martin Savitt would have made a wonderful president, simply because he was so hard working, so committed and so well liked. One thing he might not have been able to do was to quote the Torah portion of the week as his opponent did every time he made a speech or – quite remarkable this – be able, as I winessed, to be introduced to complete strangers at a dinner in Geneva and an hour later recall every name in his speech, without a single note. No, Savitt, with his cockney accent, wouldn't have been able to do that, but he had other qualities that the Jewish community was denied. He lived for many years after his election defeat, and was deeply hurt by the experience.

Needless to say, I looked forward to working with Martin, although it would have been different from working with Greville Janner, who was always ready with a news story for the programme. It suited us both. He was glad of the publicity, and I was glad of a good story.

One tale wasn't exactly anticipated. It revolved around our annual celebrations of the festival of Purim – a time when children put on fancy dress (I've known many a rabbi to do it, too) and people send round to each other cakes, sweets and other treats. It is also traditional to play the equivalent of April Fool gags. These are the Purim spiels. In 1983, soon after the end of the Falklands war, we ran an interview with a young man supposedly from the South Georgia Jewish community. Now South Georgia wasn't exactly known for its Jews. In fact, it wasn't exactly famous for its humans of any stripe. Actually, until the British army arrived to ensure that it was the Union Flag flying there, rather than the banner of the Argentines, the population consisted almost entirely of a few sheep.

But our interviewee told us about the relations between the president of the community there and Mrs Jacobs, head of the local Ladies' Guild, and their two synagogues (you know, the one you belonged to and the one you wouldn't be seen dead in). Greville was terribly excited about that. 'Give me the name and address of the president,' he said. 'I can't understand why they are not in the Commonwealth Jewish Council.' Then he saw the joke.

I am afraid that Greville was a constant butt of our Purim spiels, not least the one in which we predicted he would become the world's first Jewish astronaut. Good sport that he was, he came on the programme for what seemed to be an entirely for-real interview. Yes, he said, he was going up in space. His mother, the redoubtable Lady (Elsie) Janner was the first on the line. 'Oh, no, you're not,' she said in a very angry – and worried – phone call to her son.

The best Purim spiel of all was when we supposedly discovered a Chassidic village in Hertfordshire, which I called Brichtovich. For this, I brought in the services of the brilliant amateur writer and actor Alf Fogel.

Alf made his name writing, producing and acting in shows presented at West End theatres in aid of various Jewish charities. They were parodies of big London hits and top movies – like *Mine Fair Sadie, Morrie From Arabia* and *The Teitelbaum File*. You get the idea – in the first of these, a lady from Hampstead Garden Suburb is taught how to talk like a 'yachnah', a woman who knows how to call a dumpling a kneidel; the second had a Jewish businessman saving an Arab sheikh; and the third . . . well, it was about the dress trade (or the gown business, as its practitioners liked to call it). The company answerphone announced: 'Teitelbaum Fashions. The cheque is in the post.'

Alf, I am sure, could have become a top comedy and songwriter. Bud Flanagan once bought one of his songs. Morecambe and Wise almost decided to use another one as their signature tune – but chose 'Bring Me Sunshine' instead. Why Alf didn't choose to do it all for a living, instead of making clothes, I have never been able to understand. The fact that he had an elder brother who had been to RADA, and didn't quite make it, probably had something to do with it. But his shows were products of genius, and many of the national newspaper critics seemed to agree when they reviewed his shows at the Prince of Wales and other London theatres.

So why not adapt this concept to the radio? Alf loved the idea and brought his company into the studio. We had meetings to discuss what we should have – a pub, a hunt, a *sheitel* (wig) maker. There was also a midwife – 'I don't deliver' – and the traffic warden who made sure everyone kept to the right. Middle of the road wouldn't have suited the Chassidim at all.

For the pub scene, I got the BBC sound archives to send us a record of a crowd noisily enjoying a public bar. But we added our own effects, like the shout from the crowd: 'Make mine a 4A.' For the uninitiated, 4A is the top of the range of the Palwin brand of kosher wine.

But the real fun came from the Brichtovich Hunt. Alf was the master. 'One blast of *tekiah* and we're off,' he said. That, too, was an in joke. *Tekiah* is the note sounded by the ram's horn, or the *shofar*, on Rosh Hashanah, the Jewish New Year.

Did they hunt foxes? I put that vital question to the master of the hunt. 'Foxes? Nah. Chickens. When you hunt a fox, what are you going to get? Perhaps a collar. But with a chicken, you get soup, you get chopped liver, you get the chicken itself.' Yet there was one problem. Brichtovich would demand that the chicken was kosher – so at the front of the hunt had to be a religious slaughterer, a *shochet*. And the *shochet* would wear the traditional garb, a fur *streimel* hat and a long coat, a *kapota*. 'That gives us a serious problem. Because of the *kapota*, he has to ride side-saddle and he keeps falling off.'

People fell off their chairs when they heard our Purim spiel. We were overwhelmed with letters – at least 300 of them, people demanding to know where Brichtovich was. They thought they'd pay it a visit the following week. Amélie Jakobovits was intrigued. She and her husband pondered why they hadn't heard of the place, and then the Chief Rabbi looked at her and said: 'What day is it today?' Purim had come to the official residence at St John's Wood.

There were always frequent calls to and from the home of our Chief Rabbis. Soon after Jonathan Sacks succeeded to the office in the early 1990s, he took part in a wonderfully oversubscribed phone-in programme. A lady rang from Finchley with an important question about Jewish ritual, but we had had other questions on the same subject and she stayed at the back of the queue. Alas, when the programme ended, we still hadn't had time to include her question. Of course, if we had realised this was the Chief Rabbi's mother, we would have done things differently. The story made the *Standard*'s 'Londoner's Diary' and the following week's programme, of course. The shame was that Mrs Sacks herself didn't make the phone-in.

It was actually one of the joys of *YDHTBJ* how members of the public were introduced to broadcasting, and not just through phoning in. Men and women were constantly asking to be included in our schedules. Some were, and proved to be very good. Some weren't – like the woman who wanted to come in and talk about a series of cookery programmes. It seemed a reasonable idea – until the day that we met. She walked into the Radio London studios preceded by a chopping board, a carrier bag of ingredients and a large enamel saucepan. 'Excuse me,' I said, 'what's all this for?' The woman was incredulous that I should ever have asked. 'How else am I going to make chicken soup?' she asked. I pointed out that this was radio, not TV, and she should think of another angle. In the end, she did, but we didn't. We frequently discussed Jewish food, but radio recipes weren't for us – although occasionally we tried.

One listener who proved to be a genius (yes, another one) in culinary matters was the gravel-voiced Myer Robinson. Myer died unexpectedly, much too young, a few days after describing the ideal way to make latkes. ('You should grate the potato holding it very close to the grater. If you see the potato taking on a red colour, you will realise your fingers were a little too close.' He was a wonderful broadcaster – he had never done it before, but he was a natural. His voice did resemble footsteps on a stony path, but that was part of the fun. He told stories about things we all recognised, and was a delight.

Latkes had always been a challenge to us. They are a staple for Chanucah, and I thought it would be a very good idea to do a programme about them. At the time, London's main Jewish eaterie was Blooms, a very traditional kosher restaurant then in both Whitechapel and in the ghetto of Golders Green, where it still functions. Maybe, I thought, there could be a recipe for us from the experts in the field?

I looked up their number in the phone book. A rather stuffy-voiced lady answered my call. 'Oh,' she said, 'you had better talk to Mr Bloom.' 'Thanks,' I replied, 'that's exactly what I should like to do.' Mr Bloom came on the phone. 'How can I help?' 'I'm Michael Freedland from BBC Radio London's Jewish programme, *You Don't Have To Be Jewish*,' I explained. 'Yes?' 'And I'd like to broadcast a recipe for latkes.' 'But', he responded, 'we are antique silver merchants.' It seemed that I still hadn't learned the lesson I should have remembered from my trip to Blundells.

# 17 Contributors, contacts and correspondents

There was always the same reaction, the same gesture of apprecia-tion, to a rather older story-teller, Harry Blacker, who was principally known as a cartoonist. I most liked the drawing in which some rabbinical-looking figures were seen picketing a synagogue. The slogan on their plackards and sandwich boards was 'Repent now – and avoid the Yom Kippur rush'.

Week after week, Harry told stories about the 'Mittel East' – which to him meant Bethnal Green. There were tales about his mother, about his siblings, about synagogues, about youth clubs, and about the policeman who had a favourite stopping point on his beat – above a grating in the pavement over a baker's shop. The friendly neighbourhood bobby used to stand there like Marilyn Monroe in *The Seven Year Itch*. One cold, cold night, Harry remembered him saying: 'It's a ma-chia, mate, isn't it?' (wrongly pronouncing 'ch' as in 'chess') *Machiah* (pronouncing the 'ch' as in 'Reich' – how innappropriate can you get?) means lovely, as in the story of the differences between that word and a simiar one, *nachas*. *Nachas* is when the grandchildren come for the afternoon. *Machiah* is when they go home again.

It was a *machiah* listening to other contributors, people who excelled in comedy writing, like Harold Kirk, an optician, who thought that too many people spoke about their mothers (tape in: 'My Yiddisher Mama', Sophie Tucker) and ignored the Yiddisher father, and Eddie Summers, who used to write for *Jewish Youth* when I was editing the *AJY* magazine and showed a remarkable talent that, like Alf Fogel, he sadly never used professionally. For us, he told stories about Stamford Hill and the 73 bus, which was the favourite meeting place of the gang. (How different from the early twenty-first century, when few self-respecting gang members would admit to knowing a bus when they actually saw one).

Of all the celebrity guests, could there be anyone who was more fun than Sammy Cahn? This was the man who came up with the theory for us of the 'ethnic ladder' – in showbiz, first there were the Irish, then the Jews, then the Italians and then the blacks. He hadn't yet got round to adding, in America at least, the Hispanics.

I went to see him in his plush home in Beverly Hills. Outside were the regulatory cars with 'His' and 'Hers' number plates (they actually were 'his' and 'hers') and we talked about his six Oscars – replicas of which he carried on his keyring.

We talked about Oscars, but what I really wanted to know was more about his own particular rung on that ethnic ladder. 'Easy,' he told me. 'It was at my Bar Mitzvah. My mother said when it was all over, "I have to go and pay the band now." "What?" I asked her, these guys get paid for having more fun than anyone else at the party?"' So he learned to play the violin – not terribly well, but it didn't matter. He also played the piano while his mother sang Yiddish songs that never ceased to amuse him, like 'Ich Bin a border by mine vibe' (I am a lodger to my wife) or 'Es gevein, es gevein, es gevein' a song for the beauty parlour, 'What has gone, has gone – and will not come back again'.

He told about his first big hit, 'Bei Mir Bistu Shoen', which he first heard performed by two black singers and dancers at the Apollo, Harlem. 'I thought that if blacks could sing it, why wouldn't the Jews, who were there first?' And then, why not everyone else? He and his partner Solly Kaplan (later to be Saul Chaplin, eminent film composer and producer and multi-Oscar-winner himself) turned it into a pop song for the Andrews Sisters ('They were Greek and didn't know what the hell they were singing').

When he was in London, he always came into the Radio London studios and played his piano – and made up new lyrics for old songs for us, just as he did for Frank Sinatra and for American cosmetics firms to use for their promotions. Like 'Never feel bluish when you listen to *You Don't Have To Be Jewish* . . . with Michael Freedland.'

In the late seventies, we did an album, 'The Best of *You Don't Have To Be Jewish*' (fortunately, nobody tried to pronounce it as 'The best of you . . . don't have to be Jewish'). It featured the first of at least a dozen Sammy Cahn performances, some of which I later

26. I greatly admired Harold Wilson. When he came to a *YDHTBJ* party, I couldn't  have
been more happy – or can you see that? With us is Derrick Amore, station manager at Radio
London.

28. We did have to be Jewish. Rehearsing a family seder, which we broadcast in the early 1970s. Left to right: Dani, Jonathan, me, Fiona and Sara.

29. With Cardinal Hume. Interfaith relations did well that day. My friend Hyam Corney, Deputy Editor of the *Jewish Chronicle*, is in the centre.

30. With Hugo Gryn in 1982 – at Theresienstadt, where the rabbi found his own index card.

31. I greatly admired Chief Rabbi Lord Jakobovits.

32. With Abba Eban, the perfect Israeli spokesman who would have made a great prime minister. (He was not used to wearing a *kippar* – we were at a Jewish school at the time.)

33. The man who should have been king. With the then Crown Prince of Jordan, Hassan.

34. I never became a Thatcherite, but Mrs T. and I got on well on several occasions.

35. With Shimon Peres in 1981 – and David Ben Gurion looking on. I might have liked more security people looking on, too.

36. With Yehudi Menuhin. One of a number of interviews we did together.

37. Neil Kinnock and me. We both thought he was soon to be Prime Minister, but I was pleased to be photographed with the Leader of the Opposition (my suit fitted better than his).

38. It could be tiring work, broadcasting in the summer. Hyam Corney across the table. An Israeli journalist looks on.

39. Stuart Young, Chairman of the BBC, offered his support to *YDHTBJ*. Joining in, Martin Savitt, who would have made a wonderful President of the Board of Deputies, and Harold Langdon, then Chairman of the Board's PR Committe.

cannibalised for the Radio Two series, *The Sammy Cahn Story*. We had lunch soon after I had sent him a copy. 'Loved your album,' he said. How could I not love a man like that?

There were others who were more serious broadcasters – like Robert Rietti, as in the Yom Kippur Munich Olympics broadcast, who put slants on life that, in other hands (or voices) could have sounded far too schmaltzy, but were always just right. He talked about the Jews of Italy, where his father was born. 'Very difficult to tell us apart. See an Italian and he could be Jewish.' Or, of course, vice versa. He gave us his thoughts about the Holocaust, about going to Israel, about families. I always greatly appreciated Robert. He was *no* novice when it came to broadcasting. A professional actor of high standing, he frequently appeared on Radio Four and other network stations. He had a highly successful business dubbing foreign-language films into English (and the voices of foreign actors in British or American films, sometimes actually talking to himself in four different voices in the same scene) and plainly didn't need the few pounds he would have earned – indeed, he refused to take a fee of any kind. But he thought that any means of getting across a true Jewish message was an opportunity and a duty. I shall always be grateful to him for that – and for his weekly messages from the Talmud with which we concluded our programmes in the early days. He is a true gentleman in every sense of the word.

There were other regular contributors of whom I became exceptionally proud. Soon after the Yom Kippur War, I had occasion to ring the man who had been acting as the BBC's expert-on-the-spot during the conflict, the then General Chaim Herzog, who was a former official Israel Defence Force spokesman, intelligence chief and you-want-a-senior-job-done-I'm-your-man. Most importantly in the 1970s, he was Israel's ambassador to the United Nations. It was he who, in 1975, made his country's spirited response to the infamous 'Zionism equals racism' resolution at the UN. When we spoke, I asked him if we could make regular calls to discuss the situation in Israel and the world. He said he'd be pleased to do so. He was an impressive name and an even more impressive speaker – better than most of the people his country's embassy was fielding on radio and TV at the time.

He was born in Belfast, but raised in Dublin, where his father was Chief Rabbi, and his Irish brogue was one of his most endearing characteristics and made Jewish listeners remarkably happy.

He was there for us on all the important events of the day – and there were plenty of those. It is fair to say that if you wanted a definitive record of Israel's history – to say nothing of that of Anglo-Jewry – for the best part of the last quarter of the twentieth century, listening to the archives of *You Don't Have To Be Jewish* would be as good as any. I suppose that is my proudest thought.

In 1983, Chaim Herzog became president of Israel. Would he still talk to us? 'I don't intend to live in an ivory tower,' he said. 'Of course I will.' I have to say that the times we spoke thereafter were considerably more limited. But when I was in Jerusalem, I could call on him at his official residence – not exactly Buckingham Palace, but a nice, dignified, elegant home, just as you would hope. Jews don't like to think of their leaders being anything but elegant, certainly not showy. On one occasion, I took the then teenage Jonathan, sporting a hairstyle that would have suited a Rolling Stone (his girlfriend loved it) with me, and Mr President was pleased to pose for a picture with him. When Herzog came to London, we met at his hotel direct from his having tea with the Queen and the Duke of Edinburgh at Buckingham Palace. He couldn't get over the way the band of the Brigade of Guards mastered Hatikvah, the Israeli national anthem. Meanwhile, the royals couldn't get over the fact that Israel had a president who spoke like an Irishman. He entertained them with stories of his days by the Liffey and as a British army officer. No, they didn't have many official visitors with that sort of pedigree.

When Anwar Sadat was murdered in 1981, Herzog was our principal interviewee – discussing the amazing events that led to the Egyptian president coming to Jerusalem just a few years before. More, we talked about his legacy. He wasn't as optimistic as I would have liked him to be about the prospects for Sadat's earth-shattering trip to Israel being repeated by other Arab leaders. There was one other prominent Israeli on that programme: Moshe Dayan, since the 1956 Sinai campaign the one-eyed hero of every Jew in every country in the world. He spoke as a soldier about a soldier. Dayan said that he couldn't fail to be impressed by the Egyptian's gambling instincts – in daring to start the Yom Kippur War by crossing the Suez Canal ('We didn't like it, but it was a masterstroke of strategy. He knew he couldn't win, but he had bought himself a place at the negotiating table') and then in coming to Israel, being met by President Katzir, Menachem Begin and Golda Meir and then addressing the Knesset. The following week, Dayan himself died. It was almost as if we were bestowing a kiss of death. That thought didn't prevent Chaim Herzog from paying a *YDHTBJ* tribute.

Nor did it stop the man largely credited with reversing Israel's situation in that war, by forcing the Egyptians back across the Canal and into 'Africa', coming on the show, too. General Ariel Sharon was suitably bullish. Israel had to hold on to its gains and strengthen its settlements. When I later spoke to the Egyptian ambassador (yes, it was important to give a rounded picture of events), he was scathing about that, but he said that Egypt needed peace. I followed that up with three visits to Cairo over the next 15 years. Each time, I spoke to government people, all of whom said that the peace treaty with the Jewish state was permanent. 'Our people might not like it,' said a spokesman off the record, 'but what choice do we have? It would be stupid to think that there is any sense in continuing the war.'

I didn't just depend on 'names' to give us our Israel coverage. For 20 years, the words 'and now over to our man in Jerusalem' signalled the intelligent interpretation of the day's news in the Israeli capital that people came to expect from 'our man' – Asher Wallfish. Asher was a brilliant reporter who had contacts in high places. But, more than that, he had instincts and a nose for what was happening in his country. Week after week, we knew more about what was going on in the Jewish state than almost any other branch of the media. If Wallfish said it, it had to be true – as the British national press and other broadcastsing media discovered when they reported on our reports.

Asher was a Mancunian who had been in Israel since going there as a member of the Habonim youth group in 1949 and was a star reporter on the *Jerusalem Post*. He enjoyed the exposure we were able to give him on the programme and we enjoyed his excellent reporting.

Another place where we needed a resident correspondent was Washington. Again, we went to the *Jerusalem Post* for help. Their Washington correspondent, Wolf Blitzer, was only too happy to get some broadcasting experience – he had never done any before my call. Weekly, our 'man in Washington' talked about America's Middle East policy or other events concerning American Jews. He stayed with us for about five years – and then had to say 'No more'. The man who learnt his broadcasting skills on *You Don't Have To Be Jewish* had got a job with CNN as their White House correspondent, and they wouldn't allow him to appear on any other stations. He is now one of the network's most important commentators.

We had a man in Paris, too – Michel Zletovski, an intelligent Polish-born Frenchman who spoke perfect English and knew everything anyone needed to know about the Jews across the Channel. When I went to Paris to interview the members of the family business of Nazi hunters, Serge Klarsfeld, his wife Beatte and their son Armand, Michel organised it for me. 'I'll pick you up afterwards,' he said that day in 1988. He did – and handed me a crash helmet. It wasn't like riding on my old Bella. He had a highly powered motor cycle which he drove the wrong way up one-way streets, on pavements and along alleyways I wouldn't have cared to walk through. I have to say I wasn't surprised that soon afterwards he had had a serious accident on that machine – but I was delighted to hear he had recovered.

The Klarsfelds, however, were and are remarkable – working every day of every week, chasing Nazis and bringing them to justice. Beatte, the daughter of a Wehrmacht officer, took it as her duty to humanity to reclaim a good name for Germany – and chose to do so by breaking into the Bundestag and slapping the face of the Chancellor, Herr Kissinger. Their stories made wonderful radio – how Beatte had gone to Syria on a false passport and bearded a top Nazi in his lair, bringing him out of hiding for the first time – on the false pretext of warning him that the Israelis knew where he was, and he ought to escape; how Serge hid while his father was rounded up in his home; how Armand fronted the operation in the courts because he was a better advocate than his father. The capture of every Nazi in France was due to this amazing family.

But Israel was always at the top of our 'foreign' agenda, although it has to be said that by now Israel was no longer thought of as just another foreign country by the Jews – and this was appreciated by the people who now ran Radio London. In 1986 John Demjanjuk, a Ukranian living in America, was taken to Israel to stand trial as a war criminal, a concentration camp guard known as Ivan the Terrible. Derrick Amore, then the station manager (he had formerly been producer of the award-winning and ground-breaking TV news programme, *Tonight*) suggested that we cover the trial nightly. That actually never happened – it seemed more than we could cope with. Four years later, Demjanjuk won an appeal against his life sentence (the decision of the Israeli Supreme Court was a wonderful example of the country's jurisprudence principles). But we did cover Israeli elections – live. There was a lot of excitement about giving results as they came through, – 'Here comes Petach Tikvah South, Likud wins...Now, Haifa North East. Labor again.' It was our plan to bring this to the *YDHTBJ* listeners. Alas, Israeli elections are not done that way, but it was exciting, nevertheless, and I was always grateful for Radio London's interest.

I was also, by the way, grateful to Merle Kessler, who helped organise things for me, first when she worked for the British Zionist Federation and then when she became my assistant. Later, when she emigrated to Israel, she provided us with regular 'Letters from Israel', our own version of Alistair Cooke's *Letter from America*. She did the job superbly, developing a style that fitted in perfectly with what we wanted.

Incidentally, my son cut his broadcasting teeth when he himself was in Israel with Habonim during his 'gap' year between leaving school and going to Oxford. It was he who wrote the first of these letters. There were charges of nepotism which I treated with the contempt they deserved. Jonathan did them wonderfully and had he not done so, he would never have got on the air. While I was working on the programme, that was all that mattered. 'Chip off the old block,' people inevitably said. 'Are you Michael Freedland's son?' they asked him. Today, I am asked if I am Jonathan Freedland's father. The block from which came the young chip.

# 18    A foreign minister, a president and a prince

Of course, for us on *YDHTBJ*, 'names' still counted. And if there was any individual Israeli who saw the world picture into which his country fitted it was the man who was married to an Egyptian-born woman – the sister of Chaim Herzog's wife. Abba Eban was, without much doubt, Israel's finest diplomatic export and probably its most brilliant government figure before or since.

The Israelis didn't go for him all that much. He was, for them, too clever by half. That has always been one of the country's biggest faults – a determination to show that if there is a Sabra (or, failing that, a Central European or even a Sephardi) to occupy a position of power, anyone else should be reckoned as second best. What they disliked about Eban was that he not only had the brains of an Oxford or Cambridge don (he had been educated at Cambridge), he spoke like one. In fact, he spoke almost any language you could think of.

Before Herzog became ambassador to the UN, Eban was Israel's foreign minister. I first came across him when I was in New York in 1967, four years before *YDHTBJ* was born. He was in the city to address the world body on the effects of the Six Day War. I was in a taxi as he made his speech, generally regarded as one of the most erudite in the history of the UN.

You can't argue with New York taxi drivers, who may not always know where they are going, but are certain of their attitudes to life and the rectitude of what they are doing. Today, most of them come from the Indian sub-continent or from Russia, but in the 1960s, they were usually Jewish native New Yorkers. The driver of this one, who was supposed to take me from the St Moritz Hotel to Riverside Drive, decided that it was more important to hear Eban's speech than to get me to my destination. As the foreign minister spoke the language of Shakespeare as though he were Laurence Olivier at his most eloquent reciting the words of Winston Churchill at his most stirring, the driver pulled his cab over and stopped. The speech drowned out the screeches of other taxis, truck drivers shouting abuse and pedestrians who believed they had diced with death walking in front of my cab. 'Gee,' said the driver, turning his head back to me (it was before the days of the Perspex screens now in use; then, the most dangerous passenger was one who didn't have change for a ten dollar bill), 'ain't it great what a swell education can do for a guy!'

I had to agree and so did most American and British Jews, who were so proud of an Israeli foreign minister who not only spoke the Queen's English, but probably knew it better than did the Queen herself. But there were Israelis who mistrusted him as being not really one of them. They resented the comfort he felt in London and Washington, where he had been the country's most eminent ambassador. The Americans loved the fact that he had been born in South Africa but came to Britain as a baby and stayed there, and served, too, in the British army.

That was not a pedigree that the average man in the Ashkelon street thought much of. The fact that he had worked for a Jewish state during the difficult days of the British mandate, that he had served the British Zionist Federation and been the right-hand man of Chaim Weizmann, the first president of the state, cut little ice. That he had been Israel's UN representative at the very beginning, and as such had hoisted the blue-and-white flag outside the New York headquarters while still in his thirties, didn't matter as much as it should have.

There was never any chance of his being prime minister, although he dearly wanted to be and would have been the best spokesman on international television that the Israelis could have wished for. (He told me he had been offered the presidency twice but had rejected it as having too little power.) He tied opponents into knots that would have done credit to a sailor. But there was another factor that didn't exactly endear him to the Israeli voters. They were not sure they appreciated his love of the fine life. He may have been a member of the Israeli Labor Party, but it was difficult to think of him as a socialist. He always stayed at the best hotels. Invariably when I met him at one of them, there would be a shopping bag from Harrods or Saks Fifth Avenue by the typewriter which went everywhere with him. As he said, 'I can't allow a day to go by without writing something.' I appreciated that.

If there were few people who knew as many languages as he did, very few could translate them into an English vocabulary they hardly knew existed. His tongue twisted around words that he might easily have made up, but you knew they were real because he said them. Richard Nixon once remarked to Golda Meir, at a time when Henry Kissinger was secretary of state, that they both had Jewish foreign ministers. 'Yes,' said the redoubtable Golda, 'but mine speaks better English than yours.'

I witnessed his gift of languages at first hand at a reception in the Israeli capital following a session of the World Jewish Congress. He was at the centre of a coterie of delegates who wanted his ear – and his opinions. One by one they came to him and to each he spoke in their own language. To a group from Switzerland, he talked about their concerns about a fascist revival – in German. A delegate from Argentina was given his honest opinion on the chances of a Likud government taking power – in Spanish. He was introduced to a refusenik and spoke to him in Russian. When a French friend came up to him, he held out his hand and, of course, spoke in French. There were no natural breaks between these conversations. It was like a crowd gathering around a speaker after his lecture, but most lecturers have to deal with questions in only one language.

I won't forget that evening easily. For one thing, my rather hefty portable tape recorder was left by a door. Security men went crazy and were about to thrust a cordon across the room, ready to blow it up, before I rushed over to claim it. (I had seen such a thing happen on the bus that skirted Ben Gurion airport just the day before. A religious gentleman had left his attaché case on the bus – which was stopped while an army patrol came aboard, took away the case and blew it up in the middle of the road. In the midst of the explosion, you could plainly see that the case contained an orange, a banana and a packet of sandwiches, all of which flew up in the path of oncoming traffic. I've often wondered what the poor man had for lunch that day.)

That tape recorder, a state-of-the-art Uher, which was standard BBC issue of the time, was not my friend that night. I had an interview arranged with Mr Eban, who came into the room, wiping the sweat from his brow, his treble chins wobbling as he did so. I switched the machine on and...nothing. I knew it had problems with battery connections, but thought they had been sorted out. The statesman watched in horrified fascination while I first took the back off the machine, then removed the batteries and adjusted another part whose purpose I was never really sure about. It was all rather like that film in which Laurel and Hardy try to get a car moving by opening up the bonnet, removing and then throwing away every part, as though they were surgeons in the midst of a major operation.

Mr Eban was not amused. Finally, he said: 'Would you like me to lend you a tape recorder?' The indignity of all that implied was not calculated to put me at my ease, but I said something like: 'Nothing could record as well as this one – when it's working.' I think he laughed at that. I didn't, but I did manage to give the machine one last kick and got it going long enough to get a pretty good interview.

I wouldn't say that he and I were ever close friends. But he knew me, knew my name and agreed to talk on the programme whenever I wanted him to do so. He introduced me to his wife and said something like, 'You'll never guess the name of his radio programme.' She didn't, but I was pleased that he had remembered it.

Eban was, as well as being erudite, a brilliant wit. He told me once how glad he was to be in London – 'the city where you hear my two favourite languages, English and Arabic'. That could, of course, be one reason why Hebrew-speakers didn't like him. His fellow Knesset members certainly didn't go much for the fact that his Hebrew was also better than any of theirs. I caught up with him soon after the 1977 Labour defeat by Menachem Begin's Likud. Begin had been in power for three weeks. 'What do you think of the new government?' I asked. Eban didn't take ten seconds to give me his response. 'Three weeks ago,' he said, 'I remarked that we ought to give them a chance. Well, they have had that now and it's time for a change.'

The most notable programmes he did on *YDHTBJ* were a series in which I asked him about his life and the people he knew. He talked about leaders of the then present. He admired Yitzhak Rabin, was infuriated with Golda Meir, and saw Richard Nixon at his very worst – 'He gave us arms in the Yom Kippur war and this helped to turn the tide, but as we walked in the rose garden, I realised that he was an anti-Semite.' And he didn't leave the icons of his country unscathed. Chaim Weizmann was under the thumb of his wife – a terrible snob. Of course, people have said that about Eban himself. Personally, I just think he knew how good he was.

The great irony was that when Eban died in 2003, it was Alzheimers disease that felled him. The notion that that amazing brain could be turned to mush is too terrible to contemplate. And what does that say to those who insist you must keep your mind active by doing a daily crossword?

Most of the Israeli leaders of the late twentieth century appeared on our programme. I went to the country often and every prime minister from Golda onwards was featured. I would like to have interviewed her predecessor Levi Eshkol, who led the country during the Six Day War, the only prime minister whose first language was Yiddish. I liked what I had heard about the man who was diplomatically deaf when the occasion demanded – he was particularly hard of hearing when Americans were calling for ceasefires. The only cloud on the horizon was that I had met his wife and didn't enjoy the experience. Mme Eshkol in 1967 was young and attractive, and came to Britain to launch an Israeli passenger ship, the *Nili*, at the Glasgow shipyards where it had been built. The Radio Four *Woman's Hour* programme had sent me to interview her. She had agreed. But when I got to Glasgow on the specially chartered plane for Jewish leaders and journalists, she decided to change her mind. 'But I've come from London to meet you,' I pleaded. 'How nice for you,' she replied. In the end, the very charming wife of the current British ambassador to Tel Aviv agreed to speak to me, and delightful she was. The programme producer loved our talk.

Yitzhak Rabin in his first term of office was dour but interesting, and pulled no punches in condemning Israel's enemies. Menachem Begin had, I always thought, a messianic streak about him, but Anglo-Jewry loved him almost as one of their own. At a service at London's St John's Wood Synagogue, he spoke from the pulpit before talking on *YDHTBJ*.

Then there was Shimon Peres. I had first interviewed him when he was minister of defence. I saw him at the ministry, which looked vaguely like a prison camp. Armed guards at the gates, lots of barbed wire and a search for hidden bombs inside my famous tape recorder. When I was introduced to the minister, then at the height of his powers, he wouldn't talk until he was sure that his spokesman was in the room with a tape recorder of his own. He caused a bit of a stir by saying that he hoped and believed that the PLO, then a proscribed organisation in Israel, could under certain circumstances be recognised.

Later, in opposition, I called at his office at the Tel Aviv head-quarters of the Labor Party. A man wearing a beret, a rather untidy blue jacket and reading a paper as he smoked a cigarette looked my way and then looked in the opposite direction. 'Mr Peres?' he asked. 'Upstairs.' Upstairs, sitting at a large desk with a painting of his idol David Ben Gurion hanging behind it, was Shimon Peres, leader of the opposition. The door was open. I could have been a terrorist, my Uher a bomb. It was a lapse in security that I still find incredible. Even in 1981, before the advent of the suicide bomber, Israel was a country that knew all about terrorism.

The strangest of those Israeli premiers was Yitzhak Shamir, a little gnome of a man who had been active in the extreme right-wing Lehi organisation and always seemed to think that he had to be belligerent to be effective. He and Peres had an arrangement that was probably unique in politics – they shared the premiership, or, rather, they had an agreement that after Peres had sat in the prime minister's chair for two years, Shamir would take over. Amazingly, it happened. I interviewed the then Likud leader at the Knesset, when he was surrounded by so many security people that you could barely see the man himself. 'I am always willing to go to the table of negotiations,' he said in our talk, and then proceeded to explain that it would have to be on the condition of Israel holding on to all it had gained in war. A recipe for peace? I asked. 'It is my recipe and Israel's recipe,' he replied.

Binyamin Netanyahu was totally different. His politics were surely never mine, but he was an attractive personality – in his younger days, just *how* attractive the women working with me would always be willing to testify – and a marvellous communicator.

It seems that representing Israel at the UN has to be the spring-board to greater things. When the American-educated Bibi was in New York, he was following in some pretty remarkable footsteps – and leaving his own prints in the sand outside the big East River building. Not since Eban had there been an advocate for the Jewish state's cause who had been so impressive on television – and in America and Britain, too, that was even more vitally important. It wasn't that Israel had learned its lessons as far as PR were concerned. More by luck than judgement, Netanyahu occupied a role that lent itself to the small screen and he was available almost by default.

He and I first got together when he came to London on a private visit and I met him at his hotel. His wife (there have been another two since then) was busy in their bedroom, so it wasn't a good time for an interview. That being so, how about going to the studio? So I drove him through the streets of London and we talked at Radio London's Marylebone High Street headquarters. No security men, no hangers-on. It was a fascinating talk. A few years later, I was in Israel and desperately trying to get a meeting with the then foreign minister. Not easy, I was told. I then bumped into him as he sipped a drink in the bar of the Tel Aviv Hilton. He recognised me and agreed to talk – the following day. There were other times and other chats. By then, however, it was difficult for us to agree on much, apart from the priority of protecting Israel and its borders. How the state did that was a different ballgame altogether.

Yitzhak Rabin came to London in the late 1980s at the time that his former deputy Shimon Peres had taken over the leadership of the Labor Party. He came into the studio and we talked about the international situation, even about his personal lifestyle. Then came the question no one had yet thought to ask him: was he going to try to lead the Labor Party again? The former prime minister, who had lost his job as the result of a smallish financial scandal while ambassador in Washington (both he and his wife had American bank accounts), was now considered to be cleaner than clean, but as yet had done nothing that would make people think he was about to reclaim the leadership. 'I don't rule out anything,' he told me, 'but I have no plans – at present.'

That answer caused a huge brouhaha in Israel. The next day, I met him on the El Al plane that was taking us both to Ben Gurion Airport from London (he was in first class; I wasn't). 'You set the cats among the pigeons,' he said. 'All the papers are saying that I opened up my leadership election campaign on the BBC yesterday.' He laughed. I smiled. It was the beginning of his campaign – and he won. When he became prime minister again in 1992, he set in motion a peace onslaught that got the whole world buzzing and we covered it all – for as long as our programme lasted. Sadly, we were no longer there to pay him tribute when he was gunned down by a *Jewish* assassin in 1995. Ironically, that death could have paved the way for everlasting peace – had it not been later dashed by muddled political thinking on both sides. For the first time ever, an American president, a British Prince of Wales and prime minister and Arab kings and princes (even from Saudi Arabia) had landed on Israeli soil, throwing away all previous inhibitions about doing so. It could have been the start of a great change. Unfortunately, it wasn't.

Nevertheless, it wasn't the old Arab–Israel world – and hadn't been since the day that Begin and Sadat signed their peace treaty on the White House lawn in 1979. (We did a programme that day from Jerusalem, which also coincided with Israel winning the Eurovision song contest; I was never sure which was the more exciting event for our listeners.)

Back in 1972, when the Olympic athletes had been massacred, Jordan's King Hussein had expressed his horror. I thought it was an opportunity for a scoop. I wrote to the royal palace in Amman requesting an interview. The request was turned down, but extremely nicely – 'wishing you well in your work'.

Asher Wallfish in one of his dispatches said something about Jordan that was not totally flattering. It was an intransigent society that was saying nice things but doing nothing to improve the chances of peace. That week, a letter arrived from the Jordanian information bureau. It was signed 'Naomi Glubb' and said, very politely, that we had got it all wrong. I was so struck by the fact that the Jordanians were listening to *YDHTBJ* that I wrote back to say thank you, and that if we had got anything wrong, I'd like to know about it and possibly put matters right. Ms Glubb turned out to be the adopted daughter of Lieutenant-General Sir John Bagot Glubb, who, as Glubb Pasha, commanded the Arab Legion when they attacked the infant State of Israel in 1948. The first King Abdullah had appointed him, but it was his grandson Hussein who had subsequently sacked him. Ms Glubb asked me if I would like to meet her at the Information Office, round the corner from Buckingham Palace.

Of course, I went. I met her boss, the highly personable Nasser Joudah, who asked me if there was anything he could do for me.

Yes, I said, I'd like to meet the Crown Prince. What I didn't know at that time was that HRH Crown Prince Hassan bin Tallel was his father-in-law.

In November 1993 I landed at Amman airport, to be greeted by a soldier in battledress. He didn't look at all like one of his Israeli counterparts. His tunic was pressed, his boots mirror-shiny. 'Your passport, please,' he said. All sorts of thoughts entered my mind. Did they think I was an Israeli spy? Had there been a palace coup and the prince no longer had any power there (shades of what would happen a few years later)? Was I under arrest? I felt better when the soldier saluted me. I had never mastered the art of giving a salute when I was in Aldershot, now I was actually *receiving* one. He asked me for my baggage slips. I gave them. Fifteen minutes later, no baggage carousels to wait for, no trolleys to get, no passport or immigration queues to suffer, he appeared again – and saluted again. Would I care to follow him? I cared and I followed – to a waiting Mercedes. He saluted yet again, invited me to take my place in the back – it was so comfortable, I virtually sank into the seat – and we drove off to the palace complex.

I was welcomed with sweet Arab tea, served by the most polite soldiers I have ever met. The thought running through my mind was simple: if Israeli troops could be even half as smart or as quarter polite, they would indeed be the world's greatest army. (I had put that to Chaim Herzog in one of our chats. Herzog, himself a former Irish Guards major and gifted with Anglo-Saxon manners, who looked immaculate at all times (particularly when in uniform), put it bluntly: 'Yes, it would be very nice. But we have to have other priorities. I tend to think that knowing how to win wars and save lives is even more important than having nicely pressed uniforms. But, yes, it would be nice if they were a little smarter.')

Eventually another flunky came to take me to the Presence in the Palace. This was not the sort of room you would expect in a royal house – no great paintings, although there was a huge portrait of the King with his arms around his brother, the Crown Prince. There was no chandelier, no gold fittings. Instead, I was taken to a room that would have looked attractive in one of the classier suburbs. Lots of glass and french windows leading out on to a small garden stocked with grapefruit trees.

The prince entered, a short, tubby, moustachioed man whom I

immediately discovered laughed a lot and laughed loudly. So loudly, in fact, that when he chortled the building seemed to rock. Or was it some previously unknown volcano in the Amman area?

That was the first impression. The second was more than a mere instant discovery: this was a man with a brilliant intellect, which accounted for the fact that his brother, the King, had 30 years earlier named him Crown Prince and his successor to the throne – rather than his then infant son Abdullah. We didn't know at that stage that Hussein would one day change his mind and make Abdullah Crown Prince and then King after all. At that stage, Hassan, the man whose photograph next to that of the king appeared on posters all over Amman, on Government buildings, next to cinemas, even on dust carts, was the undisputed next monarch.

He was also the one man in Jordan to whom the Israelis could relate. When we met that day in 1983, he was leading his country's team negotiating with the Jewish state. He and Shimon Peres were on first-name terms. He was almost the Jordanians' Abba Eban. He had learned Hebrew at Oxford, had taken an exam in Mishnah at the time of the Six Day War. He seemed to understand the Israeli mind. All that came through in one of the most impressive interviews I had ever done on *You Don't Have To Be Jewish* (if ever the programme's title was proved appropriate, this was the time).

Hassan wanted peace, saw no reason why there couldn't be an instant agreement. There was little to separate the two sides, no notions of the hatred that existed in other Arab countries. How, I asked, did he feel when he went to Jerusalem? At that stage, he hadn't gone to the Israeli capital. But he looked longingly at the land on the other side of the Jordan river – not enviously, because he hoped that before long, there would be opportunities for his countrymen to travel freely into Israel and for Israelis to go to Jordan.

He enjoyed talking to Israelis. 'I have discovered that with them, discussions are a martial art.' That was an example of his brilliant mind. I made the mistake of putting that to him. 'Bullshit,' he replied.

There would be two other meetings with the prince. By the time the second trip came around, after the death of *YDHTBJ* (I was writing for the *Sunday Express*) he was prince regent, deputising for his dying brother, lying in an American hospital. He had taken over King Hussein's office and was saluted by armed guards as he and I moved into the king's much more formal and ornate study. Apart from the volcanic laughs, this was a more serious man, talking about the Middle East situation and the love he felt for his country. One day a week, he rode on horseback through Amman, and each cobblestone he seemed to know intimately.

On the third occasion, he had already been usurped by Hussein on his return to Amman – just a couple of weeks before his death. I asked him how he felt. Sad, he said, that his brother had not told him before writing a letter alleging all sorts of terrible things that Hassan had done and which he staunchly denied. I believed him. He was quite clearly not a man who sacked generals, who had redecorated the royal study all as part of a scheme to take over the throne before his time. 'I was unhappy that I was not able to mourn my brother as I should have wished. People were afraid to offer their condolences' – because, he suggested, they wouldn't want to be identified with the losing side. Yet he had loved his brother. 'I am of Hussein and Hussein was of me,' he said in one of those wonderful parable-type Arabic statements.

Plainly, this was a man to admire and one whom I liked enormously.

# 19    ...And other Arabs

No one could say that the Jordanians loved Israel – there were too many Palestinians (half its population formerly lived on the West Bank and in parts of what is now Israel) for that to happen. Yet I was able, on mike, to explain the emotions I felt at seeing something that too few Israelis or other Jews ever had. Ever since the establishment of the state, back in 1948, people had gone to the Red Sea port and seaside resort of Eilat and seen, as close by as your neighbourhood supermarket perhaps, the Jordanian port of Aqaba, no more than three or four miles away. What was it like? Thinking tourists, from the time when Eilat consisted of a couple of boarding houses and roads that didn't have the advantage of traffic lights, have wondered about that for 50 years. Now I could watch the lights of Eilat – from Aqaba. I met Jordanians who regularly crossed the border. One man even went there to buy his groceries.

There were plans to twin the two towns officially. At the Jordan–Israel peace talks, Prince Hassan had suggested to David Lewis, one of the most unsung but most vital friends of Israel, that he should extend his business interests to the Jordanian coast. Lewis, to whom I had reason to be extraordinarily grateful, virtually created modern Eilat. He built most of the resort's hotels. Hassan asked him to think of building one on the Jordan side of the Gulf of Aqaba (the Israelis call it the Gulf of Eilat) and he not only said he would, he actually started doing so. He had even got as far as appointing a general manager – but it all died a death with the coming of the 2001 intifada.

I could have forecast that it would be so. The Palestinian leadership, or what there was of it, didn't want any solution or any contribution to that solution that might limit its power. As Abba Eban had said:

'They never lose an opportunity to lose an opportunity.'

The idea of an Israeli-backed Jordanian hotel would not have been welcomed by Yasser Arafat. Nothing was good for the fork-tongued Palestinian leader who preached peace in English and war in Arabic. When I met him in London, he put the blame for all the troubles in the area squarely on Israel. When I asked him if he did not think he was being unreasonable in not recognising that his side had its faults, too, he looked at me squarely in the eye and concluded our interview. But it was a useful contribution to the programme.

Going to Arab countries was one of the most revealing experiences of running a Jewish radio programme – certainly of the kind I had developed. When I reported the Egyptians' insistence that they really did want peace with Israel, it was plain that if they could do without a Jewish state in their midst, they would be happy to do so. However, they were accepting realities. But it wasn't all wonderful. I went to the Cairo Synagogue and it was clear that these were its dying days. The chances of regular services being held there for much longer were remote in the extreme.

Going to the pyramids, it was fascinating to see just how many Israelis were also there, lining up to crawl up to the top of the remarkable architectural structures for which they claimed ancestral rights. Whether my great, great- (to the power of a thousand or so) grandfathers actually did build them has never been reliably proved, but tradition says that they did while the taskmasters went at them with their whips (just look at a Passover *Haggadah* to see those pictures of the children of Israel, their suffering and the pyramids always in the background).

All that was nice and nostalgic. What I saw at the local Intercontintel Hotel was not, and made an item in the programme that caused quite a stir at the Egyptian embassy in London. It appeared that the most popular volumes in the hotel's bookstore was a collection (in various languages) of that infamous forgery, *The Protocols of the Elders of Zion*. The hotel told us that the books would be withdrawn (once all copies had been sold), but I gather they never have been.

A trip to Morocco would be happier. It was 1994 and *YDHTBJ* was on its last broadcasting legs. The Moroccan government was anxious, if only informally, to establish some sort of relationship with Israel. They were looking for conduits and Anglo-Jewry seemed one that could be useful. But who do they go to? They looked to the media. We were on top of that list.

There was a good excuse for this. The minister of tourism was Jewish. Would I like to interview him in Rabat? Well, of course I would. And, I told the tourist office in London, that could lead me to do a programme on the Jews of Morocco. Wonderful, they said.

The minister was a gem. Not so much for what he said – the expected statements about Morocco offering so many places of interest, so many beautiful sites – but for his recommendations to the other people who counted in the country and in the Jewish community. The first was the eloquent and elegant Jacques Amar, administrator of the royal court. He wore a marvellously tailored blue suit, with the ribbon of a Moroccan knighthood on the lapel. If you wanted to be in the presence of an impressive, dignified man who knew what was going on in this country that traversed the world of Arab North Africa and the Middle East, no one could be more helpful. He spoke beautifully and knowledgeably.

He spoke about relations with Israel. I wasn't sure what he would say. 'Of course, I have very special feelings about Israel,' he said. 'I am a Jew and the Jews of Morocco do feel very close to the Jewish state – without compromising their patriotism and their citizenship of their country.' As I looked out of the huge windows in his book-lined office, with pictures of King Hassan on his desk, it became a more and more fascinating story. This man was the King's financial adviser. As Sara remarked as we left, 'This man is a twentieth-century Joseph – adviser to a king.'

The story got even better. Back to the tourism minister, who said he had someone else he would like me to meet – the King's doctor. He was happy to meet me, too. 'In fact,' he said, 'he'd like you to come to lunch. He'll meet you at your hotel and take you.' Sara and I looked at each other. There would be problems. How do you insult a man and tell him we might not be able to enjoy the restaurant he would take us to? We were strictly kosher. More than that, this was the second day of the festival of Succot. We didn't really want to go to a restaurant.

The doctor was waiting for us in the hotel lobby as we returned there – resplendent in the uniform of a Moroccan army colonel. 'I'd like to take you to our home,' he said, once we had introduced ourselves and I had told him that I wanted to interview him for my radio programme. 'You are well?' 'Yes,' I said, 'thank you, we are.'

'Well, I'm glad,' he answered. 'I thought you were ill and needed some treatment.' He took us to his car. 'It's about half an hour,' he said. We drove through the city into a leafy suburb. Into the drive of a detached house we went, one that would have looked good anywhere, in Radlett as much as it did in Rabat. His wife and his two sons were waiting for us. 'Sit down and have a drink,' he said. The wine was delightful and his wife and his sons were, too. 'You come from London?' his wife asked. His sons said they were going off to Paris soon – to study medicine so that they could compete with their father.

'Come,' said Colonel Victor Ohayon, 'it's time we went in for lunch.' This was going to be very difficult indeed. We followed, both of us trying to find polite, kind words for restricting what we were going to eat. The doctor opened the double doors of the room where we were sitting – and led us into his...*succah*, the 'tabernacle' in which strictly Orthodox Jews sit and eat (and in some cases sleep) during Succot. We looked at each other – and then at the table. An embroidered cloth covered two *challot*, the loaves eaten on the Sabbath and festivals. Next to it, a bottle of wine and a silver goblet, the traditional *becher*.

This was more than we could ever have hoped. A delicious kosher meal awaited us. Succot in Morocco. His sons told us why they were going to Paris – not just to study medicine, but in the hope that they would find brides. It was difficult to meet Jewish girls in Morocco. They did not want to marry out of the faith. So it wasn't just the food that made us think that Jewish life in this Arab country was so familiar. 'Would you like to go to the synagogue tonight?' our host asked. We said we would. That night, we *davened* the festival evening service in one synagogue and then went on to another. It all made a wonderfully unexpected programme. More important, this was a marvellous human experience, a chance to meet people we would never have imagined. A chance to see Jewish life in a corner of the world so often ignored by other writers and, indeed, by most of the Jewish world.

## 20  The never-to-be-forgotten – the Holocaust as we did remember it

Those visits to Russia had given an impression of a community that was beleaguered, of people desperate to go to Israel, of Jews who knew they were Jewish and wanted more than anything to be able to practise their faith and take part in their culture. The other countries of Eastern Europe offered a different scene. Here, there were tiny pockets of Jewish communities, people both young and old who in their own way did still practise Judaism, even if it was merely a sort that had to look over its shoulders.

In 1983 I was in Warsaw, to join in the commemoration of the fortieth anniversary of the ghetto uprising. *YDHTBJ* listeners heard the sound of muffled drums from Polish soldiers and of a group of British Jews singing 'David Melech, Yisrael', 'David King of Israel', a song that might well have been last heard in that city in 1943. I talked to a middle-aged man who in between tears and piercing screams listed the names of his entire family, murdered by the Nazis 40 years earlier.

A party of Jews from all over the world took most of the rooms at one of the few luxury hotels in the city – on Friday night, the Chief Rabbi of Tel Aviv waited patiently in the lobby for a lift to take him to his floor. He was hoping someone else was going there, too, or preferably to the one above. The Sabbbath regulations wouldn't allow him to press a button himself. If, on the other hand, there was someone on his floor, he could get out the lift and then go to his room. If there was someone who then got out at a higher floor, he could be merely joining an elevator that was travelling in any case, with someone else pressing the buttons. Such circumventions of the Jewish religious law hadn't been known in Poland for 40 years either, and our listeners probably wondered if they would ever be heard of again.

We went to the home town of Holocaust survivor Ben Helfgott, who survived Auschwitz, Buchenwald, Schlieben and Theresienstadt to come to Britain – and eleven years later represented his new country at the 1956 Olympics. Diminutive Ben was a weight-lifter. A weight he could not lift from his mind was that of seeing his family wiped out – and of watching most of his local community, including his mother, being herded into the synagogue, which was then set alight.

We walked through the streets and saw house after house with signs of – well, missing signs: the spaces that could never be totally eradicated which had contained the *mazuzot* on the doorposts.

Before the Holocaust, Poland had had the biggest Jewish population in Europe, some three million. Now there were just 3,000. Yet they had their own Yiddish theatre and, again, I recorded it. The theatre was packed, mostly with Jews there for the commemoration. If anyone went to it during the rest of the year, they were simply watching an ancient culture and listening to a language no one in Warsaw spoke or understood any more. But I was told over and over again that that culture and that language were revered as part of the history of Poland – a country where anti-Semitism had been rife even before the Nazis moved in, where there had been pogroms organised by the Poles themselves while the Germans looked on approvingly and where there had been a massacre when the war was all over. A government minister told me for the programme: 'How can we ignore the great contribution that the Jews made here? It was their country as much as ours.' A country where the wheels of the Nazi murder machine spun to a crescendo of horror.

It was in Poland where the stench of the death camps pervaded the atmosphere for more than four years – some would say it does to this day. It was in Poland that was sited the one place that has served as a metaphor for the Holocaust – Auschwitz. We went to Auschwitz – Greville Janner, Martin Savitt, an Israeli member of the Knesset, who was also a rabbi, and I. It was almost a half century since the end of World War Two, but I swear I could still smell that stench of death. There were, incredibly, still ashes on the roads leading to the sign proclaiming 'Arbeit Macht Frei'. The Israeli rabbi said Kaddish over what we took to be a mass grave. All the soil of the Birkenau section of Auschwitz had been part of a mass grave, even if it was only because the ashes from the chimneys fell there. As the prayers were being recited, I allowed my feet to scrape that soil. Underneath, I found a spoon. Who, I wondered, had once used that spoon? What food had it ever helped into that unknown mouth?

It took a long time for the memory of that terrible place – the sight of piles of children's shoes, of suitcases, of miles of human hair – to fade, for the stench to be replaced by something more pleasant.

This was, though, just one episode in our campaign to bring the Holocaust to people's attention. Amazing though it now seems, when we spoke to the man who gave a title to the hitherto unnamed catastrophe, Elie Wiesel, on that second edition of *YDHDTBJ*, the Holocaust was not on every (or at least every Jewish) mind at that time. To us, there was just one person who acted as a kind of representative for all the other survivors of Hitler's death camps – my dear, much-missed friend Hugo Gryn.

Hugo was later a regular member of the team on Radio Four's *Moral Maze* programme – after the producer had heard him on *You Don't Have To Be Jewish*. He constantly held high the survivors' banner – but, more important, that of the victims. On one *Moral Maze*, he confronted a Holocaust denier, who could not have known what sort of match he had met in Hugo Gryn. The gas chambers were all a lie, said the man. Hugo looked into the man's eyes and you could almost feel the vibrations of those eyes being pierced by the Gryn mind. 'Look at me,' he told him, 'and tell me I did not see my little brother go with my grandparents into the gas chamber. Tell me I did not see it happen...' The man was destroyed. On our programme, Hugo told us the background to his period in Nazi captivity. It had to be among our most moving broadcasts. 'What about those who say the time has come to forgive?' I asked him. 'I have no right to forgive on behalf of six million people who cannot be offered that opportunity,' he replied.

In programme after programme he told the story, a new episode here, a new event to recall there. He put it all into a new human perspective. He told how the people of his little Czech town first realised that things were getting drastic. His grandfather, who owned a nearby farm, discovered that his cows had been attacked – all had their bellies cut open. Before long, human beings in that area would suffer similar fates. He talked about the subtle ways in which the Nazis, when they arrived after the cursed Munich pact, made their presence felt. They took local Jews prisoner, but said they would release them after the payment of a colossal ransom. For a weekend, the leaders of the community went round collecting gold, jewellery and coins. The Jews were released. 'That was very clever, because it meant that the Nazis kept their word – and we could trust them to do what they said. When they said that people were going to be resettled in a nice new area, they were believed.'

Jews in Czechoslovakia were among the first to be put on 'transports', but his town had been given a new nationality. It was now part of Germany's ally Hungary – which meant that it would take time before the citizens of Berehovo were told that they were going somewhere nice where they could find new homes and work. A train arrived at the local station. Hugo, an inquisitve youngster, went to investigate. 'There was a label on one of the cattle cars. It bore a name nobody had ever heard before. It was 'Auschwitz'.

The future Rabbi Gryn was a schoolboy at the time – one who had won a scholarship to a school with a tiny Jewish quota. Before long, however, he had been moved along with other Jewish students in Hungary to an exclusively Jewish school.

'What the Hungarians did not realise was that they were helping us, because we had some of the finest teachers and university lecturers in the country, men who had lost their job in other schools and colleges.' And, as he also said, among them were outstanding athletes and physical training experts. 'They taught us self-defence. It would prove useful.'

He was also useful to the people from Berehovo. 'On Sunday mornings, we used to get film shows – and they always included a newsreel. One of these showed the gallant Hungarian guys knocking the hell out of the Russians. In the background, we could see refugees being captured and marched to the camps. I recognised some of these people – they were from our town. So I quickly sent off a note home warning people to get out.'

Before long, Hugo would be sent to Auschwitz himself, after doing the horrific round of other camps, other forced marches, other indignities. One of those other places was Theresienstadt, not a concentration camp as such, although Jews were huddled together in less space with less food than would have normally been possible for an animal, let alone a human. It was the establishment set up by the Nazis as their showplace – photographers and movie cameramen were there for a Red Cross visit, to see happy faces of inmates walking in the streets, sitting in cafés, watching shows and operating sewing machines. Happy-looking people, all with Stars of David fixed to their clothes.

In truth, Theresienstadt was a way-station for Auschwitz and the other factories of death. In 1982 I went there with Hugo, just as I had gone to his home town and to Prague, where we stood by the grave of his ancestor, the famous Rabbi Loewe, around whom the story of the *golem* (the monster created to do the manual work in the rabbi's house) was woven. But it was in the Theresienstadt offices – just a stone's throw from where children painted pictures now on display and wrote unbearably touching essays and letters home – that, in an example of the superb Nazi bureaucratic efficiency, we saw the card indexes containing the names of all the inmates who had gone through its gates. Hugo found his own.

This was a man who was as loved as much as he bestowed his own love. When he died in 1996 at the early age of 66, he was missed as probably no other leading member of our community had been. Hundreds of people attended his funeral – alas, not the Chief Rabbi, Jonathan Sacks. I wrote an obituary in the *Guardian*. One deep regret was that there was no longer any *You Don't Have To Be Jewish* in which to pay tribute to a great man, a great Jew – and, not least, one of our most popular and most respected contributors.

There were similar survivor stories in other countries that the programme visited – in Hungary, one rabbi was described as the community's 'treasure'. We were warned about rabbis and officials being communist stooges, but there was no question about the honesty of Rabbi Abraham Schreiber, this charismic character. We went to the various Holocaust memorials, we spoke to survivors – like the brilliant Stephen Roth, head of the Institute of Jewish Affairs in London, who recalled the time when he and his family had joined other Budapest Jews lining up to try to get a Swedish passport care of Raoul Wallenberg, the diplomat who alone saved thousands of Jewish lives simply by giving them an instant transplant of nationality. 'We all took refuge in that house,' he said pointing to a nondescript structure. 'All day, we queued up for the toilet – joining the queue at the end once we had finished, because we knew that by the time we got to the front again we would need it once more.'

In Romania, the Chief Rabbi, Dr Moses Rosen – or, rather, 'His Eminence' Chief Rabbi Rosen – had, for reasons that no one was willing to publicly say at the time, managed to keep Jewish life alive – and at the same time be very friendly with the dictator, Nicolae Ceausescu. He said that by keeping that friendship more Romanian Jews left for Israel (which he seemed to visit monthly, stopping on the way to shop in Paris, London and New York, buying his wife a mink coat on one of the trips) than from any other Eastern European country. The trouble was that a lot of people wondered if there was more to it than that.

What was really interesting was not so much what was going on in Budapest as the situation in Transylvania. Here were places that were closer to the *shtetlach* of old than anywhere else in the world. There were doctors, dentists and tradesmen living in what appeared to be abject poverty – but in virtual cloistered Jewish communities. There were rabbis who still circumcised baby boys and slaughtered chickens for kosher consumption. They gave the group of British Jews with whom I travelled food that they had stored for special occasions, near-rotten apples, which were their big treats. We went to a Yiddish theatre, which was outstanding – this was the part of the world where that very theatrical tradition had had its birth.

There was, after every one of these visits, a feeling of Jewish brother and sisterhood, that very small Jewish world, a benign international conspiracy of love and friendship. I saw it in Berlin, where a then tiny community was trying to re-establish itself and prepare for the influx of Russian Jews who were about to arrive. It wasn't all that marvellous there, however – despite the fact that synagogues were being rebuilt, others restored, including the main shul, which had escaped Kristallnacht because it was so close to other 'Aryan' buildings. A small fortune was being spent on regilding its magnificent dome. There were places where Jewish history was being relived (not least in the former Gestapo head-quarters) and when I was there in 1992 they were already planning the Jewish museum, which is now one of the great tourist attractions. I spoke to a rabbi who had previously lived in London. Did he feel safe? I asked him. He produced a Luger pistol from his desk. 'I'm never without it,' he said. When he went out, he carried it as though it were a mobile telephone.

It was my – and the programme's – second visit to Germany. In 1985 I had gone to Hanover, the nearest place to the former Belsen concentration camp. It was where Gina Goldfinger, an inmate at the camp, had fallen in love with her interrogator, Norman Turgel, a British army sergeant. They were later married in Lubek, near the camp. The officiant was the man who later became minister of the Hendon Synagogue in London, Leslie Hardman.

I interviewed all three – and ran the interview along with a recording from the archives of the first Jewish service on German soil in five years, conducted in 1945 by Hardman for the pitifully few survivors. We heard two of them singing the concluding hymn, *Adon Olam*, Lord of the World. They were sisters – one of whom died a few days later.

But there was one other interviewee on the programme from Belsen who caught the imagination of our listeners – Chancellor Helmut Kohl, who told us, on this fortieth anniversary, how not only must it never happen again, it would *not* happen.

America and its huge (comparatively speaking) Jewish population always fascinated me and, I think, fascinated our listeners. We did numerous programmes from what I described as the biggest Jewish city in the world. I asked people to decide whether I meant Jerusalem or Tel Aviv – and then admitted I was talking about New York.

It always struck me just *how* Jewish that city was – every lawyer's and doctor's nameplate seemed to be Jewish, you walked down Fifth Avenue and every other person seemed to be a co-religionist. I spent an evening (a long but fascinating Saturday evening) listening to Menachem Shneerson, the Lubavicher Rebbe, addressing thousands of adoring disciples. (I liked what he said about professional students – it was the duty of every Jew to work for his family.) I went to a commencement exercise at Yeshiva University, an almost incredible institute that offered a synthesis of religious and secular studies. I spoke to rabbis who worried about the 'edifice complex' of their community, which was building too many new synagogues. And I met show people who confirmed the power of Broadway – and of its Jewish producers. In a theatre, you had to look far to find a gentile face. In the midst of an interval (sorry, intermission) a shout from the gallery to the stalls (sorry, orchestra) was as entertaining as the show on the stage. 'Sadie, how did you get those seats?' came the noise from upstairs. 'Me, I got twofers,' her friend replied. 'Twofers' – two for the price of one – have become a way of life in New York, and are almost, just almost, catching on in London.

## 21  Of prime ministers

Audience reaction showed that people enjoyed hearing about Jewish communities hundreds and sometimes thousands of miles away from their neighbourhood synagogues or delis – perhaps almost as much as they enjoyed listening to the great political figures of our world in that last quarter of the twentieth century. The Israeli prime ministers I mentioned earlier were not the only government leaders who appeared from time to time. Harold Wilson was something of a hero of mine, a fact that I didn't allow to influence any of the numerous occasions on which he appeared in the programme. The first time he appeared was in the period between his second and third administrations. Wilson and his wife Mary had just come back from Israel, where his son Giles was working on a kibbutz.

The Wilsons had joined him at a typical kibbutz dinner – at which the members seemed to be having a great time. 'I loved the way they ate their meat, Henry the Eighth style,' he said – and said it affectionately. 'So we did, too.'

Wilson loved the way of the kibbutznik just as he loved the way of the Israeli. They were the kind of socialists of which he counted himself one. It had been Giles's own idea to go to the kibbutz – 'and his mother's, and I thought it was a wonderful thing for him to do.'

We spoke in that first interview in his office as leader of the opposition in the Palace of Westminster. I had decided not to risk the Elstree-to-London traffic, so caught the train. I was going to be early, very early – which was quite a decision on my part. The train came, I settled down, looked at my watch and was comforted to know that I still had plenty of time. I *was* comfortable. I had had a good lunch. Languidly, I looked out of the window and saw the stations pass. First Radlett. Ah, plenty of time. Then St Albans. Yes, still plenty of time. Then I felt the blood drain from my face. St Albans! I was on the wrong train, going in the wrong direction. I managed to jump on to the platform just before it took off for Harpenden. Amazingly, I also managed to cross the bridge to get the next train going the right way. I have never been more grateful for this uncharacteristic demonstration of punctuality. The second train got me to the House of Commons with about five minutes to spare.

We met next when Golda Meir died. It happened early on a Sunday morning and I knew that Wilson was the man I wanted to pay tribute to Israel's first woman prime minister. 'Come straight away,' he said. There were about two hours till the broadcast – just in time to get our chat on the air. The interview was at his farmhouse in Buckinghamshire. I was ushered into his den, dogs sniffing around us, all the Sunday papers piled up on the floor next to his chair. Golda was one of the great statespeople of the world, he said. She was a towering presence in the Middle East. But what about his personal relationship with her? He recalled the meeting that I had witnessed myself, at a dinner given by the Labour Friends of Israel. When Harold arrived, he walked straight over to the guest of honour – and, as the assembled gathering of Labour and Israel supporters, by no means all Jewish, stood to cheer, Wilson plonked a massive kiss on her cheeks.

'The Foreign Office went crazy,' he recalled. 'Telegrams came back and forth between us and our embassies in the Arab world. I told them that I wasn't in the least worried. I said that I'd kiss who ever I liked and if they want to know why I kissed Golda, just say it was sex.'

It was a compliment that the less than beautiful Golda Meir had rarely received in her lifetime, and I felt a little sorry that it had to come after her death.

Later, he and I met at events like book fairs, at which he spoke and I presided. In 1981 *YDHTBJ* celebrated its tenth anniversary with a party at the ever more gloomy Woburn House (I like to think we brought a rare moment of jollity to that terrible place that night). Various BBC officials came to drink weak kosher wine and eat a morsel of smoked salmon on a salt biscuit. I was happily surveying the scene when, to my total amazement, in walked Harold Wilson. I was overwhelmed. 'How can I thank you for coming?' I asked – a question I really meant. 'You don't,' he said.

'I've always admired your programme and am pleased to appear on it – when I'm invited, that is.'

His successor as prime minister and leader of the Labour Party, James Callaghan, was featured live on the programme on the day that he addressed the Board of Deputies. I have to say that I never felt quite the same affection for him that I had for Harold Wilson – maybe because I caught the *right* train to get to our meeting.

We were, however, always pleased to invite him on to *YDHTBJ*. I was also always glad to welcome Margaret Thatcher, who was delighted to come on the programme and pay tribute to her favourite Jews – notably Chief Rabbi Jakobovits and Shimon Peres.

I had first met her during the first 1974 election campaign. As education secretary in Ted Heath's monstrous government, she had become known as 'Thatcher the Milk Snatcher' – because, as education secretary, she had abolished the time-honoured practice of supplying schoolchildren with their daily bottle of milk. She had already proved herself to be a dab hand with the media, so when I met her I suggested that this previously little-known Tory lady with a rather high voice had been the real success of her party's election campaign. I could see the look of gratitude on her face – the appreciation radiated from her. 'Do you *really* think so?' she asked, as if my comments were *really* important. Well, I suppose they were. Whatever, I left her presence convinced that I had a friend.

When she became leader of the opposition, the first woman to get to that position, I went to see her again. She and Dennis lived in the not exactly down-market Flood Street in Chelsea. Although it was close to the Thames Embankment, the only flood you were likely to experience there would be of cash rolling into bank accounts and into the nearby stockbrokers' offices.

I asked her about her plans for living in Downing Street, by no means a certainty in 1978, even just a few months before the election that saw her in that famous blue suit quoting St Francis of Assisi. That day, though, she didn't show any signs of needing the help of Francis or any other saint. She knew, as a matter of certainty, that before long she would become prime minister. So, in addition to small matters like the dreadful economy and the strains of the slightly warming Cold War, how was she going to deal with the real priorities – like remodelling the living quarters and having enough room to cook in the Downing Street flat?

'Oh,' she said, certain of her answer to this as to everything else, 'I won't live there. I could never afford to.' It wasn't the only thing she couldn't afford. Just a day or so before, she had been featured on a BBC news programme on her visit to Northern Ireland, where she had been seen looking admiringly at Waterford crystal and pure Irish linen table cloths. 'Oh I could never afford the crystal,' she said. 'But I did buy a small table cloth. I would have liked the big one, but it was too costly for me.' She then proceeded to show me the very small one she *had* bought. The readers of *Woman's Own* magazine for whom I did the interview were not the only ones to be impressed by her answers. I am sure the folks who bought every daily newspaper which quoted the interview also started taking a collection for the poverty-stricken future PM.

The next time we met was in Downing Street, just before the 1987 election. I had gone to the House of Commons on behalf of my programme to interview the then opposition leader Neil Kinnock, a man I liked immensely – even though his extraordinarily long answers to the simplest questions provided numerous editing problems. I also spent time with David Steel and David Owen, the leaders of the Liberals and the Social Democrats. All of them spoke sympathetically about the important role played by the Jewish community in Britain and, in varying degrees, about their admiration for Israel, although the two Davids were careful not to be seen to be too sympathetic to the state. Mrs Thatcher, on the other hand, was all love and devotion for both the community and the country.

I asked her about the Jews in the cabinet, notably Lord Young, her one-man think-tank, who was secretary of state for trade and industry. It was to me that she made her now famous remark, 'Other people come to me with problems, David comes with solutions.' She also found time to talk about Nigel Lawson, who was to be her chancellor, and Malcom Rifkind, later to be foreign secretary. But what about the then Sir Immanuel Jakobovits?

Was it true she had said that she wished he was her Archbishop of Canterbury? 'I wish he was,' she said under her breath – and then asked me not to use that aside. 'There are very few religious leaders who are as intelligent and knowledgeable as the Chief Rabbi,' she said. 'He understands the problems that this country faces.' It was a comment that would not endear either of them to the more left-wing elements in the country. When the then Archbishop, Lord Runcie, had issued his controversial paper *Faith in the City* in the late 1980s, Jakobovits took what was generally regarded as a Thatcherite stand, totally opposed to much of what was in Runcie's report. As he told me once more, 'The trouble with people in this country is that they don't work hard enough.' Thatcher said she loved that and totally approved of what he said – so much so that in 1988 she made him a member of the House of Lords, which meant that he was the first rabbi ever to sit in parliament, let alone the first to take his seat on the crossbenches of the upper house wearing a *kippar*. (Jonathan Sacks took a rather more left-wing view, which, of course, he revealed in his own comments on *Faith in the City* for the first time on *You Don't Have To Be Jewish*.) Naturally, we covered the Chief Rabbi's historic introduction to the Lords on one of our specials.

As for Israel, Thatcher told me: 'I admire so much what that country is doing. As you know, I have always greatly admired Shimon Peres and I think he has worked very hard both for his country and for peace in the region.'

The Americans were more willing to appear than one would think a local radio station – we had to remind ourselves that that was, indeed, what we were – merited.

The first President Bush mumbled a few platitudes when in London to address what was then called a JIA (Joint Israel Appeal) dinner about how important the Jewish state was to his country, to the Middle East and all the democratic word. Since he had not been in the main pantheon of Israel's American supporters during his time in the White House – much less so, in fact, than his son was during his first term of office – it seemed that yon president talked with forked tongue.

I wondered, too, about Alexander Haig, who had been Ronald Reagan's secretary of state – who famously declared himself in charge when the president was gunned down in the first months of his term of office. To hear the former general talk, Israel was the most important country in the world after his own. One wished he had said so when in office.

I felt more of a sense of truth listening to Jean Kirkpatrick, who had been America's (Democrat) ambassador to the UN. You knew she was speaking nothing but her true thoughts when she addressed Israel's position on the world stage and said how vital its existence was to world peace.

I could have wished that the then Dr David Owen, who had been Jim Callaghan's foreign secretary in the years before founding the ill-fated Social Democratic Party (SDP) was equally sympathetic, but one could not accuse him of being anything but honest. Israel was vital to world security, he said, but it wasn't playing its part in the Middle East and in bringing peace to the region.

As for Prime Minister Callaghan himself, when he addressed the Board of Deputies in a speech that we broadcast live, it was difficult to know exactly where he did stand on the issue. He said the right things about the way Anglo-Jewry played its part in British life, however – but we knew that he would.

We had our share of other statesmen and women, not just prime ministers. Some just liked to say they were politicians.

And talking about that species, there was one who never made high office – as the House of Commons's resident bookmaker, he couldn't have afforded to. Ian Mikardo, sometime fiery left-winger who hd a nice line in business ventures, was one of my favourites. I always liked what I took to be his unadulterated cockney accent. 'Not cockney at all,' he told me. 'It's pure Portsmouth.' But, he said, it wasn't exactly his native tongue. No, Mr Mikardo was bred in the seaport town – speaking Yiddish. 'I still speak Yiddish,' he told me. 'And to this day I always count in Yiddish. You know, you can always tell a person's first language by the way they count.' If ever he had been interrogated – and I imagine his dealings behind what used to be called the Iron Curtain could conceivably have led to that – his counting would have given him away.

Israel's ambassadors did their best to bring the cause of Middle East peace to this country, although I often felt that the best envoys were those 'ordinary' Israelis who had gone to the state from Britain and found ways of making their homeland 'a light unto the nations'. I don't usually like phrases of that kind, although I do appreciate the sentiment. They are clichés that convey the impression of Israel being superior to any other country – which might go down well with Jews, but I thought always sounded a bit patronising.

The official ambassadors to the Court of St James were always a mixed lot.

Michael Comay, ambassador during the Yom Kippur War, was a South African who took off his jacket (his braces were a trademark with him) and was more down to earth and tolerant than most – particularly of journalists who only wanted to get to the truth.

His successor Gideon Raphael always kept his jacket on, which was why he was called a *Yekke* – a term everyone in Israel uses to describe someone, usually from German stock, who is very precise and orderly. 'Yekke' means 'jacket', a garment which in Israel's early days only they wore. Non-ultra-Orthodox men of other antecedents wore jackets only at weddings (the bridegrooms, that is – very few guests ever put them on). It took a long time for the rest of the Western world to catch up with this dress code – but when Israeli politicians started wearing ties, British MPs discarded them.

Raphael didn't like something I had said in the preamble to an interview. The talk was pre-recorded. Two days before transmission, he rang to demand that I change my introduction. I saw no reason to do this, and said so. He continued to press the matter and I continued to refuse to accede to his request. He later phoned me at home and became more and more infuriated . 'I want to talk to your producer,' he insisted. 'I *am* the producer,' I said in one of my happier ripostes. That was the end of the matter – and of our relationship.

Avraham Kidron, who took over from him, and I got on much better. He was pleased to have the opportunity to bring greetings to Anglo-Jewry. 'We are, after all, *am echad*, one people.'

He didn't stay in London long enough, but he was replaced by Shlomo Argov, perhaps the finest and, as we learned all too soon, saddest ambassador the Jewish state ever sent to Britain. He wrote letters to *The Times*, appeared on BBC news programmes and addressed public meetings, putting forward Israel's case in a way that perhaps only Abba Eban was ever able to equal. And he did so on *YDHTBJ*.

One day in 1982, I was in Israel, moaning to Sara about the usual mess in organising interviews. 'I'm going to raise this once and for all with Shlomo,' I said. 'I'm fed up with trying to find ways of putting Israel's case and getting a door slammed in my face for my trouble.' 'Good idea,' she said. I'm not even sure if she managed to get the word 'idea' out before the phone rang in our hotel room. It was Ann Kaye, by then my deputy on the programme. 'Have you heard the news?' she asked. 'What news?' I asked. 'Shlomo Argov,' she said. 'He's been shot.'

In fact, he had not been killed. He would live for another 20 years, a brilliant mind, a wonderfully charming personality, articulate and witty, locked in a wheelchair-bound body, unable to do the simplest tasks for himself.

*YDHDTBJ* was happily able to welcome Shlomo Argov's successor, in a way a very Jewish ambassador. On behalf of the programme, I was at the Board of Deputies on one wet and miserable Sunday morning, not made any more pleasant by the dark and dismal Woburn House. On the platform was a small plumpish man whom we were told was the new ambassador of Israel.

The feelings of disappointment were almost palpable. After the tall, slim, suave Shlomo Argov was this man who looked what he was – a Jewish gentleman from the provinces. When Yehuda Avner spoke, his Manchester accent made not a few of the deputies groan under their breath. But those groans vanished after the first sentence of his speech: 'This week, I presented my credentials to Her Majesty the Queen,' he told them. 'Today, I present them to the Anglo-Jewish community.'

That was exactly what they wanted to hear – and what my listeners in particular were glad to listen to. Time after time, he came on the programme to talk about Israel's problems and did so brilliantly, as he did in the other British media. We talked about the relationship between Jews and the Jewish state, about the fact that he was the first ambassador to convert the official St John's Wood residence into a kosher house, and, early on, about the day that he did present his credentials to the Queen. It was, she said, the first time she had received an ambassador who had been born in Britain, one of her own subjects, in fact. Except, to take on his ambassadorship, he had had to give up his British passport.

There were more and more numerous special programmes, many of them from Israel – ranging from the one featuring the country's first Eurovision triumph and the signing of the peace treaty between the country and Egypt to a record-request programme involving immigrants and their families in London: (I interviewed a dear family friend, in the middle of which I had a mental blackout. I couldn't remember her name.) In another, people were asked to pose questions on Jewish law to the computer at the renowned Bar Ilan University near Tel Aviv. Someone (it could have been me) asked whether, since an Orthodox Jew is not allowed to destroy a piece of paper containing God's name, could he destroy a piece of tape?

Now, that could have been a matter of vital importance to some of our more religious contributors, particularly those who were inquisitive enough to stay behind and watch inches of the material falling to the floor. The answer, our computer spat out before I had a chance to break off a piece of chocolate, was given by a rabbi in Germany in the late nineteenth century. Sorry... nineteenth century? Tape? No, this rabbi was writing about a blackboard in a *yeshiva*. You could, he said, rub the word off the board, since it was not permanent. Jewish law, so often considered immutable, had marched with the times. But what I remember most about that programme are the cheers and applause I got for my farewell greeting to Sara at the show's end: 'Ani ohev otach' – Hebrew for 'I love you.'

This was a short time after Sara had been struck down by a devastating illness. She had had a wonderfully enjoyable job, editing the *JC*'s children's page, but a series of headaches, dizziness and before long a fear that she was mortally ill ended all that. We were afraid that she had a brain tumour. To everyone's great relief, from the National Hospital for Nervous Diseases came the news that she had an encephalitis, in other words an inflammation of the brain. She was told that she would never really recover, that her lack of balance would mean the end of a normal life. And for a long time it seemed as if that would be precisely how it was. But she is – as was proved again 25 years later – an amazingly brave and determined lady. It took ten years, with most of the time our having the social life of 6-year-olds, but she recovered amazingly to an extent her doctors could never have forecast.

That she was able to do so had more than a little to do with the support she received from our children. Fiona and Dani became tremendously supportive. Jonathan achieved wisdom and a sense of responsibility far beyond his years. We had always had a wonderful sense of camaraderie, even – especially – when he was very small. His bedroom adjoined my study. Years later, he told me that he could only get to sleep with the sound of my typewriter in the background.

His bar mitzvah came soon after the devastating attack. It was held not in the synagogue but under its auspices in a marquee in our garden. Rabbi Alan Plancey, one of the finest pastors among Jewish ministers I have ever known, came to take the service, dressed in his canonical attire (if only he and his colleagues still did so). The synagogue provided a mobile ark and lent us a Sefer Torah, from which Jonathan read the week's sedra portion. Our close friend Max Dias assisted the rabbi, who began his address to the bar mitzvah boy, 'Today, Jonathan, you DO have to be Jewish.'

I found ways of bringing events such as this on to the programme, as I did when my father celebrated his eightieth birthday and later when he and my mother died, ten years apart.

I often felt it was this sort of personal touch that kept the programme in the community's affections. It was, I like to think, also because we kept in touch with the Jewish world (on an incredibly minuscule budget) as well as any major news programme.

## 22   Scoops

We had our scoops, too. In June 1976, an Air France Airbus plane was hijacked by pro-Arab German terrorists, who forced the crew to land at Entebbe in Uganda. The megalomaniac Ugandan dictator Idi Amin threw in his lot with the terrorists and came to the airport to praise their work and bring not a little fear to the 103 Jewish hostages – who, in a chilling echo of the Nazi 'selection' processes, had been separated from the gentiles on board, men and women who were, before long, freed.

No one thought they would get out alive, but early on the Sunday morning of 4 July, Maurice Davis rang our home in Elstree – he had just heard from Israel that the prisoners had been freed. In what must go down as the most daring rescue in history, Operation Thunderbolt, Israeli transport planes flew the 2,500 miles from Tel Aviv to Entebbe, over Arab lands on the way to black Africa, low enough across Lake Victoria to avoid radar detection, and got all but one of the hostages safely to Israel. One woman, Mrs Dora Bloch, was in a Ugandan hospital – she had been taken there after a choking fit – and was never heard of again. The crack team of Israeli commandos were undetected until the last minute when, in a shoot-out, Yonatan Netanyahu, brother of the future Israeli prime minister, was killed.

The whole story, or as much as we knew about it at the time, was told on YDHTBJ. That morning, the Board of Deputies was in session and we were able to air the reactions of the British Jewish community to the miracle of Entebbe.

There was another scoop – which the rest of the world failed to recognise for another five years. Arieh Handler and I used to meet for the occasional lunch. It was during one of these, in 1990, that I asked him to put on his banker's *kippar* and contemplate this thought: there must be huge amounts of Jewish money still lying dormant in Swiss bank accounts.

'Nobody is talking about this,'Arieh told me. 'I'm so glad you have now done so. It is an international scandal.' He put me in touch with people dealing with the issue – to that date, without any publicity – in Jerusalem. Merle Kessler, then my assistant in London, arranged what seemed to be a hopelessly difficult link-up with the Jewish Agency. 'How much is there?' I asked an Agency spokesman. 'About $2 billion,' he said. 'Why has this figure never been published before?' I asked. 'Because no one has ever asked,' he replied, insouciantly. I spoke to people in London who were claiming that their parents and grandparents had deposited money in Swiss accounts and yet were unable to retrieve it. There were stories of people who, knowing they were about to be put on the next transport to a death camp, handed over riches to people whom they trusted to bank for them in Switzerland – and were never heard of again.

The story was picked up briefly – a couple of paragraphs – in the *Sunday Telegraph*, but no one seemed to take much notice of a human calamity which few could get their heads around. Then, as though we had said nothing, the story broke on the BBC's *Newsnight* programme and was taken up by the newspapers from what was still called Fleet Street, several of which revealed that the matter had first been raised on a BBC radio programme. How much was involved? Two billion dollars, they discovered – the precise figure we had revealed. Before long, a settlement was arranged, and I like to think we had something to do with bringing it about.

I went to Switzerland, a heaven of a holiday destination in both winter and summer, which made some good copy for various travel newspaper columns. But what of the Jews of Switzerland? They seemed to be living in idyllic conditions, had total freedom of worship, apart from having to import kosher meat, and were able to make a wonderfully prosperous living. When they heard that I was doing a Jewish radio programme about the country, communal leaders came to see Sara and me. Their hospitality was superb. We went to the finest restaurants. They gave us small presents. And they gave us history lessons – about the country that had not been the wonderful friend to Jews we imagined, how they had had to have the letter 'J' stamped in their passports during World War Two, just as in Nazi Germany, in case, sneakily, they had tried to find refuge there, and how, in years past, Jews and pigs were not allowed to cross certain bridges in the country – a sign to that effect was still there at the end of one of them.

There were plenty of signs for the Anglo-Jewish community itself. Thanks to Immanuel Jakobovits, now Lord Jakobovits of Regents Park (I could never quite work that one out) the state of education, for one thing, had changed beyond recognition. Many more, even most, Jewish children now seemed to be going to Jewish schools – which was great if for only one thing: youngsters no longer had to spend those terrible Sunday mornings (or, as in my day, Wednesday and Saturday afternoons, too ) not only learning nothing, but in a state of purgatory attending Hebrew classes. These were all a disgrace, or at least most of them were.

Years before, I had had the idea of asking an educationalist to take a look at the chederim to see if our idea of just how bad they were was right. I gave the job to a Jewish journalist, John Izbicki, who was the *Daily Telegraph*'s education correspondent. He did a reasonably competent job, although I could have hoped for more depth. But he *had* done the job and had to be paid for it. The Board of Deputies, which, at the time, looked after the progrmme's budget, sent him a cheque at my request.

He repaid my payment – by a page lead in his paper saying that the cheque we had kindly given him proved that the BBC was broadcasting sponsored programmes. It was not at all true, of course: the Board was simply helping the corporation out financially with a programme that they could not have afforded to run themselves. Mr Izbicki didn't consult me before writing his story. But he did bank the cheque.

I considered this a kind of treachery on Izbicki's part. Questions were asked in the Commons, but nothing further was heard about it.

Things were changing. In 1989, Chief Rabbi Lord Jakobovits announced that he was going to retire. There were two *kippot* in the ring from the moment the announcement was made, although neither wearer would say so. There were subtle hints and very many suggestions that were neither subtle nor actually hints. One of the names mentioned was that of Jonathan Sacks, universally acknowledged as one of the most brilliant brains in the British rabbinate, a man who had already shown himself to be a superb preacher and who was rapidly developing a reputation both as a thinker – he had recently gained a philosophy doctorate – and as a communicator.

The second candidate who officially never was was Cyril Harris – by now Chief Rabbi of South Africa – who had a pedigree many considered perfect for the role. He had been a communal rabbi in London, was also a marvellous preacher – his Scottish accent gave him almost a non-conformist clergyman's panache – had worked with young people as head of the Hillel students' organisation (when he swapped his canonical attire for a sweater and jeans) and had been Senior Jewish Chaplain to the Forces. When he spoke, he could be spellbinding. In South Africa he was emerging as a national figure, bringing much credit to both himself and his Jewish community (later, he would be a close friend of Nelson Mandela, managing to bring him to numerous communal events). I have to say that I had thought he would be a perfect chief, the unofficial title that the heads of the United Hebrew Congregations of the Commonwealth shared with African tribal leaders. It is possible that I merely wanted to see my 1960 prediction come true – that I had just witnessed at work the next Chief Rabbi but one (after the retirement of Brodie and his successor, Jakobovits). But I also sincerely believed that the community would benefit from his preferment.

I had that thought long before Jonathan Sacks entered the picture. I admit that at the time, I thought I might be able to help Harris before any other candidate emerged. It turned out that my good intentions via *YDHTBJ* did him no good at all. It all started with my memory of asking the then Chief Rabbi if he would consider debating with a Reform rabbi and his turning it down – in favour of his meeting with the Archbishops. How would Cyril like to do it now? 'Against whom?' he not unreasonably asked. 'How about Hugo Gryn?' I asked.

Naturally, he had the greatest respect for Hugo, and who could blame him? Hugo himself liked what he knew about Cyril, a man like himself who had intelligent ideas of his own and who stuck to principles for which he deserved respect, too. He didn't agree with him, but defended his right to hold those beliefs. They were both wonderful broadcasters. Both had had their apprenticeships on *You*

*Don't Have To Be Jewish*. It was a recipe for a very good programme. And a very good programme it turned out to be – unfortunately. I had too much affection for Cyril Harris to be pleased with what happened, for Cyril is generally accepted to have gone too far to endear himself to the Establishment. It was a 'fight' that Hugo won – and he confessed afterwards that he was sorry he had done so.

At first, as one would imagine, they agreed on a lot. They both accepted that they had to acknowledge their differences and agree to differ. They agreed on the need for Judaism to be relevant to the late twentieth century. They didn't dispute the necessity for rabbis to be able to comment on world affairs. But then it happened. Hugo mentioned an eminent European rabbi. It was a good reference point – except that Cyril took the reference as a bait which had not been offered. 'I'm surprised you know about him,' Cyril said. It was not calculated to win friends and influence people. And then came this: 'If you've ever read a page of the Talmud, Hugo, you will know that...' The Gryn cool remained low on the anger scale, *sang froid* personified. Then came a further insult: 'There are Reform rabbis who don't know an aleph [the first letter of the Hebrew alphabet] from a swastika.' And if that wasn't enough, 'I know of Reform rabbis who stand under the *chuppah* with their fingers in a Magen David hoping that both bride and bridegroom really are Jewish.'

I think I know what Cyril intended – that the Orthodox case needed to be put forcefully. He could have also believed that Orthodox Jews, who might have doubted whether a rabbi so brilliant and so articulate could really be strictly 'frum', would have their minds put at rest: here was a rabbi with just the right credentials. Unfortunately, there were people who thought he had gone too far. When Cyril became Chief Rabbi of South Africa I was delighted. When he more obviously became a candidate for the London office, although he had countless friends – including former congregants at Kenton, Edgware and most recently at the fashionable St John's Wood synagogue – too many people remembered what he had said. It was the only time I regretted remembering a *YDHTBJ* broadcast. He may have seemed intemperate on that occasion, but I understood why. Certainly, I don't believe there had ever been a better communal rabbi in England, and I doubt that we would ever have had a better Chief Rabbi.

This had become apparent when his dignified figure appeared in ceremonial uniform at the annual Jewish Remembrance Day parade and service at Whitehall's Cenotaph. This was always – and is still – one of the most remarkable Jewish days in Britain. Thousands (still thousands) of Jewish ex-servicemen march past the memorial to the country's dead from two world wars. There the Chief Rabbi and the senior chaplain – after Harris, Malcolm Weisman, a judge, a barrister, minister to Britain's small Jewish communities, a member of the panel on numerous inquiries and committees and a find-a-job-and-I'll-find-time-to-do-it man – conduct a service to the accompaniment of massed Guards bands. It always made very good radio and I enjoyed being able to do a running commentary ('a regular Richard Dimbleby', wrote one listener).

Cyril was perfect for those occasions. As it turned out, our loss was South Africa's gain – and it was a triumph for him and for his wife, Ann, a lawyer who did brilliant work running a legal 'clinic' in the black townships. He made an indelible mark on the country, right from the time he first went there and launched a series of calculated attacks on apartheid. It was not the Jewish way, he said – and he thus built bridges few people had thought possible between the organised community and the majority population. Jews like Helen Suzman, Joe Slovo, Helen Joseph and Abie Sachs had been at the forefront of the anti-apartheid movement. So had the man who would soon be known as an international jurist, Justice Richard Goldstone. He would later head the war crimes trials that followed the Balkan troubles of the 1990s. There were other Jews who were leading members of the African National Congress – one of them had been arrested along with Mandela. But the community as such had remained uncomfortably quiet until Cyril came along and made a stand. When I did one of my overseas focus programmes on South African Jewry that fact became very clear from speaking to people on both sides of the racial divide. At first it seemed that Jews might be locked in the middle of what everyone expected to be a black-versus-white conflict. Plenty of people thought that would happen, and were prepared to say so. Others said they planned to ensure it never did. That it didn't happen had more than a little to do with the work of their Chief Rabbi.

In Britain, Jonathan Sacks was the delight of every Jewish woman. They smiled admiringly when this handsome bearded man, then in his forties, spoke in terms that made them very proud. When it came to finally choosing the British 'Chief', Sacks won.

He was a marvellous ambassador for the Jewish community to the outside world. His troubles here, however, were huge. He would say one thing and then change his mind. He promised Jewish women a greater say in communal affairs and instituted an inquiry – which was never acted upon. He refused to attend Hugo Gryn's funeral, but then spoke at a memorial meeting praising him and his humanity. The Reform community were grateful – until it turned out that he had written a letter, in classical Hebrew, condemning Hugo to an ultra-Orthodox rabbi.

I later dubbed him a weapon of mass retraction. It is a pity that his brilliance and the marvellous work he does for inter-faith relations, to say nothing of the impact he makes on the non-Jewish population as one of the outstanding brains of the age, has to be clouded by those changes of mind and indecision.

That could have been said to be the fate of Radio London, too. In 1988, the BBC decided that London's oldest local station should die. It was going to be replaced by something called Greater London Radio – an idiotic decision.

It was idiotic because the name Radio London was just about the best you could get. When I went abroad, it was as though I was talking about Radio Paris or Radio Moscow. How the BBC didn't see it in its wider context has always amazed me. What also amazed me was the way it decided to make the change – by insult as well as by ignorance. The position of station manager would be replaced by that of a managing editor – 'Derrick Amore will not be invited to apply for this,' a faceless BBC official declared at a staff meeting called to discuss the issue. Amore was sitting next to him, looking stonefaced at the assembled staff members. Everyone knew that he was not well, or rather that he had a severe drink problem, but he was still a brilliant manager at times – and editor – and his earlier work for the Corporation didn't deserve that sort of treatment. (Before very long, he was dead.)

Then, said the faceless one at that meeting, he had some papers to distribute. 'John, please pass them round.' 'John' was John Murray, Amore's deputy, who, in truth, did most of the work, a dedicated BBC man who deserved more than being delegated to pass round papers. He left the BBC soon afterwards.

I then had to decide what I would do. The idea of the change was to bring the audience figures up. Therefore there would be a lot more music than ever before. But there would be some speech items and I was invited to remain. Naturally, I was delighted. Except, as far as I could see, I would be remaining under sufferance – and mainly because *YDHTBJ* didn't cost the BBC anything.

The new editor, Matthew Bannister, had come from Radio One, not my sort of station at all. He was a young man, full of enthusiasm, and was very welcoming. When we had a party at the Marylebone High Street studios to celebrate our 1,000th programme in 1989, he said some very kind things – as did people like the then Chief Rabbi and the president of the Board of Deputies. But it soon became clear that we were less than welcome – we didn't fit in with the stars of the station, like Tony Blackburn and a very young Chris Evans, eventually to become the bad boy of radio and television, who suffered the fate of turning into a multi-millionaire for his trouble.

There were other executives on the station who plainly didn't like me or what I did. One of these, who walked around all day with a baseball cap (I thought he was a painter and decorator) on his bald head, insisted that I record a programme for Kol Nidre night, the eve of the sacred Day of Atonement, which I had never done before. I played cantorial music that I am sure no one ever heard. To make matters worse, we were no longer *YDHTBJ*. I had to find a new name and a new signature tune. I chose Mahler's Fourth Symphony, which I thought encompassed my less than happy feelings about being shunted to late on a Sunday evening – a time when virtually nobody bothered to listen to what was now called *The Jewish World*.

There was one other insult that they obviously didn't know suited me very well – had they known, they would probably have done something to change things. The programme had to be recorded at the BBC's satellite studios at Elstree. It was a five-minute drive from home – if there was a lot of traffic, that is. However, nobody would ever agree to come to Elstree to be interviewed. Plainly, this wasn't going to work.

It was then that London's commercial station, LBC, came to my rescue. They had a question that amounted to: how would I like to be privatised? A meeting was called, thanks to a great deal of work by the Board of Deputies PR committee chairman Wally Leafe, a dedicated public servant who became a great friend. The LBC executives were all assembled to welcome me to commercial radio – before I realised I had actually been invited to join. They had a scheme up their sleeves – an independent outfit was looking for programmes and wanted to take us on.

Once more we were going to be called *You Don't Have To Be Jewish*, and once more we would be at an accessible time, early on Sunday evenings. Programmes would be recorded at some rather impressive private studios, just a stone's throw from my old familiar territory of Carnaby Street. What was more, we could have as many guests – and as many sandwiches, which were provided on the house – as we wanted. The money would no longer have to come from the Board of Deputies (which pleased them enormously) and we would go on the air in January 1990. Which we did, to great joy all round, not least that of my new and extraordinarily dedicated assistant Sue Krisman, who came down from Reading every week full of enthusiasm – especially for being called 'producer'. I didn't mind. It meant she took some of the strain off me – in fact, a lot of it. I was in overall charge and made all the decisions, but she was at the coalface and it was an essential job.

On our first programme, Joe Loss came to talk about his life as London's favourite band leader – to say nothing of the being 'By Appointment' conductor to both the Queen and the *Queen Elizabeth 2*. In the next programme Jonathan Sacks appeared at the studios to talk about his new appointment as Chief Rabbi.

The arrangement seemed perfect – except that just a few months later, the independent producers went out of business. We could carry on broadcasting, but LBC didn't have any money. Where had I heard that before? What I hadn't heard before was that there was a man called Clive Marks, who headed a charitable trust. He loved the programme. Before long, I would love him. He agreed to finance the show and never said no to anything. The one thing I was glad he never said no to was the idea of our becoming friends.

We weren't the only good cause that he took under his wing. Indeed, if the community ever initiates a serious honours list, he deserves a peerage – no, a dukedom. He also deserves an honour from the Queen, but that hasn't yet come. Among his 'clients' was that pride of world Jewry, the ORT, an organisation set up in nineteenth-century Russia (the letters were initials for words in

Russian, but later became adapted to stand for Organisation through Rehabilitation and Training).

Together with his wife, Adrienne, and Sara, Clive and I went to see the ORT at work in South America. We went to Peru, where we witnessed two sides of the country. On a Sunday afternoon, we went to tea in the bright seaside home of what seemed a very ordinary Jewish family – the aged father, the husband and wife and their children. Except that Samuel Goldenberg wasn't in the least ordinary. He was the prime minister. I asked him if he thought this was a tribute to the country's Jews. 'Certainly,' he said. 'It makes my father *qvell*.'

He himself, on the other hand, was interested to know that he shared a family name with Edward G. Robinson. 'Do you think we could be related?' he asked – the answer to which I'd have loved to know myself.

The other side of Peruvian life that we saw was somewhat less comfortable. In shanty towns consisting of huts without roofs – families slept on shelves with chickens and other livestock running around them – an Israeli ORT official brought regular supplies of food and encouraged young mothers to take their children to the baby clinics they ran in nearby towns.

An easy job for this former Israeli soldier to do? Not if the pistol he carried on his waist was anything to go by.

It was a similar story in Chile, where the government was asking ORT to supply them with computer technology. In Argentina and Uruguay, we saw an amazing network of Jewish schools. Children in Montevideo were learning the *Mah Nishtanah*, the celebrated 'Four Questions' asked by the youngest people present at the Passover seder. It was just weeks before the attack on the Jewish centre in Buenos Aries, but even then in the Argentinian capital we got a sense of the unease felt by a community that was still recovering from the Peron era. I also got a sense of a community structure – synagogues, welfare organisations and some of the most wonderful schools I had ever seen. I talked to a rabbi who had only recently taken on the role of a congregational minister. 'Don't say it too loud,' he whispered over lunch. 'My mother still thinks I'm a doctor.'

LBC was not exactly the most prosperous business in the world of commercial radio. It was worried about its licence renewal and even more concerned about the drop in advertising revenue. *YDHTBJ* wasn't achieving the listenership it had gained in the old Radio London days, although what we had was vastly higher than the figures under which we had barely existed in the GLR backwater. It was plainly taking time for people to realise we had a new home.

The company, however, was scratching around for all the cash it could find. We had survived because we didn't cost the firm anything, but before long it turned the big guns on us, too. We weren't going to survive unless we could get a sponsor. What John Izbicki had tried to allege had been our *modus vivendi* all those years before was now coming true. What hadn't been acceptable on the BBC was now to be the norm on commercial radio. This gave me one of those moments of desperation that I suppose come to us all from time to time, but it seemed to be knocking on my door with a frequency I wouldn't have thought possible.

It was quite clear that LBC would have been pleased to unload us at the earliest opportunity. A man called Robin Malcolm, the station's editor, whom I had considered friendly enough when I first joined the station – and who had been happy with our financial arrangement – called me in to see him at 2 o'clock on a Thursday afternoon. We either got sponsorship to the extent of £20,000 for the next year or we were out. I had – and this is absolutely true – five hours to organise it.

Five hours! I got on the phone to one man who had helped various communal organisations, but to whom I had spoken just a couple of times over the years. What I knew about David Lewis was that he was a successful businessman – he frequently appeared in the *Sunday Times* 'rich list' – and that he had a heart that was probably as golden as his bank balance. What I didn't then know was that he was out of the country more than he was at home, running the Miss Chelsea shops and a chain of European hotels and – this was the real operation that endeared him to the Jewish community – that he had virtually built up Eilat with an ever-growing number of those hotels there, too.

David was not just in his office in Ealing, he was able to speak on the phone to me. I gave him the gist of my appeal in an instant. There was no brush-off. 'Come and see me,' he said. 'Can you get here straight away? Hop in a taxi now.'

That was what I did. He gave me a warm welcome, and then asked me to leave his office while he made a call. Five minutes later he called me back in. He had been talking to another prominent community figure who had, apparently, vouched for me and my programme. Yes, he said, he would do it. From that moment on, *You Don't Have To Be Jewish* was brought to you by All Abroad, north-west London's leading travel agents, another one of his business outlets (set up, I am sure, to promote Israel's tourist business).

The interviews went on as before. Some of them were done in conjunction with other radio programmes or with newspapers and magazines. One such interview was with Robert Maxwell, five years before his suicide and the subsequent revelations of his being a crook. An appointment was arranged at his private sanctum at the *Daily Mirror* offices. I drove down from Bournemouth for the meeting – and got stuck in an enormous traffic jam. I knew that Maxwell was not a man to trifle with. I wanted the interview (commissioned by *Woman* magazine – the very young Jonathan could never understand why I was always buying women's magazines, until I pointed out that I was merely reading my own pieces, and there were quite a few of them at the time) and was sure it was going to collapse.

The vibrations of his PR man shaking in his shoes as he took my regular phone calls from call boxes along the way (this was before mobiles) came across the wires. 'Mr Maxwell won't like this at all,' he kept saying. I knew it was all going to be a waste of time, but, nevertheless, plodded on and got to the *Mirror* at least an hour late.

To my amazement, he granted me the interview. To my even greater amazement, he was extraordinarily polite. It resulted in a good piece. A couple of years later, after he had become immersed in his Holocaust memorial activities, I requested another interview. This time, no reply. I tried again. Once more, nothing. Then I met him at a Board function. 'Mr Maxwell,' I began, reminding him of our last chat, 'I've been writing to you, but not getting a reply.' 'My dear man,' he said, 'I can't reply to all the letters I get' – and then he walked away.

Little stays the same in the worlds of journalism or broadcasting. There was another big development in the early 1990s. The station was sold – to Shirley Porter, Dame Shirley Porter, Margaret Thatcher's protégée as leader of Westminster Council and daughter of Jack Cohen, the *Pile-'em High, Sell-'em Cheap* founder of the Tesco supermarket chain. This was not long before the said Shirley would be ordered to pay a small fortune back to her council after charges of alleged gerrymandering. I knew her, but she emphasised, when we met soon after the deal was done, that there could be no favouritism for my programme. I accepted it. There could be no reason why there should be any, but I had a sneaking feeling that, with her at the helm, we would be reasonably safe.

This was a judgement enhanced when a party was held at the station. I never used the LBC studios as frequently as I did those at RL. I wasn't the same sort of fixture. The 'stars' didn't know me, or, if they did, they didn't always recognise me. That was obvious at the party. One after the other, those stars – Angela Rippon, the former BBC *Come Dancing* presenter who had a programme on LBC, among them – formed a procession to shake my hand and make small talk. I was flattered. And then I realised why. There was I, middle-aged, greying, wearing a rather smart blue suit and a clean shirt and Jewish. They were convinced I was part of the Shirley Porter operation.

It was not such a good thing to be. In 1993, applications were invited by the Independent Broadcasting Authority for the LBC licence, which had either to be renewed by Porter or offered to someone else. Dame Shirley, naturally enough, applied to renew the licence she had just bought with the IBA's approval. It seemed only natural that it would be renewed. Refusing renewal was virtually unknown. She submitted a business plan. Not surprisingly, *YDHTBJ*, brought to you by All Abroad, London's leading travel agents, would be part of her package. But then came the blow – in a year's time the station would be under new management yet again. Dame Shirley had lost the franchise. We were not on the schedules for the new company, which was going to call itself something different.

I decided to carry on as though nothing had changed. There were still good programmes to be made. There was every reason to go to South America with Clive and Adrienne Marks – Clive had now taken over the sponsorship of the show, bringing it to our public, care of ORT – and to go to Morocco.

I tried not to get too depressed. After all, there were still my books and still there was the opportunity to broadcast on Radio Two, which, in its way, was just as satisfying and reached a wider audience for my programmes on people like Fred Astaire, Maurice Chevalier and Danny Kaye. And there was much else to be grateful for. Sara's illness had not been cured, but was being kept very much under control. We were living a contented life, doing all the things that we wanted to do, with none of the old restrictions. And our family life was perfect.

Of course, there had been the sad moments. My parents were gone. But our children were a constant source of pride. Fiona was a successful solicitor and in 1991 had married the barrister Robin Oppenheim. Three years later, Dani, brilliantly engaged in PR, married a writer, David Sewell. Jonathan had passed the BBC's news training course, top of the 2,000 applicants. He had won the Stern fellowship, working on the *Washington Post* for a few months, and then being shared jointly by the *Guardian* and the BBC's *World at One* programme as their man in the American capital.

Both girls were married in an open-air ceremony at Woburn Abbey. It was *déjà vu* for a number of reasons. Woburn was fulfilling the hope I had expressed all those years before that it would be a great place for a wedding. The *chuppah*, or wedding canopy, was even more significant for us. They were both – and Jonathan and his bride Sarah Peters would follow suit in 2000 – married under the canopy which had been used at both our wedding and that of my parents.

Dani's wedding was somewhat fraught for one reason alone. It may have been our last year, but I still ran *YDHTBJ* with as much enthusiasm as 23 years before. I still wanted to be on top of the news.

As we were leaving for Woburn, news came of the death of Menachem Shneerson, the Lubavicher Rebbe. We could not ignore it. As luck would have it, only days before I had recorded an interview with Dr Louis Jacobs about the role of the rebbe – for use some time in the future. But how could we do it? I couldn't leave my daughter's wedding.

With all the cheek of the devil, I asked Sue Krisman, at Woburn with her husband, Alan, if she minded leaving early – and doing it in my place. I now shudder at the chutzpah of it all. I plainly should never have done it. Sue wasn't thrilled, but, trouper that she is, she agreed to leave after lunch. For reasons I have never really understood, we have remained friends.

The programme died in October 1994. I left it with great regret. There were occasional forays into attempts of resurrecting it somehow. We even got close to a televised version, but the company (after taking a lot of money from the ever-supporting Clive Marks) went broke before it could go on air. Not even a reception kindly given by Chief Rabbi Sacks at his home could save it.

Fortunately, there was life after *You Don't Have To Be Jewish*, and my third life was as busy as ever.

# LIFE THREE

# 23   A Jolson story

When did it all begin? When did my fascination with that special kind of show business start?

I can date it precisely – well, almost precisely. It really started the first time I went into a cinema with my parents, or when my mother and I queued up for the ninepenny seats at the Savoy on Saturday afternoons. It was then that I began to realise that the best things in life happened in a darkened room with little lights flickering in the ceiling above. That was when I first became fascinated by America and practically everything American. As far as I was concerned, the most glamorous place in the world was the one that had skyscrapers and flew flags with both stars and stripes. But I'll be a little more accurate than that. Let's say it was 1947. I was 12, sitting in a Luton cinema watching a young star called Larry Parks miming to a song called 'Mammy'. A little old lady – really a little old lady wearing a black bonnet (this was, after all, 1947) – touched me on the shoulder. 'Is that the one who sang "Sonny Boy?"' she asked. The 12-year-old had to answer, 'I'm sorry – I don't know.'

I didn't know because, up to then, I hadn't liked music very much. I didn't like singers. But I was drawn to *The Jolson Story* by posters I saw on hoardings near my grandparents' home in Stoke Newington. They showed a small boy singing in a synagogue choir, just as I had dreamed of doing as a 5-year-old.

The film captivated me. I knew that because I immediately started regretting not seeing the movie the first time round a few months before. I knew it later on, because the film kept reappearing on the screens in Luton and I kept wanting to see it. I knew it because every time I went to see the film, I kept a mental record of the exact scene being shown as I walked into the theatre. Once it was when Larry –

Al Jolson – Parks was singing 'The Spaniard That Blighted My Life', another when he tells his pal Steve (played by William Demarest) to invite the president to his next show in Washington. 'Of the United States?' asks Steve. 'No,' Jolson replies, 'of the synagogue.'

Well, a little Jewish boy in Luton doesn't forget lines like that. But going in to see the movie after it had been on for at least half an hour? That was how stupid adults, as well as children, were in those days. There were continuous performances, so nobody seemed to bother to be sure to see pictures from the very beginning. That was OK when you had seen the movie before, but generally going to the films was something of a mystery tour. You had to work out what had gone on and who had done what with whom – and then see if you were right when it came round again. You'd leave at the point 'where we came in', an expression every movie-goer knew at the time . It was such a common way of seeing movies that Danny Kaye performed a whole routine about it – 'This is a picture that begins in the middle for the benefit of people who . . . came in in the middle.'

Three years later came the announcement that a *Jolson Story* sequel, *Jolson Sings Again*, was on the stocks. I knew, when it happened, that it was very special because I made sure of getting into the cinema at the beginning and stayed to see it round a second time.

My friends and I all sang Jolson songs and, if we admitted it, did so in front of a mirror. I knew those songs were very special because at 16, just before my 'O' level exams – the very first GCE papers ever, which was my mark in history – my parents bought me a gramophone and a set of records. The first one I played on that tinny-sounding wind-up machine was Jolson's 'I'm Just Wild About Harry'. I knew I was captivated by that voice. What I didn't know was that it would influence me for the rest of my life.

Jolson's really was a fascinating story. This was the cantor's son who chose the stage instead of the synagogue, who was a huge hit on Broadway before the World War One – earning something like $10,000 a week before 1914 – who made the first sound film, the first of the 'talkies', in 1927. It was *The Jazz Singer*, which was virtually his own story – a cantor's son who chooses . . . He had a fallow period from the mid-1930s until 1946, when the first biopic came out. From that moment on, he lived up to the reputation he created for himself as 'The World's Greatest Entertainer'. Nobody ever argued with that and just before he died in 1950, after entertaining the troops in Korea, he was voted America's top singer, ahead of Bing Crosby, Perry Como and a young upstart called Frank Sinatra.

I heard the news of his death as I was getting ready for school in October 1950. I burst into tears. I was in good company. I heard that others had done the same thing. The head of Columbia Pictures, Harry Cohn, had cried too. His movies *The Jolson Story* and *Jolson Sings Again* brought him successes and riches enough even to make a hard-bitten Hollywood mogul cheer. (When Cohn died in 1962, 2,000 people went to the funeral, which prompted the comedian Red Skelton to say, 'Just shows you – give the people what they want and they'll show up for it.')

I'd seen the films literally dozens of times – if I'd known I'd be able one day to watch them in my own home, I'd have looked forward to adulthood rather more than I did. Jolson would be the subject of my first book, my first radio programme, my first television show and the first West End and American stage production that bore my name on the posters and programmes.

The book took years to gestate. Nobody thought I'd do it. This was apple pie in the sky if anyone had ever cooked it. When Sara and I first went out together, I told her of my ambition to write an Al Jolson biography – which was why I was constantly collecting press cuttings. She decided it was a mere eccentricity, which she allowed me to pursue as a kind of marital indulgence.

You know all the stories about people carting book ideas from publisher to publisher. Of course, that was going to be my fate, too. I was prepared for it. One day, I'd write that book and get it published, but I was prepared for a long wait. Wasn't that the way it always was? And in any case, there was *The Jolson Touch* to work on, my first complete radio programme on BBC Radio Two. I was doing interviews with people like Ben Lyon, Larry Adler and the old silent star Bessie Love – 'Oh, he was like a cyclone!' – and I was writing a script that I was presenting (in Oxford-accented tones that embarrass me totally these days). Most of all, best of all, I could play all those Jolson records I had loved for so long, and – this always fascinated me – discs he had made in the 1920s and even earlier, which I could compare with the newer versions made in the four years between his comeback and his death.

It wasn't a programme that now gives me much pride, but at the time this was a child being told he could drive a train or ride on a fire engine. My very own radio programme. A programme playing Al Jolson! One of the most remarkable things about it was that I suddenly discovered I was not the only crazy man around. It brought me a new lot of friends, members of the International Jolson Society, which would one day grant me honorary membership. One of them, Dennis Sykes, who knows more about my kind of movies than any man on earth, is a dear friend to this day.

It was he who would become more helpful than I could have thought possible that day in 1971, at about the same time as Victor Mischon made his celebrated telephone call. It was then that my career took a new and parallel course and my professional life changed for ever.

Radio Four was employing me to interview a few celebrities for a programme called *Be My Guest*. I had spoken to Fred Astaire (about whom more later), George Chakiris, star of *West Side Story*, and to Walter Scharf, a man who would also play a part in my life before long. But it was in 1971 that another big one came along. Maurice Chevalier was one of the great generation – a contemporary of people like George Burns, Eddie Cantor, Sophie Tucker (whom I had also interviewed a couple of times) and, of course, Al Jolson. He was now finally retiring and had written – or at least that was what the dust-jacket said – a book about his last farewell tour. It was not a very good book, but I suppose I have to say it was the most important book I have ever read.

Coming on *Be My Guest* was part of his publicity tour for the book. What was more, he was being shepherded around various radio and TV studios by his publisher, a dour man called Jeffrey Simmonds, chief executive of W.H. Allen and Co., one of the oldest established houses, which was now specialising in a kind of show business biography – the kind into which I was convinced Al Jolson would fit perfectly. Mr Simmonds bent over backwards to be nice to me – after all, as I have said, this wasn't a very good book and M. Chevalier, the international entertainer who had taken America by storm in its golden age, was no longer top of the pops. He needed all the publicity he could get, so he was trying very hard to make this programme work.

The interview went wonderfully well. An old man, superbly dressed as one would expect, silvery white hair immaculately styled, suddenly reclaimed his middle age. He was performing again, kindly answering my questions, admitting that his French accent was perhaps slightly exaggerated to please his fans. We played his records and he loved listening to them. Was he *really* glad he was not young any more, as he proclaimed in that song from *Gigi*? He evaded the question, except to repeat his by now familiar mantra that, considering the alternative, it wasn't so bad at all. My producer called him 'Sir'. In short, we got on like a radio studio on fire. Simmonds was thrilled. 'Have you,' I asked tentatively, 'ever thought of a book on Al Jolson?'

'Al Jolson?' he said. 'A very important entertainer. Why?'

'Because I'd like to write one,' I said.

'A good idea,' he said. 'Have you ever published before?' I thought publishing was his business, not mine, but I got the picture. Almost instantly, we agreed that I'd write a specimen chapter, the chapter I'd had in my mind since I was 17 years old. Overnight, it was accepted. Suddenly, I was an author. The serial biographer was on to his first killing.

Or so I thought. The question of money came up on the chapter acceptance. 'An advance of £500,' I was told. 'When do you want the cheque?' I think I asked – it was all a little hazy by the time I got home to Elstree. 'No, we pay you,' said Yvette Morgan Griffiths, the young lady assigned to edit the book (no prizes for guessing from which part of the British Isles she hailed).

I then did some sums and worked out that the £500 would be nearly all swallowed up in the necessary trip to America, beginning in New York and going on to Los Angeles. (I didn't say that I was about to embark on the best seek-and-find holiday I could ever have wished for.) They agreed on another £300 for expenses. It was not all that usual at the time to talk in terms of hundreds of pounds – and it was, after all, 1971.

Chevalier had been the impetus in a number of ways – not just my talking to the publisher, but because in the course of our interview he had named Jolson as one of the great American entertainers he had tried to emulate 'you know, in my French way'. As he said, 'He had such great punch.' I didn't put to him something I had read, but I had little reason to doubt it. When he first went to America in the 1920s, he had seen Al and been tempted 'to get straight back on to the boat'.

That was the sort of effect Al Jolson had on his contemporaries as well as on audiences of 'civilians', the people who paid to get into a theatre or cinema. By most accounts, no one ever succeeded in dominating audiences the way he could – right from the time he played in minstrel shows at the turn of the twentieth century, through Broadway spectaculars, the earliest talkies and his big comeback (following his uneasy period) with *The Jolson Story* in 1946, which lasted until his sudden death four years later.

I found it difficult not to stress that I was going to enjoy working on this project probably more than seeing the final result. It wasn't really true. At that earliest stage, I just wanted to see the title on a dust-jacket with my name below it. I began in New York. I went to the Lincoln Center, the Big Apple's temple of the performing arts, asked for a file on Al Jolson and, when a *very* big brown folder was placed in front of me, wallowed in a feast of nostalgia. This was going to be the *real* Jolson Story, the tale told in this file – playbills and hotel bills, reviews of his revues, a letter to him about making sure that he really loved the 21-year-old girl he was marrying back in 1945. This came from the uncle of Erle Chenault Galbraith, his bride, who all but admitted he had a shotgun beside his desk as he wrote the note. (The uncle was a retired Air Force general, Clair Chenault.) There was a note from General Eisenhower's wife Mamie telling Al to kick her husband up the backside for not writing (Jolson claimed he did just that), another from his accompanist Harry Akst describing how the great man died. And it went on and on. I couldn't believe my good fortune. This was perhaps all I needed to write a book – except that I knew it wasn't. I did know a great deal already about the *Jazz Singer* (although not as much as I thought I did before looking at that file), but I was fascinated to know more. And in addition to that, this was my first book and it was going to be good – had to be good.

Jolson had by then been dead for 21 years. There were still a few of his contemporaries alive. I had to meet them all, or as many as I could. I soon realised that this was easier said than done. There were not all that many around, and not enough of them who wanted to talk. But where to start? I thought of the theatrical clubs. The Friars was the most important of them, but that was temporarily closed. 'Try the Lambs,' someone suggested. To the Lambs I went, feeling like one myself – on the way to slaughter for my chutzpah.

It was like the scene in one of those desert island movies, *The Sunshine Boys*, where the old trouper, played by Walter Matthau, tries to enjoy a game of cards with his cronies while his nephew, brilliantly portrayed by Richard Benjamin, endeavours to get him to agree on a TV reunion with his old but hated sparring partner, played by George Burns. The room looked the same. The geezers playing cards were, I could have sworn, the same ones, and barely looked up when this young, keen Englishman walked in and said he wanted to talk about Al Jolson.

A few of them said they knew him. They all said they hated him – a recurring story. 'But', said one, 'he was very definitely the greatest.' That was when another piped up and said, 'Jolson? It's been a very long time, but I still miss him.' It was a good line and I was sure to use it. In fact, it became the last of those lines in the first edition of the book.

It was that experience which convinced me, right from the beginning, that there was more to a book than a mere assemblage of facts – even priceless facts like those in the Lincoln Center file. If you just want facts about a dead person, read the obituaries. Writing a book was getting beyond the facts, behind the stories you might or might not otherwise know.

There was another question at the back of my mind. Supposing I was given a brilliant story about my subject – how could I be sure it was true? There was always the temptation to accept good stories at their face value and later blame the teller of the tale if it was proved wrong.

Very early in my research, before going to America, Jeffery Simmonds introduced me to Stephen Longstreet, the man credited with writing *The Jolson Story* (credited, although the actual writer of the film was Sidney Buchman, alas by then dead; Buchman, who, like its star Larry Parks was to be a victim of McCarthyism, was the real writer and producer of the picture, but gave production credit to Sidney Skolsky, the columnist whose idea it originally was). Longstreet, who had written a W.H. Allen book himself, had some valuable advice for me: 'Just ask yourself if the story fits.'

He said no more, but before long that became my mantra. I realised that a biographer is presented with a jigsaw puzzle without a picture on the top of the box. He has to shake up the pieces and then try to assemble then. Before long, you get to understand which are the ones with straight edges, which are part of a tree, which form the house in the corner. Eventually, the right ones fit. The wrong ones had been in the wrong box.

It took a little time, but not too long. One man spoke about Jolson's generosity. Somehow, it didn't fit. Another of his clubmates took me aside and said: 'Take no notice of Jake. He just likes telling stories. He never knew Jolson. Ask him about anyone and he'll invent a story.' I didn't put it to the test, but what he said plainly didn't fit.

What happened the next day clearly did. One of the stops on my pilgrimage, for pilgrimage indeed it was, had to be the Winter Garden Theatre on Broadway. It figured in every Jolson story I ever read. It was the centre point of *The Jolson Story* itself – every time I hear the theatre's name, I picture the scene as a young Larry Parks playing a young Al Jolson takes a telephone call and gulps out the words, 'Winter Garden!...Broadway!'

So I went to Broadway – well, I had to, didn't I? – and went to the Winter Garden, which was then playing the Stephen Sondheim hit *Follies*. Broadway was a disappointment. It was tacky and tawdry. The lights were glittering, but it didn't have anything like the glory of the Great White Way featured so often on the screen – the lights that were shut off as a mark of respect when Jolson died. But it *was* Broadway and if the place itself didn't seem as wonderful as I had dreamed, the name itself was enough.

The big sign for *Follies* outside the Winter Garden wasn't quite the way I had remembered the ones in *The Jolson Story*. But this was the Winter Garden. And it was there that I met Fred Kelly, its star. Fred was Gene Kelly's brother, a dancer of superb talent who probably could have been a big star, but was always hindered by the fame of his sibling (Harry Jolson, Al's brother, I would soon learn, suffered the same fate; he was billed as 'AL JOLSON's brother Harry').

'What's the magic of the Winter Garden?' I asked Fred. 'Well, it's a particularly beautiful theatre,' he explained. Indeed it was. This was the kind of theatre featured in a thousand Hollywood movies: plush seats that still looked plush, white pillars and a stage so big that you almost had to wear special glasses to see from one end to the other.

But I wanted to know more. One of the great stories about Jolson's early days was the fact that he could stand on an empty stage and make the theatre rock – without the help of a microphone. How did he do it? Kelly said, 'I'll show you.' He climbed down from the stage and walked to the back of the house. 'Now whisper to me,' he shouted. I whispered and he answered my question.

As is already clear, I wasn't yet making any money from this trip, so I had to try to find other ways of helping my finances. BBC Radio Two had come up with some help by commissioning a few showbiz interviews from me for their *Late Night Extra* programme. The fees involved were ludicrously low, justifying the adage about the BBC tartan – 'small cheques' – but it helped, and also helped keep my name before the public. Fred Kelly was an invaluable subject and so were a couple of the other stars – old Ziegfeld girls who fitted beautifully into *Follies*. After all, they had been in the original *Ziegfeld Follies*.

Did they remember Jolson? 'Remember him?' said one. 'I went with him. My, did he know how to use his hands!' So one theory was blown sky high. Jolson never had children. Was he gay? A question rarely asked in those days – and now I knew the answer. 'Not a chance,' said the now very elderly lady.

New York and Jolson was a connection from the past. Los Angeles, however, still had a lot of the present about it. On the way from the airport – LAX, as it is known locally, after the labels attached to the luggage bound for the city – you can't avoid seeing the giant white rotunda under which Al Jolson is buried. It had to be an early visit. It was a huge tomb, if such it could be called. The ceiling of the dome, supported by white pillars not unlike those of the Winter Garden, has a picture that one must take as Moses with the Ten Commandments (although Jewish tradition has it that one must not create a human representation as part of religious ceremony) and the words 'Sweet Singer of Israel'. Underneath, a bronze bust of Jolson. It is a marvellous tribute, seemingly intended to keep his memory alive, for the 'sweet singer' to be still there in a world and a time when other singers, not yet born, were to top the pops.

It later turned out that the people behind the Hillside Memorial Park had just opened the cemetery, and had provided the tomb to Jolson's widow free of charge. They were convinced that Al Jolson was a big enough name to bring the place to the public attention. That gave a lot of comfort to all those other crazy people who, like me, couldn't finish a day without playing a Jolson tune.

That was the dead Al. But what of the present? I desperately wanted to meet Larry Parks, star of both *The Jolson Story* and *Jolson Sings Again*. I wanted to meet him because I couldn't conceive of writing a book about Al Jolson without meeting him. Was it true that the two men hated each other? How reasonable was it really to believe that Jolson resented Parks for having the chutzpah to play him in a role he wanted to play himself? The other reason was a very human and perhaps childish desire to meet in the flesh someone I knew so very well, from seeing him all those countless times on the screen. In years to come, I would get to know his wife, the bubbly and intelligent comedy actress and singer Betty Garrett. But I didn't know her then – more's the pity.

As much as I wanted to see him, Larry Parks didn't want to see me. 'Larry has been living in Jolson's shadow for 25 years,' said his agent. 'He's had enough. He doesn't want to talk about him.' I protested about how much I admired Parks, how well I thought I knew him, but the answer was still no. I would have to write my book without him. It was a virtual calamity. If I had known Betty Garrett at that time, she would have fixed it for me. Shortly before a new edition of the book was published, I got to know a man who has become a close friend, Melville Shavelson, writer, director and repository of anything you might ever want to know about Bob Hope, whose chief writer he had once been. He was also a close friend of Larry Parks. Yes, he assured me, Larry would see me. Except that before I could get around to having the meeting, Parks would be dead from a sudden heart attack, aged 60.

There were, however, others who were involved in that film and were involved with Jolson. Like Sidney Skolsky, a tiny myopic man who wrote one of those simple Hollywood columns so popular in American journalism that I've never been able to understand, with unmissable statements like 'Clark Gable wears striped pyjamas in bed'. I kid you not, but he was popular and when he had the idea of making a film about the life of the man whom he regarded as 'the king' (before Elvis succeeded to that throne), the studios took note. Jack Warner, boss of Warner Bros., said no. He remembered Al, worshipped him, but wasn't willing to spend enough money on a film about his life. At least, he didn't want to do it in colour. Harry Cohn, iron dictator of Columbia Pictures, loved Jolson, too. He was a former Tin Pan Alley song plugger and remembered how important it was to get Al to sing one of his tunes. Now, taking up Skolsky's idea, there was a chance to bathe in his idol's glory and his spotlight.

Skolsky's office was Schwab's drugstore, the place where a girl wearing a tight sweater was discovered by a talent scout who said, 'I can get you into pictures.' He could and he did. Her name was Lana Turner. That was where I met Skolsky, who was delighted to have the opportunity to tell the true story of how he was originally responsible for the most spectacular comeback in movie history. As I have said, the star of that first talkie, *The Jazz Singer*, was no longer American's most popular entertainer. He had a radio show and had been the first entertainer to go to front-line danger spots to entertain the troops – 'Ask your grandmothers about me,' was his usual line – even frequently stopping a couple of lonely GIs on a street corner and saying: 'My name's Jolson and I sing. Do you want to hear me?' They always did, and he always would. Skolsky told me about that, about how keen Cohn had been on the idea and how he had constantly increased its budget – which, unlike most films at the time, had gone into the millions of dollars. As a result, the troop entertainer had suddenly become America's favourite singer.

But there were others who remembered the real Al Jolson long before those days. I wanted to see them all. I did a short interview with Fred Astaire, who remembered seeing Jolson on a vaudeville bill and thought he was great. It would be the first meeting with a man who would prove to be my favourite interview subject. 'How are you getting back to your hotel?' Astaire asked me. 'I'll get a taxi,' I said. 'No need,' he replied. 'I'll drive you.' The first time I ever rode in a Rolls-Royce, it was a big black car driven by Fred Astaire.

I had spoken to Fred principally for the BBC *Be My Guest* series. There were other people I met with little more in mind than talking about Jolson. It became very, very clear that a great many people who knew Jolson didn't like him – and that was putting it pretty mildly.

One of those I most wanted to talk to was George Jessel, his showbiz contemporary, the man who had starred in the stage production of *The Jazz Singer*. It was Jessel who gave the eulogy at Al's funeral. It was a staggering performance, a marvellous tribute written by himself. It was easy to see why he was known as America's Toastmaster-General – a superb way with words, humour, dignity, schmaltz...In that oration, he spoke of how Al had given just that kind of dignity he was now offering himself to the Jews of America. Before Jolson, 'The Jews in America were a poor lot, old before their time.' Al had told them to walk with their heads held high, and he himself proceeded 'like a Roman emperor'. Jews of his generation had come from the ghetto, yet Jolson could sing about 'The Night Boat to Albany and about a girl in Avalon'.

All that gave the impression of a love affair between two men who always spoke about each other on their radio programmes, who teased each other at dinners and charity benefits. So I was ready to hear more when he suggested that I have lunch with him at the Hillcrest Country Club. The club was the Jewish showbiz centre in Los Angeles, set up as an answer to all those 'restricted' clubs that barred not just entertainers, but people who went to synagogues and temples rather than churches. On every table at the Hillside club was a box of matzos. More importantly, you couldn't join until you had paid a small fortune to the United Jewish Appeal. It was one of those plush establishments that only America could dream up. The superb buildings looked out on a golf course that could be calculated to turn the least athletic person into a player. The greens not only looked lovely, they were historic and very symbolic – soon after Hillside had been established as a response to prejudice, they struck oil there. It was poetic justice.

In the dining room, as luxurious as that of a five-star hotel, with intricate drapes, the sort of carpet with a pile so deep you wondered if you would ever see your feet again, and giant picture windows looking out at the golf links, Jessel was sitting at his favourite table – and blowing his nose on the crisply laundered table cloth. I told him I wanted to talk about his pal Al. Pal? It was a red rag to a still angry bull. 'Jolson,' he said in a story that would recur again and again (the jigsaw puzzle was being thrown in the air and the obvious pieces were going to be fitted into place), 'he wouldn't do anything to help anyone. He wouldn't mail a letter for anyone. He was...a no good son of a bitch. But – ' and this was the main point which would be echoed again and again – 'he was the greatest entertainer I ever saw.'

Yet what about *The Jazz Singer*? He surely had a proprietorial interest in that product. At the time Warners were about to shoot their movie, he was starring in the Broadway version of the tale and doing very nicely, thank you. The story – one I still believe – was that he himself had turned down the role of Jack Robin, the star part of the cantor's son, because he wasn't prepared to risk his career on a new invention. It was also said that Eddie Cantor had rejected it for the same reason. Not true as far as he was concerned, said Jessel. The truth, he said, was that he and Al had been staying in the same hotel overnight. Early on a Sunday morning, Jolson said he was going to go out for a little while. 'I learned the next morning that he had signed to make *The Jazz Singer*. Are you surprised that I was angry?'

It was wonderful stuff. And sad, too. 'I was on a plane with him one day, flying back from Florida. He knew that his little boy, the one he adopted with Ruby Keeler, would be waiting for him. He couldn't wait to see the kid. When the plane landed, he trundled down the gangplank, saw the little boy waiting for him, lifted him up in his arms and said: "Who am I, sonny boy?" "You're the Jew," said the kid – and Jolson blanched under his suntan.'

Just what a biographer wants to hear – one of the stories that provides the background a writer craves and would never be found in an obituary. No one had ever before suggested that Al was a victim of anti-Semitism, let alone in his own home.

Of course, his Jewishness was an essential part of Jolson's make-up, as I found from digging through the clippings and, even more, from meeting people. One of his contemporaries remembered a story that I had read about, but he had witnessed from the audience at one of the Sunday night concerts that Al gave so that people in show business could see how great he was (only a supreme egoist but also a genuinely brilliant entertainer could get away with both that excuse and the exercise itself). Jolson talked about his father, the cantor Moses Yoelson, about how he would rush home from the synagogue on Saturday nights so that he could hear his son Asa Yoelson's radio show. Asa, or Al Jolson, had just achieved his first successes when he walked into one of New York's most expensive men's wear emporia and spied a magnificent cashmere overcoat. It was priced at $200. What a marvellous present for his father, he thought. But he knew what the older man would think about his son spending so much on a coat. This was, after all, before World War One. Two hundred dollars was a hell of a lot of money. So he got the sales assistant to put a new price-tag on the coat he was buying for his Dad – one for $12. A few weeks later he called on his father, during one of the breaks in the love–hate relationship between the two – the cantor had desperately wanted his wayward son to follow him into the synagogue or, at least, follow an Orthodox Jewish life, yet he had abandoned both – and married out of the faith, to boot. But Yoelson was undoubtedly proud of his Asa's success, and the two plainly still did love each other.

'What did you think of that coat, Papa?' he asked. 'Oh, what a wonderful coat!' the cantor responded. 'You know what? I sold it to Uncle Moshe for $20. You didn't know your father was a businessman, did you?'

That was a nice story, one that was another gift to a biographer. But there were a number of other tales that weren't so nice – and always the conclusions were the same. Like the yarn spun by Saul Chaplin, who was vocal arranger on both *The Jolson Story* and *Jolson Sings Again*, and before that the songwriting partner of Sammy Cahn. (His name was originally Kaplan; Cahn's was Cohen. Sammy persuaded him to change his name. 'Cohen and Kaplan sounds like a firm of dress manufacturers.') It was the perfect example of how a story would 'fit' into the general picture, and I have never doubted its truth.

Chaplin knew all the Jolson records from old, and sat at the piano as Al went through numbers like 'Mammy', 'California Here I Come' and 'April Showers' once again, rehearsing them before going into the recording booth, while Morris Stoloff, the musical director, conducted the orchestra in another part of the studio.

It was, apparently, 'April Showers' that gave the first signs of trouble. In the classic recordings, Al sang the last word in the song as 'whenever April Showers come a–l–o–n–g', wobbling on the last syllable. When he sang it now, he did it straight, no wobble. Chaplin had the audacity to bring that point to the star's attention. Al's reaction came without an apparent moment of further thought. He took out a wad of dollar bills and said to the musician: 'Now show me yours.' (My dear friend Melville Shavelson, who was Bob Hope's principal writer, had a similar experience when Jolson was on the Hope radio programme. He dared to suggest a change of emphasis in a comedy line. Al took out his money and hit him over the head with it.)

Saul Chaplin and Jolson co-operated on the number 'The Anniversary Song', which was a last-minute choice for a scene at the end of *The Jolson Story* when Larry Parks as Al is entertaining his parents on their wedding anniversary. A song was deemed necessary for that moment and Jolson said he knew one that would fit the bill perfectly: 'Waves of the Danube'. It needed a lyric, however. Chaplin came up with one, he told me. He was never very proud of it. 'Just imagine,' he said, 'those words "the world was in bloom, there were stars in the skies, except for the few that were there in your eyes". I wanted to change it. 'Don't,' said Harry Cohn, the boss of Columbia. 'You'll improve it out of a hit.' He was right. The song was the biggest song success of the year and Al did very well out of it. 'He promised to share the royalties with me. I never got a cent.'

So, not a pleasant memory. But there was a corollary to the story. 'When he performed,' says Chaplin, 'it was just wonderful.'

There would be other great stories from the man born Nathan Birnbaum.

He was a small, bent man, with a grey wig (he insisted he had to have a haircut, which caused a certain amount of fun in the office in which I was then sitting). He was speaking in that familiar voice that I mentioned earlier – the one that sounded as though he ate sandpaper for lunch. And he had changed his name about 70 years earlier – to George Burns.

This was one of the greats of showbiz. When I had gone to the Hillcrest, he was the centre of attention, at the head of the bridge game, sitting in the place of honour at the club's round table, the one at which Jolson had sat like a king on his throne, surrounded by people like Burns and his close friend Jack Benny, like Jessel, fawning over the man whom he said he disliked so much, like Eddie Cantor – that incredible generation of American entertainers.

In 1971 Burns was loved by his contemporaries, but as far as his audiences were concerned, he was just the surviving partner of their favourite vaudeville and black-and-white TV comedy team, Burns and Allen. Gracie Allen was dead, and he visited her grave every day and told her he wouldn't be long and would take his music with him. (In fact, it would be almost 30 years before that happened.) He wanted to talk about Gracie, the Irish dancer he had met when he was on one of those vaudeville stages (he had been working with an old performer who had a performing seals act; it was a time when he found it difficult to get a girl because he always smelled of fish).

'Gracie was the real star. All I did was point my cigar while she talked. I asked about her brother and I asked her why she always put the pepper in the salt pot. "Oh, that's obvious," she said with her illogical logicality. "Everybody takes the salt when what they really want is the pepper. So this time when they're wrong, they'll be right."'

We talked about Gracie and we talked about his childhood – how he had started singing with the Peewee Quartet when he was about 7 years old. 'We used to sing on riverboats and people threw coins at us. Sometimes, the coins would go overboard and we'd jump over to get the money. It got so we could only sing with water in our mouths.' We talked about his father, who, like Jolson's, was a synagogue cantor. 'He wasn't a very good cantor. He had a disappointment act. You know what a disappointment act is? When a cantor got sick, he used to substitute for him.'

The only singing he himself wanted to do was in show business. 'What other business can I be in and make a lot of money, smoke my cigars and put on lipstick like your secretary?'

How could you not like a man like that – especially when he talked about his contemporaries? I mentioned Maurice Chevalier. 'I once went up to him and said, "Maurice, would you do me a favour?" "Of course," he said in that wonderful French accent. "What would you like?" I said, "You know my sister, Goldie?" He took out his fountain pen. I said, "No. She doesn't want your autograph. Would you have an affair with her?"'

That was great, but he knew I wanted to talk about Jolson. He had a similar view about Al as Jessel's, although he was a lot kinder. 'I knew he wasn't the nicest man around,' he told me. 'But there was never a better entertainer. I saw him on stage and it was wonderful.'

He proceeded to tell me *how* wonderful. 'There was no one like him – at least, I don't think so. He stood on stage and was amazing.' He remembered the time he was waiting for Al to appear at a Broadway theatre. 'It was very late before he showed up. There was two or three feet of snow outside. But the audience wouldn't go away. He eventually came in from the back of the theatre and walked to the stage while the customers went crazy. 'He sang for a couple of hours and then he said he had to have dinner. "There's a restaurant next door and they've got a swell piano player there, why not come over in a few minutes?" He then passed candy around the theatre while they waited. I think it was 2 o'clock in the morning before he got off.'

During World War Two, he passed portions of sturgeon around the Hillcrest Country Club, said Burns. Sturgeon – a distinctly non-kosher fish – was a rarity at the time and is still a protected species. 'Jolson somehow managed to get hold of it and was pleased that his friends liked him for getting it for them. Then came *The Jolson Story*. We knew Jolson was doing well again – because we stopped getting the sturgeon.'

Burns remembered sitting with Gracie in the balcony of the Metropolitan Opera House for a bond-selling rally. 'Caruso had just got through singing Paliacci, and Jolson tumbled on to the stage, threw out his arms and shouted, "You ain't heard nothin' yet." Imagine saying that – after Caruso. In Caruso's own house, yet. He was somethin'. That little Jew, wearing a blue suit, what a nerve. But he looked great, always suntanned – because he spent so much time in Florida.'

He knew how popular Jolson had been – only he could have got away with dismissing an entire cast during a show by calling out to the audience: ' Do you want me or do you want them?' They all wanted him. 'You know, he used to sit in the box office selling tickets. But you couldn't ask him where you'd be sitting. If you were going to see Jolson, you were lucky to get in. If you asked where you were sitting, he wouldn't sell you the tickets.'

It was just the stuff a biographer wanted to hear. But what was he like off the stage or out of the film studio? Was he happy? 'Oh, it was easy enough to make Jolson happy. All you had to do was cheer him for breakfast, applaud wildly at lunch and give him a standing ovation for dinner.'

He remembered the famous parties. 'I gave a party one night for Damon Runyon. And when you give one of those parties and you have a piano player with a great left hand, everybody wants to get on. But I like to sing and didn't want anyone else to sing, too. Why the hell should I let anyone else perform.? Hell, I'm playing the piano player! So I was giving Jolson a pain in the ass. Eventually, he said, "Do you mind if I sing?" Imagine that, Jolson asking to sing.

'I said, "Sure, Jolie," so he sang and I joined in. He grabbed Ruby [his wife, Ruby Keeler] took her fur coat and left the house . As he walked to the car, I stood in front of it and sang, "Rockabye your baby... ".'

*

Burns's closest friend was Jack Benny. I had met him before I began the New York and Hollywood troll. It was for another BBC Radio Two programme and he agreed to give me a couple of hours, with my producer, to talk about his own amazing career.

I had always loved Benny's dry humour and was, frankly, flattered by his attention. He was then 78 years old and looking tired. After the couple of hours were up, my producer said we had to go, it wasn't fair to take up any more of his time. As we left, I mentioned my Jolson project. Would he be willing to talk? 'Sure, I have the whole day. I've got nothing else to do.' I was grateful for that. I came back in the afternoon and we talked about his close friend Jolie. He lay down on the couch in his suite at London's Dorchester Hotel, introduced me to his wife and comedy partner Mary Livingstone – and we talked.

There was a lesson in that – in what was, I suppose, the first real interview I had ever done for a book. The bigger they are, generally speaking, the nicer they are. None of that too-busy-to-talk-to-journalists stuff that many of today's stars maintain. No nonsense about giving every paper, TV or radio station just ten minutes to ask precisely the same questions (which have to be approved in advance). It was as James Stewart had once said when I asked him why he, a great star who needed no more publicity than did the Royal Family, bothered to talk to people like me. 'I've always considered it part of the ballgame,' he said. To Jack Benny, it was a courtesy he returned to someone whom he thought was nice enough to want to see him.

Talking about Jolson, the man he had honoured at the dedication of that memorial in Hollywood and whose story he had told in a movie documentary, was part of Jack Benny's ballgame, too. (He said that he actually couldn't remember the film commentary – I was terribly impressed. Just *how* could someone be so busy that they didn't remember something as important as a movie commentary about Al Jolson? But it was, as George Burns put it, a case of big things only ever happening to his best friend.)

Talking to him about Jolson wasn't so much the usual collection of stories and anecdotes as a psychological assessment from a contemporary, a man who had played with Jolson, eaten with Jolson and, most important of all, had seen him perform. To him, as to all the others of his generation, Al had been the greatest.

'You know,' he said, 'they say that Jolson was the greatest singer of them all. Singer, my eye! When someone can make you laugh for a couple of hours, he's something very special.' And that from a man who made a living out of making people laugh. They had made each other chortle with the most inane jokes when Al had been on the Benny radio programme. 'You're not a very good driver, Al, are you?' he asked on one show. 'No, Jack,' Jolson replied, 'I may not be a very good driver, but have you seen the way Larry parks?'

What struck him was the difference between a Jolson performance in blackface and one without makeup. 'When he was nervous, I'd plead with him to put on the blackface makeup,' he said. 'He was much more confident with his face black – it was as if he was hiding behind the makeup.'

That was something I had suspected myself. I never went along with the modern concept of blackface being an insult to the African-American population. On the contrary, when Al appeared on stage in his stock character of Gus the butler or Gus the groomsman, he was speaking up for those African-Americans at a time when slavery was still for some Americans a personal memory. It was a time when a black man was not allowed on to the Broadway stage – and when, eventually, a few exceptionally talented people did get on to shows like the *Ziegfeld Follies* they were told to black up themselves, because none of them could look black enough for Mr Florenz Ziegfeld.

It was the age of the minstrel show – of Sambo shaking his tambourine and trying to answer the age-old question of why the chicken crossed the road. Al Jolson would have none of that. He was, after all, Broadway's biggest star, and he had to be the one who got the upper hand. When he did so, he was performing a service to a downtrodden race. In his 1930 film *Big Boy*, he is ordered by the wicked plantation owner: 'Boy, dust my boots.' 'No, sir,' says Gus. 'I don't dust nobody's boots no more. I is free.' That, and the way in which he would usually manage to rescue the white maiden in distress from the hands of the professional gambler, gave black people a dignity that they struggled to find for themselves – sufficient to have the movie banned from the Deep South for 40 years. It was an answer to all the complaints of Jolson himself being a racist that I have tried to combat for three decades.

Benny knew that and knew, too, that I was going to present the case for Al Jolson as had not been seen or heard for 20 years.

He pulled no punches. Plainly, he saw the sad side of the entertainer, particularly during the so-called fallow period, although it was all relative and not so fallow – he still had that radio show when radio was king, even though, for the moment, there were no new movies and even no new records. Jack didn't tell the story about the sturgeon, but he had his own memories of that period when even Jolson himself no longer would call himself the world's greatest entertainer. 'He would sit in the club in the corner by himself, looking very dejected.'

He said he was going to try to get me to see his close friend, Erle Krasner, Jolson's widow. But she said she was too shy to meet an interviewer, let alone a biographer. Years later, when she came to London's National Film Theatre, Dennis Sykes did manage to see her and tried to persuade her to change her mind. 'It's too late,' she said, 'but I wished I had seen him.' Such are the perils of biography writing.

The other person he was going to put me in touch with was his pal George Burns. Benny had signed to play one of the two warring vaudevillians in a movie version of Neil Simon's *The Sunshine Boys*. But he died before he could move into the studio. So Burns took his place – 'I couldn't argue with the Man Up There,' – and, he told me, 'I've been a Sunshine Boy all my life.' A Sunshine Boy who at the age of 79 suddenly found himself with a brand new career – and an Oscar for his trouble. I wanted to give both him and his friend an Oscar for making one biographer very happy.

A younger Jolson contemporary (which gives you another idea of how long ago the early seventies were) was Bob Hope. He and I had a good relationship. I had done a BBC chat with him in London, which he liked, so much so that when he returned the following year, he was only prepared to do one new interview – 'How about the fellow who spoke to me last year?' I generously agreed to take up the new challenge. We met in one of the swankiest suites at the Savoy, all antique furniture with large windows looking out on to the Thames. A huge barge went by while we talked – 'It's carrying Crosby's money,' he joked.

But it wasn't Crosby, his old *Road* film sparring partner, that he wanted to talk about. It was mostly about Hope himself – who had turned down the chance of running for the presidency because he wasn't born in America. There was, however, he told me, another reason: the house that went with the job was too small. He also genuinely wanted to talk about Al. I recalled the fact that on his radio show he had teased Jolson about being in his early sixties. Now he was even older than that himself. 'I said that about Jolson!' he laughed. He also recalled quipping that since Al was the guest on so many radio programmes, it would be a lot simpler if he just had one of his own – the line was drowned out by unanticipated applause from his audience.

You wouldn't have picked that up from the clippings. Neither would I have experienced the power of the Jolson voice. Of course, I knew about that already. But I saw it in a new perspective when I met a certain Mr Morris Stoloff. Stoloff was the musical director of both *The Jolson Story* and *Jolson Sings Again*. I had been looking forward to a man whose music I had grown up with. If I couldn't meet Larry Parks, which I still regret to this day, he was almost the next best thing.

But the day didn't begin so propitiously. I was sitting in a taxi taking me to the music man's home on Wilshire Boulevard, the main drag in Beverly Hills. I looked down at my brown right shoe. 'That's funny,' I thought. 'I was sure I put on black shoes today.' I thought no more about it, paid my fare and walked through the lobby of the apartment building. As I talked to the concierge at the front desk, I looked down at my feet again – at my left foot and its black shoe. I had put on odd ones. As I rang the bell at Stoloff's front door, I tried desperately to keep one foot behind the other.

He later said he hadn't noticed. I was grateful for that. But certainly we had other things to talk about – notably Al Jolson and the songs he had recorded for the two biopics. He said it had been a long time and he really couldn't remember much about them. It had been so long since he had last heard them. It was all I wanted to hear. I had with me my tape recorder – and a generous supply of his tapes, the songs Al sang to Stoloff's accompaniment, the singer in a booth while the conductor and arranger waved his baton in front of the band, yards away.

He prepared to listen attentively, almost, I thought, indulgently. Until, that is, Al began singing 'California Here I Come'. It was a number on which Stoloff had plainly worked hard, but it wasn't his own music that stunned him. As he listened to the Jolson voice, I could see the colour drain from his face. Turning from red to white, he shook his head at the end of the number and told me: 'You know, that gives me the chills.' It was not an expression I had heard before. But ever since, playing those songs another thousand or two times each, that's what it does for me still: gives me the chills. If that's what putting on odd shoes does for you, I might do it again some time.

The book finally came out in 1973 and had respectable enough reviews. Some of them were gratifyingly very good. Not all. One of the worst – in fact, I can think of only one other that wasn't totally complimentary, and it *was* reviewed in every national newspaper in Britain – came from the man who would soon become a close friend, Larry Adler. He said the book was 'pedestrian'. I wasn't happy about it, particularly since he had more than one honourable mention in the work, but that didn't mean I had to return the meanness. Indeed, when I had reason to, I interviewed him on *YDHTBJ*. 'For a Jew, you are a very Christian gentleman,' said this Jewish kid from Baltimore who once had to be persuaded by Fred Astaire to break the kosher laws.

I appeared on radio programmes and the biggest thrill of all was seeing the black-jacketed volume in the shop windows. One shop in Edgware, a couple of miles from my home, had a whole window full of them. As I think I told the proprietor, I might have been even happier had they all been sold. Not quite. I more than just liked seeing them in the window. The cameras came out and the family was transported to the shop as though it were one of the sights of London. As far as I was concerned, it was.

The book was well enough reviewed to be bought by an American publisher. Stein and Day of New York did their own lush version, which they called simply *Jolson*. Their book was bigger than the London one and the typeface and paper quality were better, although the way the pictures were reproduced left a little to be desired. But the jacket was a work of art, an art deco work of art that gave me a thrill I had not known since my children had been born. Sara and I spent hours just looking at it.

There were enough people in the American media showing interest for Stein and Day to send me on a national publicity tour. I was busy for three weeks, going from radio station to TV show – something like 70 of them, being ushered into each one by a young dynamo of a PR lady called Sheri Safran. I went from Manhattan to

Chicago to Washington, DC, to Dallas and Houston Texas to Los Angeles, and dozens of stops in between.

I had hardly been in New York for an hour or so after arriving on the red-eye before I was on TV, following a woman displaying the art of making split peas. It was morning television, a novelty to an Englishman in the 1970s. 'What was so amazing about Jolson?' the presenter asked. 'Well,' I remember saying, 'he did everything in show business before anyone else. In fact, he did everything but split peas.'

In Washington, DC, the host said he had always had a very soft spot for Al Jolson – because he himself had been circumcised by Jolson's father, the cantor.

I went from bookshop to bookshop. At the famous Doubledays store on Fifth Avenue – alas, no longer there; I suspect the owners found it more profitable to let the store to a fashion house – *Jolson* volumes were piled up on the floor, on the counters and in the window. I went to the shop and signed dozens – which my publisher encouraged, since, once signed, they could not be returned. I was there when a middle-aged couple started fingering one. The assistant told them it was a signed copy. 'Mabel,' shouted the man, 'these books are signed by Al Jolson.' I didn't feel like disabusing him of the notion.

It was exciting, and nice because a number of expat friends saw or heard me, rang the stations and made contact. One said: 'Who would have thought it when you were on the *Luton News*?' I didn't say that I for one had *thought* about it.

Another old friend, Ivor Davis, then the *Daily Express* man in California, wrote a piece about the tour in his daily column.

'Schlepping the book,' as the trade called it, really was exciting. It was also exhausting. Sara had expected me to be away for a fortnight. The two weeks stretched into three and then three and a half. Finally, I had changed my ticket home for the last time and was looking forward to going back to my beloved and our young children. On that last night Sheri Safran rang: would I go back to Los Angeles – *The Tonight Show*, starring Johnny Carson wanted me to appear. The most important show in the country, perhaps the biggest in the world. How could I turn it down? By saying no, that's how. I couldn't have imagined rejecting such an offer, but I had the family's faces in my mind's eye and I couldn't let them down again. So I didn't do the show. Would it have made a difference? Just to me, I suppose. Do I regret it? I suppose I do, even now, 30-odd years later.

There are certain other frustrations in selling a book hard. One of them, gratifying though it undoubtedly is, is when people come up to you and say they knew the subject of your biography and why didn't you include the story of . . . ?

One of the nicest such stories came from the lady who said that her father was a great friend of Al's. She said she was delighted that I had made a point of emphasising Jolson's love of gefilte fish, a Jewish delicacy that can only be tasted, not adequately described. Her father, she said, not only used to enjoy the fish, sitting next to his pal Al at a local Jewish restaurant, his mother once made a plateful of the treat and took it round to the stage door of the Winter Garden Theatre. Al liked it, but didn't return the container. 'Your friend Jolson,' said the mother to her son, 'he liked my gefilte fish so much that he ate the plate, too?'

To make the story even more tempting, she enclosed a picture of Al and her dad in a marvellous pose, one leaning on the shoulders of the other in profile. Why didn't I know about it in time? Fortunately, there would be six other editions of the book – called variously *Al Jolson*, *Jolson* and *Jolie*. And the story was in each of them. I wrote to the lady after the first one. She said her dad would have been thrilled, but he had just died.

There would be other I-wish-you-had-written-this stories, although that was one of the nicest. Years later, I interviewed the famous songwriter Burton Lane. And, as always happened at such meetings, I asked him about Jolson, because I realised he had written the score of Al's last Broadway show, *Hold On To Your Hats*, in 1940. He spoke of Jolson's cruelty, how he doctored songs – and, best of all, how he and his co-star Ruby Keeler went through the motions of their divorce on stage. As if it were part of the action, Jolson accused Ruby of ruining their marriage – and complained about the role of her mother in making things go wrong for them, while all the time the other performers and the orchestra leader didn't know what had hit them. Probably just par for the course for a man who dismissed the rest of the cast when he felt like it. I am still waiting for another edition so that I can include the Burton Lane story.

Of course, it *could* happen. In 1985 there was *The Real Al Jolson*, my first TV documentary on the prestigious *South Bank Show* on Britain's independent television. And in 1995 the show *Jolson*, about which more later.

What is undoubtedly true is that a successful book is the first stage on the way to an addiction. I couldn't wait to get on to another one. I liked the idea of a new book with my name on it, I loved the thought of going back to America for more research and I enjoyed the new lifestyle of not having to rush out on a Friday afternoon to write about Harrow Council for the *Evening Standard*. Joe Dray was very kind and indulgent and I wrote my thanks to him in the acknowledgements pages.

It was also true that I enjoyed the money the first book bought – not a fortune, but enough to place in the coffers of a building society, a deposit on our flat in Bournemouth, which more than 30 years later is still much more than just a second home.

# 24  *Irving Berlin – always*

There was one question from my publisher when we met at this time: 'When are we going to get Irving Berlin?' Berlin was my next subject because I thought he fitted in with my nostalgic kick, a member of the same generation as Jolson, a charismatic personality of a totally different kind, now quite old, by reputation extraordinarily crusty and about whom anecdotes had gathered like song pluggers around entertainers in Tin Pan Alley.

Berlin had virtually invented the music business. In fact, the man who wrote 'There's No Business Like Show Business' could easily have also penned 'There's No Business Like The Music Business'. He not only wrote both words and music, but he published his stuff – and that of countless other songwriters, too. There was one lovely story told me by the veteran Hollywood music man Saul Chaplin, sometime partner of Sammy Cahn and the man who had worked on 'The Anniversary Song' with Jolson. He recalled the time when the citizens of Tin Pan Alley would gather on a Saturday night at a particular bar to which was attached a music store. For weeks, his colleagues couldn't understand why Berlin would go over to the shelves where his own music was stacked and then run his fingers over the tops of the sheets. When one of the other writers plucked up sufficient courage to ask what he was doing (and you needed courage to query anything Berlin did – at least to his face) he was happy enough to provide the answer: he was feeling for dust; if there was too much of it, the shop wasn't selling enough of the music.

He was a phenomenal character whichever way you looked at it – and look at it I did. For one thing, he wrote 3,000 songs, all but about half a dozen of them both words and music. For another, he wrote some of the greatest standards of the twentieth century –

from the song he gave his bride on their wedding day, 'Always', to 'Let's Face The Music and Dance'. To say nothing of 'White Christmas'. He had written his first big hit, 'Alexander's Ragtime Band', in 1910, and was still writing them when I started work on my book 60 years later. As a 5-year-old, I had seen him standing on the stage of the London Palladium, singing a tune that I could have taken as my own theme song – 'Oh, How I Hate To Get Up In The Morning'. When I heard that he had said, 'When I'm in love I write love songs. Because I don't like getting up in the morning, I wrote that one,' I knew that we must have had some joint ancestry.

He had written the scores of a huge swathe of Broadway shows and movies, not least one of the very first I had seen, *Annie Get Your Gun*, which contained probably more hits than any show before or since. 'There's No Business Like Show Business' was always talked of as the national anthem of the theatre. More than that, he had written a song that was hugely important in the pantheon of patriotic music, but I had no idea then, in the 1970s, just how significant it would become. Ever since Kate Smith had sung 'God Bless America' in 1939, it had struck a national nerve at a time when the United States was dithering about entering World War Two. People stood to attention when they heard it and put their hands to their hearts. It was the most patriotic song America knew. Steps were taken to make it a new national anthem, but it didn't happen. Yet enough copies were sold for it to make a fortune for the Boy and Girl Scouts of America, to whom Berlin had given the royalties. He couldn't have known that it would be played even more often than 'The Star Spangled Banner' at commemorations for the victims of the September 11 massacre. It was almost as if he had written it in 9/11 time.

There was a point about Berlin that made him journalistically fascinating – he seemed to live his life as though chasing headlines and the songs that would follow them. His first wife died as a result of catching typhoid while on their honeymoon in Cuba in 1912. To express his intense sadness, he wrote a song, 'When I Lost You'.

In 1926, he fell in love with Ellin Mackie, the heiress to a silver fortune. When her father, Clarence Mackie, opposed the idea of his Roman Catholic daughter marrying a Jewish boy born Israel Baline from what was decidedly the wrong side of the New York tracks, they eloped – while the world's press focused on them day after day.

He was the bespoke songwriter, producing songs for individual performers the way a tailor cuts cloth to fit a cherished customer. That was how he could write 'We're A Couple of Song and Dance Men' for Bing Crosby and Fred Astaire or Jolson's *cri de coeur* 'Let Me Sing And I'm Happy'. In Berlin's hands they were almost folk songs, numbers that seemed as if they had been there for ever.

Then there was his habit of never letting a good song die, no matter what the music-buying public thought or did. He had a trunk in which he put failed songs, ready to dust them up and sell them all over again when he judged the time to be right – with, of course, certain changes. In the early thirties he had written a flopperoo called 'To My Mammy', for Jolson, naturally. It went up the music charts like a snail with arthritis. But it contained the line, 'How deep is the ocean, how high is the sky'. Looking for a new song with a catchy title, he cannibalised that line and it became a huge hit. In 1918, he had written another classic flop called 'Smile and Show Your Dimple'. Unfortunately, nobody smiled and not a dimple was creased. But a few years later, Berlin was looking for a song for the Easter holiday. He came up with 'Easter Parade' – to the tune of 'Smile and...'

That was another thing about him. He was teased about wanting to corner the market in American holiday songs, which he probably did. But what about the biggest holiday of them all? He pondered that one when he was commissioned to write the score of a Bing Crosby picture called *Holiday Inn* in 1943. He gave the matter Mr Berlin's personal attention and – according to some sources that I dispute – brought another tune from out of the trunk, the most successful popular song of all time. That was *White Christmas*. At one time, it was just the most successful ever Christmas song, eclipsing 'Silent Night' in a handful of years. But soon afterwards it had beaten everything else, too, to the tune of about 400 million copies being sold. It didn't do Bing Crosby much harm either.

None of this was bad for the son of a synagogue cantor – yes, another one – born in Siberia in 1888. And that was where I began my quest, not in Siberia itself, but my story. I wanted to know the truth of it all. I had made a few forays into the research. I saw Ethel Merman in a restaurant and asked her for an interview to talk about all the Berlin songs she had performed, not least of all 'There's No Business Like Show Business'. She told me how Rodgers and

Hammerstein, the producers of *Annie Get Your Gun*, had anticipated an extra song and he had come up with the anthem. 'He didn't have it on Friday. Monday, it was there. But he didn't include it when he played a selection. When Dick Rodgers asked him about it, he said, "I didn't think you liked it."' As I got to know, Berlin was a bundle of insecurities – he was a victim of insomnia most of the time. Once, a friend said, 'Irving, you look great. You must have slept last night.' 'Yes,' he replied, 'but I dreamt that I didn't.'

(Incidentally, I did a radio interview with Ms Merman. She said that her big problem was keeping her legs together when she sang. 'I always find someone shouting, "Look, there's Ethel again – with her legs wide open."' The *Woman's Hour* producer cut the line out.)

Bing Crosby was in town and agreed to see me at his London hotel. We had met on a previous visit when I attended a press conference before his show at the Palladium, but this was being laid on specially for me.

At first, it looked as though it wasn't going to happen. Like the appointment with Harold Wilson, there was trouble with trains. I didn't get the wrong one, but the right one was late – and so was I. When I rushed up St James' Street, sweat pouring from my brow, microphone flex dragging from my tape recorder, he was standing outside, smoking his pipe, little hat on his bald head. 'Are you the guy who's coming to talk to me?' he asked as I panted my way up to him. 'Yes,' I puffed, fortunate that I didn't have to manage more than a one-syllable word at that time. 'Well, come inside.'

He chewed on his pipe and talked about his pal. Inevitably we got round to 'White Christmas'. 'Yes,' he said, 'White Christmas. I was on the set of *Holiday Inn*, and knew that Berlin was working on something new. Before long, his secretary came to me with a sheet of music and played the tune on a piano. I remember saying, 'I don't think you need worry about this one, Irving.' Needless to say, it was the showbiz understatement of the century.

There were so many legends about music men and entertainers generally that I wanted to go to the source of it all, Berlin himself. That was much easier said than done. He hadn't given an interview for ten years and made it very clear he wasn't going to do so any more. But I had greater confidence in my powers of persuasion than most other people. At the same time, fortunately, I had been commissioned by Radio Two to do a programme about him. That was a good way of broaching the subject. I took a sheet of Radio London notepaper – I know I was right when I said it was the best name a radio station could possibly have – and wrote to ask for an interview. I knew it was a tough one, but was amazed when the reply from his secretary came: he would talk to me. She asked me to phone to organise a date and time.

I phoned. We fixed a time and a date. 'You do realise', said the redoubtable Ms Schneider, 'that he will only talk on the phone.' This was a disappointment. It turned out to be only the first, but it did mean we would be able to talk. A time was fixed. I would go to the BBC studios at the Rockefeller Center on New York's Sixth Avenue. The engineers were apprised of the situation. They would put me through to his office and then Ms Schneider would transfer the call to Berlin's home (actual number withheld). When we were connected, the recording machines would be switched on. I would be allowed 20 minutes.

It all happened. I spoke to Ms Schneider. She put me through to the Berlin home. A little voice started croaking at the other end. I knew then why the comedian Joe Frisco had said about him, 'You have to hug him to hear him.' I was ready to start hugging across the phone lines. 'Thank you so much for talking to me,' I said in my best polite BBC voice. 'Well,' he replied, 'you wrote me such a nice letter.' Game, there. Set and then match to come. Or so I hoped. There were more pleasantries. 'Just a minute,' I said, and added a 'Sir' for good measure. Very good measure, I was convinced. 'I'll just ask the man to put on the machines.'

'What machines?' he squealed. 'The recording machines,' I said. 'No recording machines,' he ordered. As a result, then, in a demonstration of integrity I have regretted ever since, I told the engineer to forget about taping our 20-minute conversation. Twenty minutes that turned into two hours. Two hours of journalistic gems. Two hours of material that would have been wonderful on the air, but were still marvellous for a book. Two hours that disappeared into the ether, even though he would never have known if I really had turned the machines off. I could never have used the interview for this particular programme, but it would have been marvellous for the archives. He was already in his mid-eighties. Would there not come a time when it would be useful? There would. Dozens of times in my life since then.

Nevertheless, human memory is a powerful thing – and so was the shorthand I had learned so painfully at Luton College of Further Education. I repeated my thanks for the great honour I was being done – which, apart from the big, regretted test of my integrity, I genuinely thought this was – and he said, 'You're not writing a book about me, are you?' I spluttered. 'I'm talking to you for this BBC series,' I said obliquely. 'Well,' he said, 'I read in *Variety* today that you're here to write a book about me. No books. I'm old now, wait until I'm dead, then all my archives could be opened for you.'

I didn't have a chance to answer that before Berlin, as though he had a deadline for a new song to be thumped out on his piano en route to being rushed to the printers, said: 'What do you want to know?'

True, I asked, that he had been born in Siberia? 'Sure, sure,' he answered. 'We weren't all convicts there, you know.' And his father was a cantor? 'Yeh. I used to sing in shul with him. That's how my musical career started.'

And then, was it true that his name had been changed from Israel Baline simply because the printer of his first published sheet music, 'Marie From Sunny Italy', had spelt it wrongly? 'Sure. He didn't have room for the whole name, so he just printed "I. Berlin" He spelt "Baline" "Berlin", so "Berlin" it became.'

He confirmed the story of the dinner to which he had been invited by Winston Churchill at Ten Downing Street. 'Do you think America is going to pull out all the stops to beat Hitler?' Churchill asked him. He said he was sure that he would. What about the relationship between our two countries? 'Oh, they couldn't be better.' And what about Roosevelt? Would he be re-elected? 'I really hope so,' said Berlin. 'I'll certainly vote for him.' 'What,' countered Churchill, 'you mean you think you will actually have a vote? Marvellous!' As he left Number Ten, Churchill shook Berlin's hand warmly. 'Good night, thank you for coming, Professor.'

The prime minister was delighted because he thought his dream of a permanent link with the United States – to be followed by his hopes of a United States of Europe – was coming true. He also thought he had been entertaining I. Berlin, but Professor *Isiah* Berlin. Just before he died, I asked the then Sir Isiah Berlin about the celebrated meeting. 'I don't believe it,' he said. Well, maybe, but his namesake plainly did. He had been there.

Then there was the matter of his piano. Was it really true that he had one made specially for him that had a handle underneath to change key because he could only play on the black notes? 'Absolutely. You're not writing a book about me, are you?' Before I could answer again, he went on: 'You know, that piano was made for me by a firm called Weiser.'

(All that would have later significance when Benny Green, the late Radio Two presenter who went out of his way to say nasty things about my work, denied any of those facts, facts I obtained from the horse's mouth.)

For instance, he laughed about Berlin being born in Siberia. 'No Jews in Siberia,' he said 'not in Berlin's time.' I wrote to him, quoting the *Encyclopaedia Judaica*, which recorded that there were several hundred thousands living there at that time – a fact that was later confirmed for me by Berlin's daughter when we spoke on a TV special I presented. She not only knew her father's story, but had gone to Temun in Siberia to see his birthplace. But Green didn't reply. Of course, he had never spoken to the songwriter himself. Nor did he acknowledge my correction to his statement that 'How deep is the ocean' was a line from "Let Me Sing And I'm Happy', which, of course, it wasn't.

I started to tell Irving about seeing him in his all-soldier show *This Is The Army*. 'You're not writing a book, are you?' he began. But he didn't even bother to finish the sentence. 'You know I was having trouble with your paper rationing at that time,' he said. 'Couldn't get enough paper to print the song I'd written specially for the London show, *My British Buddy*. But Lady Mountbatten heard about that and sorted it out.'

Every now and again, although less frequently, he would punctuate his sentences with 'You're not writing a book, are you?' And then before I could answer, literally, there would be, 'Did you hear the story about...?' When the book was published, a *Guardian* writer described this performance as 'an invitation to be raped', which maybe was a little unkind. Certainly, I had little doubt that the two hours in which we spoke was a demonstration that he wanted the book published but some inbuilt modesty prevented his admitting it. (I sent him a leather-bound copy of the book, which wasn't acknowledged – one way or the other.)

'Who have you spoken to?' he asked. I told him, among others,

Bing Crosby and Ethel Merman. 'Have you spoken to my friend Fred Astaire?' I said no, I hadn't. 'Well, he's my *best* friend. You must speak to Fred. Are you going to California?' 'Yes,' I replied, 'tomorrow.' 'Well, you must see Fred. I'll phone him and tell him you're going to come.' I was looking forward to that, a chance to renew our previous brief acquaintanceship.

Would he have been so keen for me to see Mr Astaire had he not wanted the book that he knew full well was forthcoming? I doubt it.

Mr Astaire himself opened the door to me with the words 'I remember you,' and we talked for a couple of hours about his friend Irving, the man with whom he had spent the night as he waited for his baby daughter to be born – playing gin rummy. He showed me some paintings that Berlin had worked on for him – all birds wearing top hats, but with no feet. 'He said he started painting a bird and thought of me. But I asked him about the lack of feet. "I can't paint feet," Irving told me. I treasure those paintings very much.'

As Berlin told me, 'As a painter, I'm a very good songwriter.'

Note that word 'songwriter'. He never called himself a composer. For him, audiences were always 'the Mob' – and he didn't mean the Mafia. But Astaire was the man he liked to sing his songs more than any other – 'because he gets the phrasing exactly right. That was why I wrote for him so often. I would never have written "Top Hat, White Tie and Tails" if Astaire wasn't there to sing it.'

I left the man they all called 'Mr Astaire' – the only show business personality allowed to join the posh Los Angeles Country Club – certain I wanted to see him again. Perhaps another book.

For the moment, the Berlin book was the one I was thinking about – and Jolson, too, since there were still TV and radio programmes on which to appear.

Before leaving America, I went to see one of Berlin's very few contemporaries in the music business who was still alive. I heard that Eubie Blake would be happy to talk. He was the much-admired black pianist and songwriter who had written the first tune I ever had spinning at 78 revolutions a minute around the turntable of a gramophone, 'I'm Just Wild About Harry'. I wasn't sure if he was just wild about Irving. He agreed to see me and I took a taxi to his apartment in the Bedford Stuyvesant district. There wasn't much he either wanted or could say. 'Izzie will kill me,' he said, using Israel Baline's original familiar name, now unknown outside the music industry. But I was delighted to see him, one of the few remaining jazz greats. I called a taxi to take me back to my hotel in Manhattan. 'Watcha doin' here?' asked the very Jewish, very New York cab driver. 'Doing an interview,' I told him. 'Well,' he said, 'all I can say is you have some very big balls.'

I didn't realise that white people didn't venture into Bedford Stuyvesant without thinking about the journey very seriously. This was a white no-go area. But I was safe and glad of the adventure of it all.

One songwriter I met was another Irving – Irving Caesar, who had penned the lyrics of 'Swanee', George Gershwin's first hit – for Jolson, naturally. He also wrote his 'Is It True What They Say About Dixie?' to say nothing of 'Tea For Two'. He was also very old now and showing his age, as well as being virtually blind. What was Berlin's message? I asked him. 'No message,' he replied. 'Just to write good songs.' I told him that Berlin had told me that he never understood what he called 'the science of music' and that he had once attempted to take music lessons – 'until I thought after two days, "Heck, I could have written three or four songs in the time I've wasted here."' 'Very good,' said Caesar. 'Very good. I like that.'

Back in London, a lady was in town who had seemed to be in virtually every movie I saw as a child – Alice Faye, still blonde, still lovely. She had sung Berlin's 'Alexander's Ragtime Band' in the movie of that name and had starred in his *On The Avenue*. 'Never saw much of him,' she said. 'He seemed to keep out of the way.' So she was fairly indifferent to Mr Berlin. But she said she wouldn't have felt that way about me – because she had so liked an interview I had done with her a couple of years before. As I left the Dorchester Hotel, she gave me a big kiss.

# 25 The Dirty Rat and Mr Twinkletoes

The one thing you learn about writing biographies is not to be swayed by popular conceptions – or indeed not to be a victim of hero worship. I would have loved Al Jolson to be the kindest man in American show business, but he wasn't. And because he wasn't, I got my flat in Bournemouth. People like stories about unpleasant characters, just providing they have the redeeming features of talent, excitement and ... yes, let's say it, star quality.

The image of James Cagney was that of a tough guy you loved to hate, which meant that you didn't hate him at all. He had a coterie of friends who admired him for himself and just a few million fans who saw him in everything he did. They could quote all the lines from his best movies. Most of them thought he said 'Dirty rat' – which he maintained he never did. They could all remember the crying scene as he was strapped to the electric chair in *Angels with Dirty Faces*, and the way he greeted his pals with the phrase, 'Whatda ya hear, what da ya say?' in the same movie. None could forget the last moments of *White Heat*, in which he climbed to the top of the gasometer, shouting 'Made it Ma, top of the world' before it all goes up in flames. I thought he was top of the world, too – which is why he became my third biography subject.

Like my previous book, it began with a BBC radio series. My publisher knew what I was doing on the radio and thought, as I did, that good programmes would become good books, too. It was as simple as that. Or at least, that was what I thought.

Cagney was one of those people who had gone into a retirement that people thought well earned, and was not interested in publicity. He had, after all, nothing more to publicise. He was out of show business and had been for more than 10 years when I started the project in 1974. The only time he had been tempted out of that retirement was when Warner Brothers filmed *My Fair Lady*. There was talk of his playing the role of Alfred Doolittle, Eliza's dustman father, but he pulled out of negotiations. All he wanted to do was breed horses in Martha's Vineyard, New England. Occasionally, he went to his home in Coldwater Canyon, close by the famous Beverly Hills Hotel, but that was private.

And that was the world into which I ventured in early spring that year. This time, I had three BBC commissions – a programme about him on Radio Two, a programme on him and his gangster pals for the World Service and another about him on Radio London. The idea of a book had not yet arisen. There would also be a reason for featuring him on *You Don't Have To Be Jewish*. In fact, on this occasion, I hadn't even thought of doing a Cagney biography. My editor asked me why I had been in Los Angeles and, when I told her, suggested I repeat the Berlin exercise.

I met a number of his contemporaries, delightful men – perhaps the nicest are the ones who stand out, Pat O'Brien, the perennial good guy, the one who played the priest in *Angels With Dirty Faces*, the one who persuades Cagney to act the coward and not make himself a hero to the Dead End Kids. Then there was Ralph Bellamy, a frequent fall guy of the early talkies, who of late had made a living out of playing Franklin D. Roosevelt. We all got along splendidly and they provided wonderful sound bites for the programmes. Every time I met anyone, they emphasised that getting to James Cagney was like obtaining a season ticket to the vaults at Fort Knox.

But Bellamy said he liked what I was doing so much, he would try to see if the great Mr Cagney would break the habits of his recent lifetime and see me. He phoned me next day. 'Jim'll see you,' he said. 'Give him a ring. This is his number.'

I rang, spoke to a secretary and a meeting was arranged for the next day at 2 p.m. I arrived on time, not always my usual habit, but I wanted to be a good boy. For one thing, I wanted to get my interview. For another, I didn't want to let down the kind people who had helped arrange the meeting. And then there was Cagney himself. I had always admired the man who danced to and sang 'Yankee Doodle Dandy' in a way that still excites the juices more than 60 years after he made a movie of the same name – the biopic of the life of George M. Cohan, which had been so good that Al Jolson wanted Cagney to repeat the experience and play him in *The Jolson Story*.

I was greeted at the huge, dark, mock Georgian house on Coldwater Canyon by a big man, stripped to the waist. I later discovered that he was Cagney's bodyguard. 'Mr Cagney will see you now,' he said. 'Please follow me.'

I was taken into a large room, one of those huge sitting rooms so familiar in Hollywood homes, so big you are tempted to ask for a pair of opera glasses with which to see the other side of the lounge.

The supposedly great man waddled into the room. Walking wouldn't be an accurate description of what he did. The lithe frame of the *Yankee Doodle Dandy* dancer and of the gangster who could terrify a whole neighbourhood had gone to serious fat. He plainly had difficulty in walking. As he sat down, he motioned for me to follow suit and asked the big burly bodyguard to bring us something to drink.

I thanked him for his kindness in seeing me. 'Well,' he said, 'I have heard so much about you from dear, trusted friends who say you are a nice fellow.' Right, I thought, we were at the start of a good thing.

We got down to business right away. The bodyguard stood sentry behind the giant couch where we sat, frequently interrupting our talk to ask if Mr Cagney was OK, and did he want another drink. I asked 'Jim' about his early days, about life in Yorktown, one of the less salubrious parts of New York City.

He was good about that. He even talked about learning to speak Yiddish – which was why I wanted him on *YDHTBJ*. It had been immensely helpful when it came to dealing with the Warner brothers, who spoke to each other in the language. Once, when he was in the midst of a pay negotiation, Harry, the eldest of the brothers, was talking to his youngest sibling, Jack, while Cagney was in the room. 'Schveig, schveig,' he suddenly broke in. 'Der Goy vershtatyt Yiddish.' 'Quiet, the gentile understands Yiddish.' He laughed at that and I did, too. He talked about the real boy whom he knew at Yorktown, who really did begin sentences with the phrase, 'What da yer hear, what da yer say?' 'He went to the chair,' Cagney commented, *sotto voce*. As I left, he said, 'Thank you for a very enjoyable talk.'

It was all very good stuff and made very good radio. When I got back to London, Yvette Morgan Griffiths and I met in the exquisite offices of W.H. Allen in Mayfair. 'Are you going to do a book on Cagney, too?' she asked. It was an offer too good to turn down. Stein and Day in New York thought so, too.

Any book that I wrote would be strictly accurate, based on actual recordings that were either my copyright or in the public domain now that they had been broadcast on at least three occasions (not including the World Service repeats, their placement in the BBC archives and the frequent use I made of the Cagney Yiddish story in *YDDHTBJ*).

I was fully entitled to write the book, hand it to my publisher and wait for the royalties to come in. It didn't quite work out that way. Again, it was my integrity that got in the way of a smooth publication story. Instead of just going ahead, I did what I took to be the gentlemanly thing and wrote Cagney a letter, thanking him for the interview, telling him that the BBC were delighted with what I had produced and that my publisher now wanted me to turn it into a book. I heard nothing. No reply. No complaint either.

Seven or eight months later, I did an even more gentlemanly thing: I sent him a set of galley proofs. Within days, all hell was let loose. Christmas 1974, there was a telephone call from Saul Stein, head of the American publishing firm. In those days, transatlantic telephone calls were a rarity, at least in the social circle in which I moved. The one from Stein on Boxing Day soon lost its novelty status. He was telling me that James Cagney Esquire had taken out an injunction in the New York courts to stop my book. It was only a temporary injunction, but the Cagney law suit was putting a stop on everything until it came up in court again the following Wednesday. Would I come to New York to help them defend the case? Of course I would. Despite everything – all the anguish, all the worry, all the fear that the months of really hard work that I had put into the book (now actually published in London; the injunction could not extend to Britain) it would come to nought. Even so, there was a rush of adrenalin at being asked to give evidence in a court in New York. I really didn't think there was any financial responsibility incumbent on me, but there *was* that worry, too.

I flew to what was just beginning to be referred to as the Big Apple, with my cousin David Natali, one of the country's most respected libel lawyers, who already represented such publications as *Newsweek* and the *Observer*. I was very small beer compared to what he usually did, and the fees he and his firm, Herbert Smith and Co. – he was to retire as senior partner – normally collected. He was also used to flying first class (indeed, he would make a virtual career out of it) but he didn't mind snuggling up in the tourist section of our Pan Am flight and I remain eternally grateful for his kindness and cousinly friendship.

It was snowing when we got to our hotel and stayed snowing for the rest of the week. I remember being fascinated by the sight of the snowflakes settling on the windows of the skyscraper offices of the American lawyers jointly retained by Stein and Day and W.H. Allen. Their team was led by Nat Dershowitz, brother of the better-known Alan M. Dershowitz, about whom films and movie mini-series had been made and who had written classic works like 'The Best Defence' and 'Chutzpah'.

I was getting more and more uncomfortable as the days wore on. David and I ate together every day, we went to the theatre and the cinema. I couldn't get over the fact that he didn't seem nearly as concerned about the whole thing as I was. There were two reasons for this – just as I wouldn't have been that concerned had he been in my position (joke) – it was essentially my worry. But he also believed that we had to take our minds off the case whenever we could. There was a third reason, too. We had a very good case.

It turned out that Cagney's lawyers were accusing me of misrepresentation, in effect claiming that I had gone to see him under false pretences. They had very little to go on and cited only one precedent – that of a shop that sold one particular item of goods, while it claimed to be selling something else. Even I thought that was a pretty flimsy piece of law to go on.

Eventually, we got to court. It was like every American court scene you have ever seen in the movies – from the hugely steep steps leading from Center Street to the court house (built that way, I am sure, to emphasise the majesty of the law and the fact that it is above everything else) to the crowded, noisy courtroom, the judge sitting on his dais, seemingly miles away from the 'audience', shuffling papers while almost everyone else was deep in the midst of a hundred conversations.

Dershowitz told him that the author, Michael Freedland, was in court and would give evidence. The judge waved his hands. 'Oh, for God's sake, no,' he said. He would contemplate the other evidence and give his verdict in two days.

The evidence was amazing. On his side, Cagney said that he had been suspicious of me from the first. He didn't like me and the pity of it all was that he had been alone throughout our talk or he could have brought evidence to show how unpleasant our chat had been. He would never have spoken to me had he known it was for a book. He thought he was talking to the BBC, the most honourable or – so he thought – broadcasting organisation in the world.

Our case was equally straightforward: far from speaking to him under the guise of pretences that were manifestly false, there had been all those broadcasts – for the BBC, just as I had promised. Far from disliking me and my interview, he had, of course, welcomed me warmly and, at the end, had said how much he enjoyed our chat. And, far from being on his own throughout the talk, his bodyguard had been in the room and we would be prepared to subpoena him. But, really, that wasn't necessary. For, of course, because it was to be broadcast (as promised) the interview had been recorded. A transcript was therefore handed to the judge, together with a copy of the tape. It included his welcome and the fact that I had been so warmly recommended by his 'trusted friends', his polite goodbye in which he said how much he had enjoyed the chat and the bodyguard constantly asking us if we required a drink. There was one other point to our case – the plaintiff was about to publish his own book, called *Cagney On Cagney*. Could that have had something to do with his obvious flouting of the famous First Amendment to the American constitution guaranteeing freedom of the press?

I went home, confident, but still extraordinarily worried. Two days later there was a phone call at my Elstree home from Nat Dershowitz. All he had to say was 'Congratulations': the judge had thrown out the case. The injunction was lifted.

Jeffrey Simmonds rang the next day to offer his own congratulations. Stein and Day, he said, had a plan and W.H. Allen had one, too. They would initiate a big publicity campaign, would make sure there were books in all the shops *everywhere*. And on every dustjacket there would be a paper slip bearing the word: 'Banned'.

Great. Except there was another call the following day. Cagney was appealing the judgment. Chances were he wouldn't succeed, but

40. You Ain't Heard Nothin' Yet. Al Jolson – subject of my first book. I told people, 'You ain't read nothin' yet.' I always think I owe him a great deal.

41. My favourite book subject, Fred Astaire. He was about to give me my first ever ride in a Rolls-Royce.

42. Gregory Peck and me. We got on like a studio on fire. The trouble was he liked to use his black felt-tip pen a little too much.

43. Leonard Bernstein wished he had co-operated with me on my book. I'm told he liked it – enough to be photographed reading it, with his daughter.

44. James Cagney on the night I met Ronald Reagan, who plainly liked him more than I did. 'You dirty rat' – he claimed he never said it. I, on other hand, thought he was just that.

45. Peter Ustinov was one of the greatest wits of our time, but denied that he was a conversationalist. I enjoyed our conversation, even so.

46. Eric Morecambe. Working with him on the book what I wrote.

47. Those were the days. Three of my books in one display – *Jack Lemmon*, *Al Jolson* and *So Lets Hear the Applause* (no apostrophe).

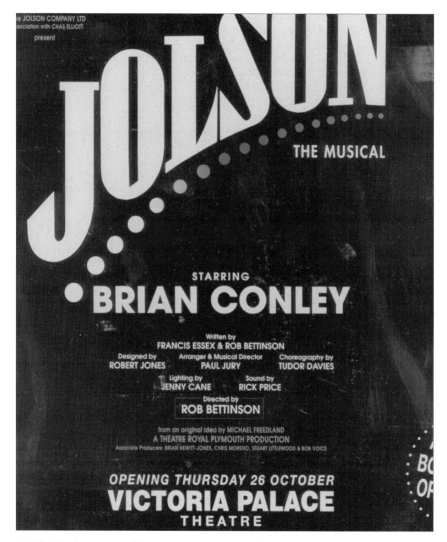

48. The big show – one of the great moments in my life.

he was going to tip up a great deal of money. He could afford it. We couldn't. So he won. The terms of his 'victory' were that we could carry on with selling what copies we had – providing we didn't publicise them. The publicity would be left for *Cagney By Cagney*. Game set and match to Mr Cagney. The so-called justice system became an atrocious injustice.

Was this enough to disillusion me? It could have been. The pain of that event, the – yes, I repeat it – the injustice of it all could have been enough to make me change my profession, or perhaps go back to what I had been doing all along, being a journalist and a broadcaster. Indeed, it was as a broadcaster that I was now best known. When I gave talks to local organisations, particularly Jewish organisations, it was about my broadcasting that people wanted to hear. I talked to women's groups and was constantly being told that I looked so much younger than they had expected. They flattered me and, I am pleased to say, sometimes flirted – like the very lovely lady, beautiful would not be an exaggeration, who informed me that I got into the bath with her every Sunday morning.

Despite the Cagney episode, life was sweet. We weren't rich, but Sara and I were very happy – and so, it seemed, were our children. Fiona and Dani were nicely settled in their primary schools, although we began to think about moving when Dani's teacher admitted that she couldn't place her. 'She must be one of the good ones, or otherwise I would know who she was.' Jonathan was about to go there, but we decided that we couldn't subject him to that, and in any case he was ready for school before he was old enough to be accepted. Our solution was to break all our cherished principles and send him to a private school. We later did that for the girls, too. When your own children are concerned, you tend to think of only their welfare, not political dreams. Sad, but an established fact. All three were on their way to satisfying and productive futures.

And so, I thought, could I be. My own programme was seemingly going splendidly and BBC Radio Two thought I was worth engaging to work on a massive 13-week Sunday afternoon series to be called *The Fred Astaire Story*. Yvette was tempted by that. 'Do a book, too,' she said. If the original blessings came from the BBC and with none of the doubts that lingered with Mr Cagney, I was only too pleased to accept – and so, I discovered to my tremendous relief, was Mr Astaire.

The path had been smoothed in advance by Fred's daughter Ava, then living in London. She had told some wonderful stories about life with her famous father, about the embarrassments of that relationship – like the time they both took part in a fathers-and-daughters ball. Naturally, all eyes were upon them. Not just because this was Fred Astaire and his little girl but because they were the only couple out of step.

She talked about her family, especially about Fred's elder sister Adele, Lady Cavendish (her husband, heir to the Duke of Devonshire, had been killed in the Second World War), the first of the pair to take dancing lessons (Freddie, as his intimates still called him, saw that Delly, as she was known, was having so much fun and was allowed to join her). She was, Ava advised me, a very elegant lady – who could swear like a drunken sailor.

Ava sent a note to her father to say that I seemed a reasonably nice guy and he could do worse than see me.

A few days later, with my BBC producer, I knocked on the door of the beautiful Astaire bungalow at San Ysidro Drive, one of the most prestigious Beverly Hills addresses. It was the street where Danny Kaye lived, although I am convinced that should he have ever wanted to buff up his reputation, which he manifestly never did, he would have been the more likely one to talk about his neighbour, Mr Astaire.

The door was opened by a butler and Fred came into the living room, looking out on to the swimming pool and an occasional palm tree, and welcomed us warmly. 'I remember you,' he said again, looking at me closely. 'And I remember you,' I said with all the chutzpah at my command. He laughed. I was glad that he did because there could have been some awkward days ahead, had he not. And he had a reputation for not suffering fools gladly should the occasion or fool indicate such behaviour was called for.

As it turned out, we got on exceedingly well. Day after day, I called at the fairly small (by Hollywood standards, where homes are likely to make the most prosperous property dealer feel inadequate) bungalow and day after day we sat and reminisced. We talked about his father, Frederic Austerlitz, who had fled his native Austria after being court martialled in the Imperial Army for not saluting a superior officer – his own elder brother. I heard again about Fred's days in the dancing school, about his and Delly's first days in vaudeville, how they conquered Broadway as a double act, with shows like *Funny Face* and *The Gay Divorce* – a title that would have a totally different meaning today.

We talked about their being the talk of London's cabaret circuit when they came to Britain, the favourites of the then Prince of Wales, 'Edward P' as he called him, and his younger brother, the Duke of Kent, 'George P'. When Adele left the act Fred wasn't sure he could carry on without her. Somehow he did and went to Hollywood – where he had a screen test that was seen by a studio executive who declared that Astaire 'can't act, [is] slightly bald, can dance a little'. Fred himself told me he thought he looked like 'a knife'. There were the tales of his deliriously happy but short-lived marriage to his society wife Phyllis, who was definitely not in show business.

Phyllis wasn't sure about her husband's roles, although he made sure that he did nothing to upset her – like kissing his leading ladies of the time, even the ice-cool Ginger Rogers. They did have one kissing scene, although it was very short, but was technically extended for the screen (amazing what they could do with what was called 'trick photography' in those pre-computer days). 'Well, at last we got that out of the way,' he sighed. Phyllis said that he seemed to be enjoying it. 'I should say you did.' As he recalled that event, Fred gave a husky laugh. I got to realise that that was something of a trademark, and one I am glad to say that he used very frequently.

Fred, as his daughter had told me, wasn't entirely a pussy cat. He could be difficult, especially when he felt that cameramen or directors were not doing exactly what he wanted or if a leading lady didn't shape up. He admitted all that and said that before he approved a female co-star, he had to be sure that she wasn't taller than he was.

We talked about the other parts of his life. For years, he was a fashion icon. His suits were made in London's Savile Row, his shoes created from his own lasts, his shirts exquisitely tailored. He wore the finest silk ties – around his waist instead of a belt.

Then there was the one other love in his life – horse racing. As he reminded me, he once owned a superb thoroughbred that won every race it entered, called Triplicate, a good name for a nag owned by the man known as 'Mr Twinkletoes', who did everything in at least three takes and up to 20 times that amount. He had a driver who took him to the track every day, but never put a cent on a horse himself. 'I can't understand why, if you don't bet on a horse, you bother to come,' Fred remembered telling him.

We talked about the tragedies in his life, notably the death of Phyllis from a brain tumour in the early 1950s. He hadn't yet met – or he hadn't announced that he had – a 40-year-old jockey called Robyn, whom he would marry shortly before his death in 1987.

His music was very important – well, of course it was. We discussed his relationships with all the great composers of his generation, his favourite bird-painter Irving Berlin, who dedicated so much of his output to his top-of-the-list singer, tunes (Berlin never called them anything else) like 'Isn't This A Lovely Day', 'Top Hat, White Tie and Tails' – to say nothing of 'Easter Parade', his close pal George Gershwin who had written 'A Foggy Day' for him and Jerome Kern, who wrote 'Lovely To Look At' for his *Roberta* as well as 'You Were Never Lovelier'. Cole Porter produced 'Night and Day' for him as well as the score one of the last great musicals, *Silk Stockings*, which had started life as the Garbo film *Ninotchka*. Astaire told me how much he enjoyed writing songs himself – one of which became a big hit, 'I'm Building Up For An Awful Let Down'.

There were days of talks. One day, it was very hot and the air conditioning was on the blink. All the doors were open. 'Would you like a drink?' he asked as I looked out on to the perfectly manicured lawn and the immaculately kept pool and its surrounds. I said yes, it would be appreciated. 'Champagne?' he asked. I was not one of those people who had champagne regularly and the thought of sampling Chateau Astaire was too tempting to turn down. He came with a bottle, newly taken from the ice, and one glass into which he proceeded to pour the sparkling, cold liquid. As he passed it to me, I asked if he wasn't going to have one himself. 'No,' he said, 'I'd rather have a Coke.'

Once more, he took me to my hotel in his shiny new Rolls-Royce.

In between those sessions, there were other people to interview. Some were wonderful. Occasionally, there was an experience that was less than delightful. It was like that when I met Rita Hayworth. The girl with the flame-red hair, whom I had remembered as exquisitely beautiful both on and off the dance floor, now looked nothing like it. The hair was the same colour – but plainly thanks to the work of a less than accomplished hairdresser. The body wasn't the one I remembered and her words were slurred as she remembered the time that Astaire had spotted her – and discovered that her father was one of the famous Argentine dance team The Cansinos, whom he admired. And she told me that her career was still vibrant – she was about to make a Spanish film that no one would ever hear of.

When you do interviews of that kind, you are expected to have a 'release' signed, one that grants you the rights to use it when you wanted to. I had forgotten to get this signed. So the next day, I went back to the house, which was close to Astaire's own. I arrived at the door to hear screams coming from inside, loud piercing screams and cries. A maid answered the door. I explained my errand. 'I couldn't ask her for anything,' she said. 'Can't you hear that?'

I spoke to Astaire's dance assistant, Hermes Pan, who, after years of working with Fred, had begun to resemble him – a similar voice, a strangely familiar laugh. There were others of his leading ladies, like the stately Irene Dunn, who managed to move the signed photograph of Richard Nixon so that I could place my tape recorder next to her. I saw the then still exquisite Cyd Charisse, whose memory of Astaire centred around her audition. 'As we talked, I saw that he was circling me. I realised what it was all about – he was trying to see if I was too tall.'

People often talked about Fred and Cyd, two generations of dancers who seemed to go so well together, two exquisite specimens in their own way. It was the choreographer Michael Kidd, who worked on the film *The Band Wagon*, in which the Astaire–Charisse partnership scored perfectly, who put it in a nutshell. He went back to one of their first rehearsals – and this was another perfect example of how by working on a biography you discover things never to be found from press cuttings. 'If a visitor had come down from Mars and watched Fred and Cyd dancing, you would have noticed that all eyes were on the beautiful Cyd, who looked so exquisite. But then, after five minutes, you would notice something else – that all those eyes had switched to Fred and stayed on him.'

Quite clearly, just watching Fred was enough. The film director, Dick Quine, who worked with Fred on one of his last films, *The Notorious Landlady*, told me: 'He even chews gum in time. I love to watch him play pool – just to see how he moves.' Jack Lemmon, who co-starred in that film and, in any case, was reputedly quite a lousy golfer, said that he played with Fred and always lost. His excuse was that he couldn't concentrate on the game – because he was watching the way Fred danced around the course. No more than he should have expected from a man who had one of his most famous routines in the film *Carefree*, performing miracles with a club and a set of golf balls.

But there was a secret side to Fred Astaire that his friends were now willing to talk about – like Ann Miller, no mean dancing sensation herself. She said that she would have dinner with Fred – after which they would go off to watch what were then, in the pre-video, pre-DVD age, X-rated movies. Once, though, as his daughter Ava revealed, he had gone to see one of those movies by himself. He walked down the long, long approach to one of the more down-at-heel cinemas on the now sleazy Hollywood Boulevard. He had a hat down over his eyes, the collar of his raincoat up so that it almost concealed his face. There were sunglasses to complete the disguise. He took a five-dollar bill from his wallet and handed it over to the girl sitting at the cash desk. 'Are you a member?' the woman asked shrilly. 'No,' he mumbled. 'You have to be a member for 24 hours,' she said. Fred slunk away, going as fast as the Astaire legs could take him. But not too fast for him to hear the woman say to another standing next to her: 'Did you see who that was? It was Fred Astaire.'

To Phoenix next – to see Adele, Ava's favourite Auntie Delly. She lived in a lovely apartment looking out on to a golf course. The room in which we sat was exquisitely furnished and decorated – although the cushions on her couch made one think. One said simply: 'Fuck Off'. 'Isn't it great?' she asked as we talked about those Broadway shows, their childhood in Omaha, Nebraska, and of life in London during the war where she helped to man the famous 'Rainbow Corner' club for American servicemen. Yes, she could swear (and had cushions to match) like that sailor, but she was an elegant, fun lady whom I liked enormously.

I did some of the other interviews in London. One was with Larry Adler, who recalled how Fred given him his first break in the show *Smiles*. And then, one of the most memorable – with the name that will for ever be linked with Fred Astaire, Ginger Rogers.

We met over lunch at the Dorchester Hotel in Park Lane. We both had scrambled eggs while we talked about those films with the man she always called 'Mr Astaire'. It became quite clear that they didn't get on terribly well, or at least that Ms Rogers wasn't all that impressed with him. What was the magic, I asked, for the 'Astaire–Rogers films?' 'Excuse me?' she said. 'What,' I repeated, 'was the magic of the Astaire–Rogers films?' 'Excuse me?' she said again. 'Don't you mean the Rogers–Astaire films? It is customary, is it not, to have the lady's name first?' Well, I thought, excuse *me*. And I mentally challenged anyone else to think likewise.

Fred had told me that he didn't like being considered part of a team. 'That always sounds like a pair of horses,' he said. '*And I* certainly didn't want to have a partner all the time,' she countered.

I interviewed a total of 64 people for the Astaire programmes and book. The first person I spoke to said that he was a 'perfectionist'. The second said, 'such a perfectionist as...'. The third said, 'As a perfectionist, Fred...' It became something of a game. I began to wait for each interviewee to use that word, perfectionist. Everyone did. Even Ginger, who recalled the 60-odd takes Fred sometimes took before he could get a routine into the cameras satisfactorily. 'Well,' she told me, 'I'm a perfectionist, too. I wouldn't let anything get by until I was happy with it.' She didn't mind any of the hardships that insistence on perfection brought, even when the cleaner moved in to polish the mirror-like black and white floor at the RKO studio after each take. At the end of one of those takes, the man noticed a long red smear on the floor. He traced it, as if he was searching for the target at the end of a fuse. He found the source – Ginger's white satin slippers, which were now red satin slippers. Fred had worked her so hard that her feet were bleeding.

There was one other woman who was less than enthusiastic about him. Of course, she used the required word 'perfectionist', but this was a very different interviewee. 'I don't know what the fuss was all about Fred Astaire. He wasn't nice to me,' said Nanette Fabray, one of the stars of *The Band Wagon*. And she proceeded to tell me how he had been rude to her, how he had complained about her work and compared her with Betty Hutton, who had been less than an easy co-worker. Naturally, I wrote about that in the book.

I spent months on the book and didn't complete it until after the radio series was broadcast – narrated by David Niven. I sent Fred a copy of the manuscript, which included Nanette Fabray's complaints.

He spent three weeks reading the manuscript. I like to think that he did it sunning himself while he sat by his swimming pool, the one alongside the palm tree. He wrote the occasional correction in red ink, and then posted it back to me. It was long before the domestic use of computers and before emails. 'I think you have done an excellent job with a long and arduous task,' he wrote. That was music to my ears, particularly after the Cagney fiasco. Now there was no fear of being called a dirty rat or of a hired gun coming my way. There was, however, one thing that he did *not* like – predictably, the comments from Nanette Fabray, and I couldn't honestly say that I minded too much. After the accolade and the approval of 300-odd pages without Ms Fabray's comments, I couldn't really argue – especially since there was no summons to the court in New York, or Los Angeles for that matter.

'Please take out the Nanette story,' he wrote in the accompanying letter (the actual story had a diagonal red line slashed through it.) 'It didn't happen,' he added. But the following day came another letter. I recognised the address on the top of the envelope, which had been sent by express air mail. Mr Astaire had had second thoughts. No, he wasn't taking back the kind comments, but he was withdrawing his objections to Nanette Fabray's complaints. 'If she said that, it must be true, so you had better put it back.'

Is it any wonder that when people ask me the name of my favourite book subject, I say Fred Astaire? This was a mensch, to use one of those Yiddish words that have no and need no translation (it's a wonder that it hasn't joined 'shtuch', 'schlep' and 'shmooze' into general circulation, to say nothing of 'shlemazel'. Maybe it's because the word begins with the wrong couple of letters. People ought to know that it is just about the best thing one could say about a man, and that's how I like to think of Fred Astaire.)

The following summer, the book was finally published and I came to Los Angeles to publicise it. I rang Fred to say I was in town and would like to hand him the first copy hot from the press. 'Come along whenever you like,' he said. I told him that my wife was with me. Could I bring her, too? 'Sure,' he said, 'come for tea, both of you.'

We did. The first thing he said after noting a few nice things about meeting Sara and welcoming me back to a house I had got to know quite well was to apologise for being, as he said, 'old and crochety'. I must say that we found him to be neither. He was pleasant and funny – especially when he said (oh, if only I had had it for the first edition of the book!) that he never went to Hollywood parties any more. 'There's always some old dame there who wants to be able to go home and say that she just danced with Fred Astaire.'

When we left, he stood in the doorway and waved. 'Bye, kids,' he said.

Fred and I talked again in the years to come. When I was writing a book about Gregory Peck, with whom he had worked in one of those what-if films about life after a nuclear attack, *On The Beach*, I rang him for a few memories of his co-star. I didn't get any. The thought did enter my mind that he wanted *his* biographer to remain *his*. 'How many more of these books are you going to write?' he asked me. I skirted round that one as deftly, I thought, as he had his replies to my questions about Peck. In December 1986 I had been asked by the ITV arts programme *The South Bank Show*, with whom I had done the programme on Jolson, to try, as I was in Los Angeles again, to persuade Astaire to agree to a TV interview for a show on him. He was married to Robyn now and had had his phone number changed from the days when I could just ring him up for a chat. But, of course, I knew his address and so drove up to the house on San Ysidro Drive. I knocked on the door. A housekeeper in the requisite white overall came to the door and gave every impression of not being too pleased to see me. There had undoubtedly been others knocking on the door. She said that she wasn't sure that Mr Astaire would want to have anything to do with me. In any case, he was out, so forget it.

I wasn't willing to forget it and asked her if she minded if I scribbled a note. And I do mean scribbled. I found an envelope and pencilled a message.

I drove away, disappointed, but not really surprised. I hadn't been back in my room at the Hyatt on Sunset Hotel for more than a few minutes when the phone rang. A notably elderly voice was at the other end of the line. 'Michael,' said the man, 'this is Fred Astaire. What do you want?'

I told him about the *South Bank Show* idea, but he wasn't interested. There was no way I could persuade him to change his mind. 'I'm *very* old now,' he said, 'and I just haven't got the time or the energy. And you know it's Christmas. All my energies are now devoted to shopping.' We didn't talk again. The pity is that his widow has put a virtual ban on using Fred Astaire material on television (not radio; I have done at least two Astaire sound documentaries in recent years). She won't bar using film clips, but the prices she wants to charge for them rule out any programme ever going ahead. Mrs Astaire wants to be able to control the Astaire image because, presumably, she thinks it will be more commercially viable if she does that. Instead, she has priced herself and his memory out of the market. Instead of increasing the Astaire value, she has undermined it. Sad though it is to say, people just don't care that much. When I was working on one of those radio documentaries, I went to the reception desk at Broadcasting House to ask about studio availability. 'I'm doing the Fred Astaire programme,' I said. 'Could you tell me which studio I am meant to go to?' The young lady looked at me and, in all seriousness, asked 'Fred Who?' This was a woman in her early twenties and she had never heard of him.

I'd put that down to unusual ignorance. That is not a good friend of the biographer, a person who goes out of his/her way to get the facts right, who researches his/her subject in the greatest detail. You need to know who was involved in your subject's life, who could say what and why. But before getting down to the job – not always an easy job, at that – of ringing total strangers, calling on them at their homes perhaps 6,000 miles away, taking out a tape recorder and asking the questions that personally interest me, there is other research.

There was a time when I became so well known at the British Library's newspaper section at Colindale – fortunately no more than a 15-minute drive away – that the librarians would get the huge bound books of *New York Times* papers from the 1920s ready waiting for me. At the research library at the Lincoln Center in New York, they'd smile and offer a cup of coffee, providing I didn't get it over any of the priceless documents, that is. The only person who found me difficult – and vice versa – was the gentleman who operated the photocopying machine there. I always tried to get so much done – copying pages of newspapers, reviews of shows or films or human interest stories that would form the background to the huge amount of new research I was undertaking – that I would usually leave my applications and handing over my fistfuls of dollars to the very last moment. The machine operator didn't like that. On my last trip there, the man said: 'You're always late.' I said, 'But I haven't been here for 14 years.' 'I know,' he said, 'you're always late.' He didn't smile as he said it.

Of course, you don't have those problems with authorised biographies like the one on Fred Astaire. Well, do you?

# 26   To *authorise* or *not*

Astaire was an exception to a rule that I try to observe – although very often the temptation to do otherwise can be overpowering. Audiences at talks I frequently give on the subject ask me the difference between authorised and unauthorised biographies. I should love to have done an authorised biography of Danny Kaye, the man who was proclaimed the World's Greatest Entertainer immediately after Al Jolson died. I loved Kaye's work and we had met once. His was a book I desperately wanted to write, but he wasn't interested in co-operating. I now know I should have been grateful – I might not have heard from him himself the stories I picked up while researching this project: like the tales of how he became table tennis champion of Beverly Hills, or how, as Anton Mossiman, the renowned chef, told me, he was one of the greatest cooks in America – entertaining Princess Margaret and other top-drawer persosnalities to dinner in his kitchen. Johnny Green, conductor and head of music at MGM, said Kaye was the best untrained conductor in the world – he couldn't read music and conducted with a fly swatter, but the New York Philharmonic rarely sounded better than when he was on the podium. From doctors at London's Middlesex Hospital, I heard how Kaye, a well-known frustrated would-be doctor, would attend operations and even sew up after an operation. And I heard how, having learned to fly, he got a licence to pilot 747 jumbo jets.

The Middlesex Hospital incident came at the time that he dominated the London Palladium as nobody else ever did. As people there told me – and as I saw several years after his 1947 debut at that same temple of variety – he was unlike any other performer. Other players had been known to get audiences shouting and screaming.

Danny did the opposite – the people in the stalls and circles were incredibly noisy as they waited in anticipation for the arrival of their idol. He would go to the apron of the stage, sit down and put a finger to his lips. All he had to do then was say, 'shsh sh' and the entire house came to a verbal stop. The proverbial pin was heard to drop.

Princess Margaret went to those shows every night and once brought her father, King George VI, Queen Elizabeth, later to be the Queen Mother, and her sister, Princess Elizabeth, now Queen. One of Kaye's routines was to have a woman in a white coat come on stage and give him a cup of tea. The night the royals were there, he took no notice of the woman and carried on talking, which he did with consummate ease. Suddenly a voice could be heard from the third row of the stalls. 'Danny,' it called, 'your tea, your tea.' It was the normally tongue-tied King who, afterwards, came back to the star's dressing room for a glass of whisky – which, he said, in that austerity age he didn't even get at Buckingham Palace.

Kaye, whose greatest work was twisting tongues as he sang the lyrics written by his wife Sylvia Fine, learned to fly after his friend Michael Kidd did so first. (He said he was a little put out by all the maths he had to master first. But he wasn't satisfied with merely flying. He had to get a licence to pilot a jumbo jet.)

Kidd was the choreographer of the late Astaire films and, among others, of *Guys and Dolls*, too. He became a superb source for a book I later wrote about the movie mogul Sam Goldwyn. He told me about taking Goldwyn on a walk down Broadway, the setting for Damon Runyon's stories about the racing, gambling, no-good characters who frequented the Great White Way in the hours when there were no shows playing in the theatres.

In the course of their walk, Goldwyn asked his younger friend, 'Michael, do you like Jewish food?' The mogul said he himself did. 'You know,' said Sam, 'I'm a good Jew at heart. I love Jewish food. Where can we get some here?'

Kidd suggested Lindy's. 'Can we get good Jewish food there?' he asked. 'Absolutely,' said the choreographer. Both of their mouths were watering as Goldwyn started to list the foods he loved – kneidlach with chicken soup, kreplach, potato latkes. They were really salivating by the time they reached the restaurant.

Inside, Sam Goldwyn was instantly recognised. 'Mr Goldwyn, please come to this table,' said the waiter, probably the same one who, when asked what the fly was doing in a customer's soup, replied: 'At first glance, I'd say the backstroke.' Sam, still thinking about chopped liver and kosher corned beef, asked the question he always asked in a restaurant: 'What's the special today?' 'Irish stew,' said the waiter. 'Good,' said Sam, 'I'll have it.'

It was just one of a stream of stories for my biography of Goldwyn, one of the best liked of all the moguls – the man who put all his own money into his movies, not that of the banks. His son, Sam Goldwyn Jr, talked about the famous Goldwynisms – 'an oral contract is not worth the paper it's written on', 'in two words – im-possible', which Jack Warner Jr told me he heard him say at a meeting of all the Hollywood moguls, or 'Do you expect me to put my head in a moose?' The younger Goldwyn explained: 'My father's brain worked faster than his mouth.'

I enjoyed working on that book. But then, as Sam himself said, 'We've all passed a lot of water since then.'

It wasn't an authorised biography. Well, Sam had been dead for 12 years by the time the book was written in 1986. The Astaire biography *had* been authorised and was a joy to work on. Well, of course it was. But there have been others that have proved less encouraging. Frankly, I now try to avoid them, even though on the surface nothing could be better – an authorised biography means working with the co-operation of the subject. So no legal threats as with Cagney, no suggestions possible that stories are inaccurate. On top of which, there is the cachet of a book being regarded as 'official'. That was the term that Gregory Peck used in 1979 when I began work on his story.

The trouble, as I soon found out, is that authorised biographies tend to be like autobiographies (present company excepted, naturally), the picture that the subjects have of themselves. It's as though they are looking in the mirror as they talk – and you know about mirror images, they are always back to front.

The real trouble is that people – Fred Astaire excepted – don't like criticism or suggestions that they may be less than perfect. What is more, they can influence the people to whom you speak in your research. 'Oh, please don't talk to him/her, the story they give you will be terribly biased.' Unlike that from themselves, of course.

Gregory Peck and I became very strong friends. He agreed to do the book after reading my Astaire biography, which he was kind enough to say that he liked very much. Our first meeting was in Vienna, where he was making *The Boys From Brazil*. To be fair, he didn't ask for any documentation and certainly not for any money. But we finalised arrangements after one very brief session, chatting not very seriously about anything. I then handed him a carefully worded piece of paper. Just one piece of paper in which I promised to let him see the final manuscript, not to approve it, just to see it. We both signed happily.

I enjoyed our sessions and enjoyed seeing him 'fighting' on the set with Laurence Olivier and a pack of dogs, Doberman Pinchers with which I would not have wanted to become particularly familiar. He and his wife took me to dinner. I met his daughter and we got on like a studio on fire.

Then we met again at Claridges Hotel in London. Sara just popped in to say hello. He was wonderfully courteous and pleasant. She said that she would recognise his voice anywhere and he seemed to like that. He was in his early sixties now, but wasn't immune, despite all his fame, to a little flattery.

A few weeks later, we met again at his superb home in Holmby Hills, just a stone's throw (if you would ever do such a thing in an area so elite that you have to have permission from the other residents to buy a home there, let alone throw any stones) from Beverly Hills. The connoisseurs of such things consider Holmby Hills to be considerably upmarket from the nouveau riche society down the road, which was why both Barbra Streisand and Rod Stewart decided to live in the same street, Carol Wood Drive. I also have a feeling that Mr Peck's presence had a great deal to do with it. He was by then old Hollywood, an actor who was a star in every way. He was a past president of the Academy of Motion Picture Arts and Sciences and graced with his wife Véronique every one of the big movie colony occasions.

We talked about that and we talked about his beginnings in La Jolla ('that's La Hoya,' he emphasised) a little further down the Southern California coast line towards San Diego and the Mexican border. He was a fairly poor boy, a product of a broken home, who went to New York to learn how to be an actor and had almost instant success in Hollywood. To his credit were movies such as *To Kill A Mocking Bird*, *Gentleman's Agreement* and *Duel In The Sun*, which he liked to call *Lust In The Dust*.

I spent three weeks virtually living in the Carol Wood Drive house, which was sedately furnished but had the requisite swimming pool in the huge garden. He had an ashtray from a famous Paris hotel. 'They gave this to you as a tribute?' I suggested. 'No,' he said. 'I stole it.' There were servants and a secretary in a place big enough never to meet each other. But Greg, as I was instructed to call him, and I did meet constantly. Véronique, sitting on a chair with her hair in curlers (discreetly covered by a scarf) told me about their meeting in her native France. Greg talked about his failed first marriage and about the great tragedy in his life, the suicide of his son, Jonathan. 'Who knows what a parent does wrong?' Nevertheless, he had a dry sense of humour which I appreciated.

I like to think it all came out in the finished book. I sent him, as promised, a copy of the manuscript. He telegrammed back within days. 'Congratulations,' the wire said, the words engraved on my mind. 'Véronique and I think you have done an excellent job.' So I had fulfilled my obligations to him. Not only had I sent him the book, but he had liked it. In any court of law that would have been regarded as approval, even had he had requested it, which, of course, he hadn't.

There was a slight sting in the tail. 'I'd like to dot a few "i's" and cross a few "t's",' he said. 'Do you think you could come over again?'

I should have said no, I couldn't. Or would you pay my expenses? But I didn't. I went back, paid for my fare and my hotel – and he kindly hired a car for me. Again, he told me how much he loved the book. But there were just a couple of changes that he wanted. We sat with copies of the script on our laps and he took out a big black felt pen – and proceeded to draw great big black lines across whole passages and, in some cases, whole pages.

'Don't worry, Michael,' he said. 'I do that with all my scripts.' I didn't point out that this was a slightly different operation. This manuscript was my baby. But I went along with it, and we agreed different wording. He didn't like my quoting a critic who described his work as 'wooden'. I understood that, but the whole man has to be portrayed in a biography, or it has no value.

He tried to be nice. 'Tonight, Michael, I'm going to expose you to some real Americana.' We went to a baseball game. Now, I get bored watching cricket, which I only just about understand. I couldn't draw up much enthusiasm for a game that baffled me from the start. But it was something different and I could think of a number of people who would have liked to have been in my shoes – watching a ball game with Gregory Peck and his family.

Eventually we agreed on a final version, which was not as good as the original but was reasonably so, and both my British and American publishers were happy enough. Sales orders were OK and there were paperback deals arranged.

It was then that Mr Peck wanted still more changes. This time, I refused to go back to meet him, so he came to London to see me. We were still friends and he invited me to go with him to India, where he was making a film he had first heard about in a phone call he picked up in his study while we were having one of our interview sessions. It was to be called *The Sea Wolves*.

Then he saw a copy of the American edition of my book – and a bunch of the changes we agreed had been omitted. He got in touch with W.H. Allen in London and said he wanted to stop the book being published here. They refused. There was no reason to agree. OK, he said, he'd buy the rights. How much did I want? I said a million dollars – and that was the end of that.

Had I not gone to America at my own expense at his bidding, there would have been a very good book on which he himself had congratulated me. It was a lesson I should have learned – but didn't.

There was one biography I wanted to be authorised, but just couldn't. Leonard Bernstein refused to play ball – and perhaps I should have been grateful. I loved Bernstein's music. I went to see him when he was in London and did a broadcast with him for the Radio Four *Start the Week* programme. 'Mr Berns*teen*,' I began. 'Berns*teen*?' he bellowed. 'Berns*tine*,' he virtually shouted, 'Berns*tine*. So I said, 'Mr Berns*tine*, you're quite a showman, aren't you?' 'A *show-man, a show-man! Mr Freedland*? No, I'm a musician.' Which I knew and which I admired more than I could at that time say. No, he didn't want to work with me on a book and, he said, it didn't have anything to do with pronouncing his name wrongly and calling him anything but a consummate musician. But I went on with the book and was delighted that I had. I spoke to other musicians, to show people, and to impresarios, and ended up with a biography with which I have always been reasonably proud. I had seen Bernstein conducting his last Albert Hall concert. It was very much like the story of Fred Astaire and Cyd Charisse. Here was a now quite fat, old-looking man who, though suffering badly from emphysema, was conducting the London Symphony Orchestra playing Mahler's Fourth Symphony. The last movement features a soprano solo, this time from a beautiful young girl. You couldn't help watching as well as hearing her crystal-like voice. Every eye was on her – until after about five minutes you noticed that the audience had diverted their eyes from her to him, to the old, fat, coughing man, who was charismatic – and who then insisted on going up to every one of the musicians and kissing them all.

The issue of his homosexuality was more difficult to deal with, even in the late 1980s, than it would be now. He had never officially 'come out', although his late wife (to whom he was devoted, despite a break in their relationship) and children knew about it.

But the question that had to be dealt with was how to avoid reducing the impact of his musical achievements, which were vast, by what might have been considered to be sensationalism. There was also the question of libel. Revealing some of the names with whom he had had affairs, like Danny Kaye (who subsequently also had a relationship with Laurence Olivier) could have distracted from the main story but would have involved too much time – and too much money – in the courts. I was much more worried about the second than the first. Affairs with famous people are at least part of the main story, but it would always risk the kind of legal action territory into which only the wealthiest writers could honestly afford to enter.

Of course, I mentioned his sexual proclivities. Since everywhere he went he was accompanied by handsome young men who did not exactly have indeterminate sexual desires, it was not something that could be ignored. To have done so would have made the book irrelevant – and not even the maestro himself when he read it, would, I dare say, have wanted that.

Like it or not, Bernstein *was* a showman. They loved him in Germany – André Previn told me that when 'Lennie' conducted the Berlin Philharmonic, he spoke the best German of any non-native he knew, a fact that was appreciated by the musicians. If that was love, the reaction to him in Israel was more like adoration.

When he conducted there and kissed his musicians, they kissed him back. They loved him because of his association with them at their times of greatest trouble. In the 1948 War of Independence, he flew out to entertain the troops and was responsible for one of the most notable victories of the conflict. He was conducting Mozart and Gershwin's 'Rhapsody In Blue', an event that stirred people's imaginations to the extent that soldiers from miles around travelled to be at the concert in the desert near Beersheva. They went in Jeeps, in armoured cars, in what served as tanks, so much so that it looked like a serious military operation. That, certainly, was what the Egyptians thought. Their spy planes spotted the military 'manoeuvre' and, as a result, their army retreated.

Bernstein died soon after my book came out. Later, I interviewed another Bernstein biographer, Humphrey Burton. 'You know, Lennie loved your book,' he told me. 'He wished he had co-operated with you.' Others had told me that he liked it.

That book had begun with one of the sad stories of publishing – the death throes of a once leading house, Harrap, which had put out the biography. It was my second Harrap book. I had joined it earlier when it was trying to set up a prestige list. Simon Dally, the man who had introduced me to the publishing firm of Weidenfeld and Nicolson, was now there and he rang me to ask if I'd like to join.

Sadly, he committed suicide soon afterwards. He had led a lonely life and was devoted to his work, which alone was a reason why I said that, since I had no obligations to other companies – I always refused to sign option clauses – I was free to do so. He welcomed me warmly and commissioned a book on the Warner Brothers – or rather Warner Bros., which I loved doing. It was the most fascinating of the Hollywood studios and it gave me a chance to relive old friendships.

I got to know again Jack Warner Jr, son of the mogul, Jack Sr, the youngest of the four brothers and the dominating force in the company. He talked of his estrangement from the father who had sacked him from the studio – not that he had ever told him; the gateman had handed him the contents from his desk as he refused to allow him through the barrier. 'Your father said you're not allowed to come in.'

Then there was Hal Wallis, studio head, the man who was there from the beginning, who remembered Jack Warner's awful radio shows in which he imitated Al Jolson. 'He was terrible. But he owned the radio station.' He talked of some of the crazy things that Warner did – like putting out his leg so that Wallis fell over as he went to collect the Oscar for *Casablanca*, or like trying to get rid of him by unloading horse manure outside Wallis's door and like having his best story conferences sitting on the toilet. 'I knew when he had finished talking. That was when the toilet flushed.' This was, in any case, a man who when asked what he thought of a book would say, 'Like it? I couldn't lift it.' Or whose philosophy in life was summed up by the phrase, 'Lonely is the head that wears the toilet seat.'

You had to be told stories like that. You couldn't read them any-where else. Then there was meeting Julius Epstein. He was one of the old-time Warner writers, a product of New York's Lower East Side, which was where all the good screenplays came from. He spoke like one and actually looked like one, and wrote like a dream. He asked me to wait in his living room while he went to get us a couple of drinks. So I sat on the couch and waited, looked out at the regulation swimming pool and waited some more. I then did what I always did when in a room with lots of books: I looked around the shelves, to see – as I always did – if we shared a taste in literature. We did – although I couldn't see any of my own work. What I did see, poking its head through the volumes, was a small bronze oval. I realised what it was instantly – the head of an Oscar. Before long, carrying two tempting-looking cold drinks in tall glasses, Epstein re-entered the room. 'That Oscar,' I asked, 'what's it for?'

'Oh,' he said, 'just for something I wrote with my late brother.' 'What?' I asked again. 'Just a film,'he said. 'Which film?' I pressed. 'Something a very long time ago.' 'Something had to have a name?' I persisted. 'What?' '*Casablanca*,' he said.

Warners had as their motto 'Combining good entertainment with good citizenship.' Epstein said: 'And I liked to think, "Great Chopped Liver".'

He was only partly referring to the grand dining room that Jack Warner installed with the help of the man whom he claimed was the best French chef in America – which was why he liked to invite the great and the good to take lunch there. On one occasion, Mme Chiang Kai Shek, wife of the nationalist Chinese dictator, came. Warner looked at the serried ranks of Chinese diplomats sitting with her at the other end of the table. 'Gee,' he said, 'that reminds me, I must get in my laundry.' On another occasion, the guest was Albert

Einstein. 'Professor, I'd like to welcome you,' said Warner. 'You know, I have a theory on relatives, too – don't hire 'em.'

Epstein told me a story about the film he made just before America entered the second World War. The film was called *Mr. Skeffington*, about a Jewish businessman who goes back to his native Germany, where he is arrested and sent to a concentration camp. 'Does this guy Skeffington have to be a Jew?' Warner asked. It was typical of the moguls, who were almost all Jewish but who hated the idea of making films with Jewish stories, particularly if they featured Jewish stars – which was why Emmanuel Goldenberg had to change his name to Edward G. Robinson and Muni Weisenfreund (a relative of Hugo Gryn) became Paul Muni – and why that grand old Anglo-Saxon Claude Raines played Mr. Skeffington himself.

A man who knew a lot about that sort of thing was my friend Mel Shavelson, who once wrote a book called *How To Make A Jewish Movie*, about the torments of filming a story about early Israel, *Cast A Giant Shadow*. He said: 'There used to be giants in this town, now all we have are the Dodgers.'

When I start work on a new book in Hollywood, (echoes of *Casablanca*) I begin by rounding up the usual suspects – people who know people who know people who know stories about my subjects. Not all of those suspects will have a story, but they usually know a man (or woman) who does. Mel is always my first port of call, as he was in the late 1990s when I was writing my books about Bing Crosby and Bob Hope. He knew stories about Crosby's early days, his cruelty to his sons – his son Gary said that whenever his father whipped him with his belt he consoled himself with the thought that 'the old man will die' one day. As for Hope, for whom he was once chief writer, his first day in Bob's office was one he will never forget. Hope asked him if he had an apartment. He said he had. 'Good. Leave the key under the mat and don't come back till midnight.' When he returned at midnight and had picked up the key from under the mat, there were wet footprints leading from the shower to the bed and back again. 'It was the story of *The Apartment*, long before Billy Wilder wrote it,' he noted.

None of the stories, the good ones, could be found in existing print. But stories in libraries are the usual skeletons on which to build the best books. If those skeletons have hitherto been in the closet, so much the better.

A lot of them had been that way with Bob Hope – hidden from his public. I discovered more about Hope the womaniser when researching a TV programme on him which went out when he died in 2003 – aged 100. His former secretary told me about Bob going out on the prowl every night, driving to the home of whoever he had chosen to bestow his services on that night, rather like a potentate with the inhabitants of his harem. One night, Bob's younger daughter, having just passed her driving test, followed him in her own car to see where he was going.

His Catholic wife, Dolores, had refrained from divorcing him, but had issued a number of threats – not least the one sent to him on the *Queen Mary*, on which he was crossing in the company of another woman.

There was a score of stars who told tales of his amorous adventures. There were also any number who talked about the art of Bob Hope. He was the man with the world's most famous joke factory, inhabited by the world's best comedy writers. I asked Mel Shavelson, its head, why, if the gags were so good, he didn't just tell them himself. 'Because I'm not Bob Hope,' he answered. In truth, there was no reason why Hope should use his own material – 'With all the things I do, there just wouldn't be time to write everything myself' – any more than Olivier should have been expected to have written Hamlet.

Hope's gift was his perfect timing. He knew he had succeeded when his audiences were still laughing at the previous gag while in the midst of the one that followed. But he had to have his idiot boards – wide strips of cardboard on which every word was written. One of his board handlers, a lovely man called Barney McNarty, told me he still had them in his garage. Wide, wide strips they were. So wide that I became certain that the only men who would qualify for the job were those who had really long arms.

The talk show host Steve Allen described for me an open-air birthday party that Hope attended, ostensibly by surprise. 'Bob said he would like to say a few words. He started to talk and then I followed his eye line – to the bushes, where Barney was standing with his idiot boards.' When they weren't available, as in the celebrated Miss World contest interrupted by women's rights protestors who threw the boards to the ground, he was lost.

But people don't remember those times as much as they do the good ones. He was the first American comic to play in Russia – when he entertained embassy staff. 'I saw they had a red star on the tower up there. I thought it was my dressing room.'

In a way, the whole world was his dressing room. Everywhere he went, he had an appropriate gag ready rehearsed for the right moment. We spoke on a number of occasions. In old, old age, he had given me approval to do a TV documentary on him. But then he decided he wanted a lot of money to appear himself. This from the man who was reputedly the richest in Hollywood – who owned more of the San Fernando Valley than the Washington government. I shall always be glad of our meetings – even when he said no.

Sometimes, those research ideas, so important in getting a book started, were based simply on what I personally found interesting. Sometimes, at the cost of commercial results. It's for that reason that I am particularly grateful to Frank Cass. Early on in my biography writing career, I was looking for an obvious follow-up to Al Jolson. Frank and I talked about Sophie Tucker. Not an international phenomenon like Jolson, although there had been a time when she could fill the London Palladium and during the twenties and thirties, long before both of us, she had been the darling of East London's Jewish community. I had interviewed her a couple of times – notably on the day I called at the Grosvenor House Hotel in Park Lane. I asked reception to call her. She answered the phone. The receptionist told her who was waiting to meet her. She asked for me to be sent up. 'Very good, sir,' he said. Yes, Sophie had a deep, deep voice – the one that for years had sold records like 'Life Begins At 40' and, most notably, 'My Yiddisher Mama'.

She had been dead for just a few years when I began work on the project. I went to Florida for the first time in my life and, with my shirt sticking to my back in the humidity of a Miami Beach November, called on a gentleman called Ted Shapiro. Ted knew her better than anyone. He had been her accompanist for 45 years, had travelled all round the world with her, knew of her problems with her son Bert, whom she called 'Sonny', had experienced her moods, good and bad, and knew which songs she liked, which she hated – and that went for audiences, too.

Ted was also an eminent songwriter – he had written the standard 'If I Had You' among others – and knew show business during its most interesting years. I cherished his friendship. He put me in touch with people like Sophie's younger brother Moe Abuza and William Hammerstein, son of Oscar. They all made a book I was glad to have written, even though I was probably the only person who was.

The next book owed not a little to *You Don't Have To Be Jewish*. George Weidenfeld, who had been given a peerage in Harold Wilson's famous 'Lavender List' of resignation honours, a man who knew everybody who was anybody (perhaps that ought to be rephrased: everybody who was anybody knew and still knows Lord Weidenfeld) and I got talking. Weidenfeld is big in every way, physically, in intellect and in the ability to make deals that amazed his competitors (to say nothing of entertaining and being entertained by the most important people in politics and the arts), and we were talking at Radio London about Jewish books. Suddenly, he said to me, 'Why don't you write for us?' I didn't know that he said that to lots of people whom he met at cocktail parties, at meetings of various kinds or when introduced to diplomats and politicians who somehow had mysteriously escaped his attentions to date. Through those meetings, he had published many of the great names in politics and diplomacy. To me, he said: 'Write me a letter with any ideas you might have. Just write, "Dear George, how about this...".'

I have to say I was flattered. I was not used to calling a peer of the realm 'George' – or Harry, Henry or...as Sam Goldwyn might have put it, 'every Tom, Dick or Harry is called George'. Certainly not peers of the realm who were among the most eminent publishers in the nation. We had several meetings. We always talked about his friends. 'Namedrops keep falling on my head' could have been his theme song. I went to his flat in Chelsea, where he would order his butler to produce a cigar or make a cup of coffee (in his own autobiography, called reasonably enough, *Remembering Good Friends*, he notes that he doesn't know how to make a cup of tea or coffee himself, let alone drive a car or work a video player). A few weeks after our first meeting, I bumped into him at Ben Gurion Airport, Tel Aviv. 'Good morning,' I said. 'Good morning,' he replied. There was an uneasy silence. 'Have you been here for long?' he asked. I knew he couldn't remember who I was – probably because he hadn't invited me to one of his parties. That was a situation that would before long be repaired, if unofficially. He had asked me to bring him the manuscript of my book. I called at the flat, where he was having a dinner party. 'Come and join us,' he said. It was an august gathering. I remember trying to hold my own in a discussion between Lady Antonia Fraser and Professor Ralph Dahrendorf (later Lord Dahrendorf) at the time principal of the London School of Economics. It was not an inspiring discussion.

The book I had suggested was about Errol Flynn. Not, this time, because I was a great admirer of this film star who summed up the word 'swashbuckler' as well as 'roustabout' and a lot of names not suitable for a family publication. But my dear friend Dennis Sykes was a Flynn aficionado. There hadn't been a good Flynn biography for years. 'Why not write one?' he suggested.

Why not indeed. The day after I wrote my letter to 'George' I had a phone call from Simon Dally, who was one of Weidenfeld's editors. He was a sweet, inoffensive fellow who plainly had enough problems to fill a giant-sized volume of its own. He said he had seen my letter and desperately wanted to publish a book about Errol Flynn. He then offered me an advance that today would seem to be a very nice fee for a good newspaper feature but which at the time was bigger than I had ever been offered for a book.

This was going to be good, I thought. And indeed it was. I learned so much more than had ever been published before about this Australian-born actor (not much of an actor, but undoubtedly a star) of whom his friend David Niven had said: 'You could always rely on Errol – he would always let you down.' But his story did not let me down at all. Not only did I get hold of the transcripts of his famous 1942 trial for statutory rape of two teenagers on board his yacht, the *Sorocco*, but I had a long interview with Nora Eddington, one of his wives, who was not afraid of discussing the most intimate (not excluding sexual) details of their married life. I spoke to people who had worked with him at Warner Bros., like the eminent actress-turned-director Ida Lupino, the stars of old Hollywood like Fred MacMurray, Alexis Smith, Vincent Price and Walter Pigeon and the directors Louis Milestone and his old drinking buddy, the one-eyed giant of a man called Raoul Walsh, director of such epics as *They Died With Their Boots On* and *The Naked And The Dead*.

Walsh could spin yarns like a high-speed worker in a textile mill. Except that his were a lot more fun – like the tale of how there would be regular gatherings of the drinking set of which Flynn served as chairman of the board, like an early version of Bogart's and Sinatra's Rat Packs.

Another regular at these 'meetings' was the biggest drinker, womaniser and adventurer of them all, John Barrymore. He even fulfilled that role after his death. As Walsh told it, Barrymore had been dead a couple of days when he himself had the bright idea of breaking into the funeral parlour and taking his body back to Flynn's house for their weekly drinking session. In Errol's living room, he was propped up in an arm chair. 'He doesn't look at all well,' Flynn said when he saw the body – and then realised what he had said. 'Jack' Barrymore was dead, yet sitting in his living room. In terror of the visitation he had just experienced, Flynn jumped out of the French windows of the house and hid in the bushes outside. Errol that night believed he had died before his time – which, of course, he did eventually do. Dead at 50.

The most revealing part of the book, however, was the casual discovery of a fact that would before long hit the headlines: Errol Flynn, star of patriotic movies like *Destination Burma*, *Dive Bomber* and *Desperate Journey*, was probably a Nazi sympathiser. The revelation came in an interview I had with the eminent MGM producer Jack Cummings. 'What, that Nazi?' he queried when I said I wanted to go to see him to talk about Flynn. 'I wouldn't give that bastard the time of day, he and his drunken buddies.' 'Nazi?' 'Sure,' said Cummings. 'A group of us at the Hillcrest Country Club started an inquiry into what we knew were his Nazi sympathies. We had seen strange things going on – not least the fact that we knew he had paintings on his walls that were last seen in Occupied Europe. How did they get there?' The word was passed to the FBI, who apparently did nothing. But they did establish a file on Flynn that contained a great deal of other suspicious information – not least the fact that he had been seen taking photographs of naval installations in California, which he was suspected of passing on to the Japanese.

When I give talks about 'my job' as a biographer, I speak, usually in my first sentences, about the necessity for accuracy – a requirement, I emphasise, drummed into me on the *Luton News*. I sincerely believe I have always regarded that as my own totem. If a book isn't wholly accurate, what's the point of writing it? But, since this book is called '*Confessions*', I have to come clean. On one occasion, one only, I allowed my principles to drift somewhat.

The American publishers of *The Two Lives of Errol Flynn* were kind about it. They liked it and thought it would do well – as it did, running not only in hardback, but in eight different printings in paperback in the States and serialisation in one of the country's leading digests – but they needed something more. I had written about Flynn's 'charm'. They liked that. It was a nice contrast to the usual image of the man. They wanted more examples. I went through my files, rang my contacts, searched the libraries. There was nothing I could find. So I resorted to saying: 'The sort of thing he would do was . . . ' Well, the 'sort of thing' was a fabricated story about Flynn being at a nightclub and going up to an ugly woman and asking her to dance. Only a very charming man would do such a thing. A few years later, Peter O'Toole starred in a movie based very much on the Errol Flynn story, *My Favourite Year*, in one scene in which he goes up to an ugly woman in a nightclub and . . . asks her to dance.

A year later, another Flynn biography was published – which took up my discoveries about his Nazi past. I was interviewed on BBC television. 'Are you peeved that this story has just come out?' I was asked. 'Not at all,' I said. 'I broke it a year ago.'

Clearly, Flynn was not among the great Jewish entertainers who remained a fascination for me. I thought of doing a book about this important genre. Frank Cass agreed, and so we published *So Lets Hear The Applause* (why it had no apostrophe after the word 'Let' I still don't know) but it was an enjoyable experience to write monographs on people like Woody Allen, Frankie Vaughan, George Burns, Irving Berlin, Sophie Tucker and, of course, Jolson.

The most enjoyable thing of all, however, was to co-operate with the *Fiddler on the Roof* star, Topol, who, I had discovered, was a talented portraitist. I got him to do pencil sketches of my subjects and they were quite outstanding. Topol was very popular at the time, not least with my friend Harry Wayne who, week after week, went to see the show at Her Majesty's Theatre. One week, Harry told me, he had complained to Topol: 'You know, Chaim, you're singing "If I Were A Rich Man" too fast these days. It isn't as good as it used to be.' Topol said, "Is that true, Harry? I'll have to change it." Which he did.' I came home and told Sara the story. As I told her, 'I wish Harry hadn't told me that. He doesn't need to embellish his friendship with Topol like that.' Soon afterwards, I happened to meet Topol at Elstree studios. I told him I brought him greetings from our mutual friend Harry Wayne. 'You know,' he said, 'I'll always be grateful for Harry. He came to see the show every week and then told me he thought I was singing too fast. I was so grateful and changed the way I sang "If I Were A Rich Man".' Which taught me never to doubt dear friends ever again.

Later, I went back to the world of the songwriter. Irving Berlin, in trying to dissuade me from working on a book about himself (or so he protested), said there had never been a decent book on his own idol Jerome Kern (the man who said that Berlin 'has no place in American music – he IS American music', so you get some idea why he was his idol).

I found Kern to be much less interesting, despite going to Knoxville, Tennessee, to meet his daughter Betty. She was custodian of her father's wealth and copyrights, but she seemed much more interested in her horses. To her, though, her father was a great songwriter, better than any other before or since. He was a great wit. He was highly superstitious – he had to play 'Old Man River' before leaving town or he knew he would be unlucky. In 1945, he forgot to play the tune before leaving his Beverly Hills mansion and died in a New York street. As usual, there was a whole gaggle of other people to meet. And again, the incidentals were the stories that counted. The best vignette came from the widow of the lyricist Oscar Hammerstein II, with whom Kern produced *Show Boat*. She insisted that Kern didn't write the show's biggest number, 'Ol' Man River' . On the contrary, it was her husband. 'Kern', she insisted, 'just wrote "dum-dum-di-dum … ".'

No one should ever write a book and expect it to be a best-seller. It just doesn't happen that way. Often an author will write a series of potboilers that tend to mark time between more successful titles. I did my share of those. I wrote books about Katharine Hepburn and Shirley MacLaine which, I have to admit, did little to further the careers of either – should they have needed that to happen, which they manifestly did not. The Hepburn book was notable for two things, or perhaps one was the extension of the other. Sara and I were staying at a somewhat posh hotel in Devon – sharing a dining room with a very sick and very aged Laurence Olivier. I plucked up enough courage to ask him to see me for a very short while. He didn't want to do so. But then I mentioned Katharine Hepburn. 'Oh, Kate,' he said. 'What do you want to know?' He didn't tell me very much, but it was quite marvellous to meet him again. I didn't mention the incident with the bucket of water and my scooter.

Cut then to a few months later. Douglas Fairbanks Jr. was in London. Would he talk to me? 'Afraid not,' he said. 'Much too busy.' I told him we had met before and had got on very well. It didn't do anything to persuade him to change his mind. So then I said, only partly lying, 'I saw Laurence Olivier a few weeks ago for this and he said, "You know, the one person you must talk to is Douggie Fairbanks."' 'OK,' he said, 'can you come tomorrow at ten?'

Fairbanks was staying in a swish place in Belgravia. My car was in dock that day, so I called to see him in a very battered, very old red Daf, which Sara loved driving and which was powered, it seemed, by a set of elastic bands.

He greeted me, this honorary knight of the realm, immaculately dressed as always, white hair neatly combed so that he looked like one of the more successful Tory cabinet ministers, and welcomed me with olde worlde courtesy. We talked about a couple of incidents in Kate's life in which he was involved – he desperately wanted to make love to her, but she wouldn't have any of it – and finally it came time to part. 'Got a car here?' he asked. 'Yes,' I said – it was the days before congestion charges and sixpence in a meter went a long way. 'Do you think you could give me a lift to St James's?' he asked. 'Delighted,' said I, 'but my own car is being repaired and the one I have borrowed from my wife is pretty disreputable and probably shows the effects of lots of children.' 'That doesn't matter at all,' he said. We crossed the road to where the car was parked. 'You know,' he said, looking at the vehicle, 'perhaps I'll get a taxi.'

There was another book on Jane Fonda, for which I interviewed her former husband (and of Brigitte Bardot, and common law husband of Catherine Deneuve) Roger Vadim. That was fascinating because of her position in the list of beautiful Vadim women and also because of her reputation as Hanoi Jane, one of the principal and most vocal opponents of the Vietnam War.

We met at his Santa Monica home (which he had bought so that he could be near Vanessa, the daughter he and Jane shared) and talked, sitting on the veranda. 'Jan has a fantastic capacity for surviving,' he told me. 'She learned long ago how to be lonely. For me, what was attractive was her attention to other people.'

However, that was the one thing that didn't make her attractive to the Vietnam veterans – the ones who dubbed her 'Hanoi Jane'. One told me: 'This was a traitor. I hated her before and I hate her now.'

Just how seriously people took her activities contesting Washington's war in the former Indo-China could be judged by the pages and pages of files on her held by the FBI, listing every speech she made, with anti-government statements in bold type. There were a lot of paragraphs that had been blacked out. My theory was that these were the transcripts of bugged phone calls – something that, of course, the bureau would never dream of admitting they had done.

Vadim told me of the problems of getting his wife to strip naked in the opening moments of his film *Barbarella*. 'She said she would do it. I decided to be kind and promised that the most important parts of her anatomy would be concealed by the letters of the credits.'

I thought that was especially kind from the man who had featured his then wife Brigitte Bardot in *And God Created Woman*. They called Jane 'the American Bardot'. 'I don't like that at all,' she said.

On the whole, she was popular with her fellow actors, at least with those who shared her politics. Rod Taylor, who co-starred with her in the fluffy comedy *Sunday In New York*, told me: 'I honestly believe she falls in love with the parts she plays. Therefore, a lot of that love reaches out to the people around her. But that was helped by the fact that she wasn't into her political bullshit, then.'

Soon afterwards, I wrote a book about Dustin Hoffman, which I very much enjoyed.

How could I not have enjoyed hearing from Sydney Pollack, the director of *Tootsie*, about Dustin's attempts at playing a woman? 'It was a strange situation,' he told me at the time. 'He wasn't going to do it in drag – in other words to make a caricature of a woman. He didn't want to make it look like a man playing a woman. And that was very hard.'

But not quite as hard as suffering what his star considered to be democracy. On *Kramer Versus Kramer*, Dustin had had an equal say with the producer and director on everything. 'I don't work like that,' said Pollack, who also played Hoffman's agent in the film. Dustin insisted that he *did* work like that – and lost the fight. It wasn't an easy situation. But he accepted it – and worked out the sort of woman he wanted Dorothy Michaels to be. Hers was the role he played in the film – an actor who couldn't get a job and so decides that a temporary cosmetic sex change could be the answer. The problem was dealing with the fact that there was no way Dorothy could be as attractive as the sort of women who normally excited him. 'If I met Dorothy at a party,' he told me, 'I'd turn me down.'

The real surprise in his life was the success of his first hit, *The Graduate*. He didn't think it would work. 'I thought it might make something in the art houses, that's all.'

But he had audacity, or perhaps chutzpah is a better word – and this was something that came clear in the research. He was playing a young virgin and he wanted to *feel* like a virgin when he made it. But what did a virgin feel, one of either sex? He all but had his face slappd when he interviewed young women and asked them about their sexual status. He could stop a pretty girl and ask directly, 'Are you still a virgin?' Surprisingly these days, a great many of them were. 'Why?' he asked. 'Are you saving yourself for your husband?' Equally surprisingly – in twenty-first-century terms – a lot said that they were.

As he told me at the time, that way, he was able to feel something of what they felt – if not exactly get under their skins, if you see what I mean.

There was almost a personal dimension to this. For years, people had thought that I looked like Hoffman. When my biography was published in 1984, my then little niece Lianne saw the picture of Dustin on the cover and asked: 'Why is *your* photo on this book?' My son Jonathan, a few years earlier, had seen the stills of the movie *Kramer Versus Kramer* outside a cinema and asked a similar question. But it went further than that.

I was in New York, crossing a road, one of those 'cross streets' where you toss up as to whether you want to go to the other side or live, when a taxi screeched to a halt – not because I was doing anything dangerous, but because he thought he had recognised me. 'Hey, Dustin,' he called at the top of his voice. A few days later at the Lincoln Center library, a woman looked at me and plainly was wondering whether to say anything. Eventually, she spat it out: 'Oh,' she gushed. 'I think you were so wonderful in *Midnight Cowboy*.' I tried to put her right. 'I think you've made a mistake,' I answered. 'Oh, you can't kid me,' she said, 'not with that phoney English accent.'

Not long after that Sara and I were at the London press showing of *Marathon Man*. We came in late, just as the opening credits were coming on to the screen. We found two seats. The man sitting next to me couldn't take his eyes off of me. I realised why. He, too, thought I was Hoffman. It was what stars usually did – sliding into their seats after a film starts. I mentioned all that in my book, which was probably the most interesting thing in the whole volume. No, not one of my favourites, even though there was a fair amount of interesting new material and I did manage an interview with one of the former Mrs Hoffmans (or should that be Hoffmen; never mind).

Peter O'Toole and I have never been mistaken for each other. I wrote a biography of him in 1983 which was better received than I expected. It told an interesting story without enough new revelations, but it was good to be able to go to his roots in Ireland and see the background to an incredible career that has never been sufficiently rewarded. My best memory of that was to talk to the much respected actor Timothy West about the time he had produced O'Toole in his biggest ever disaster, a production of *Macbeth* at the Old Vic – which would have made the Shakespeare masterpiece unlucky even if the very name didn't put the mockers on everything else.

Tim and I met in a rather swanky Viennese-type coffee shop in Marylebone High Street, the sort of place where the liquid comes in pots almost as heavy as the beverage itself. I always anjoy conversations with people who say they don't like the subjects of my books. All too often, colleagues of stars are frightened of upsetting them – they know where the bread is buttered and are constantly worried whether there will be any butter in future. Timothy West, one of our most successful actors, himself told me that he was always worried whether his next role would be his last. But he told me what I wanted to know. Certainly, he didn't appear to be worried about the possibility of buried skeletons – another reason why colleagues are unwilling to talk about people whom they don't exactly adore.

He didn't like O'Toole. He positively hated him. And he said so. 'He said he was going to work very hard for *Macbeth*, but he didn't,' he told me. As we talked, I was pleased to see there were no residual reservations about using the name of the Scottish play. O'Toole himself called it 'Harry Lauder', but the Glasgow comedian who believed in keeping on till the end of the road never had anything like the same trouble.

It wasn't just Peter himself. A whole slew of directors came on the scene and left again – not necessarily because they didn't get on with the star. There was, for instance, the Mexican scene designer who came up with a scheme for inflatable sets – a good idea, West thought, which would make it easy to take with the play on tour. 'The man delivered what looked like a collection of black bin bags.'

One of the big difficulties seems to have been that O'Toole took to heart his right to choose the rest of the cast. Timothy West thought that was too much. He at least had to be consulted. He wasn't. 'If I laid down the law, I was accused of unwarranted lack of co-operation,' he remembered. After all, Mr West was only the producer. 'He also told people it would be all right if they only came to the last week of rehearsal, or that they didn't have to do the four-week tour that we had planned... people were told they had really major parts – only for me to be asked by Peter to release him from the obligation of employing them. He had changed his mind about them.' The amazing thing, he went on, was that 'Peter himself didn't have any really clear ideas, although I expected he would.'

(I built up a gratifying relationship with Tim West. When a newspaper asked me to do an interview with him, he said, 'Come for dinner.' Sara and I had a great evening at his house in Wandsworth, South London, enjoying dinner cooked by his wife, the beautiful Prunella Scales. She and Sara got on like a kitchen on fire, and there was plenty to say about the talents of an actress whom we both greatly admired. It was a marvellous evening of mutual praise.)

Inevitably, the book went into O'Toole's iconic role *Lawrence of Arabia*, which he didn't appear to like that much. Their characters were so very different – and so was their height. O'Toole was very tall, Lawrence very short. But it was the difference in their personalities that struck home. Being in the open air, perching on a camel wasn't much fun to a man who said that his idea of heaven was sitting in a smoke-filled room.

He didn't much believe in suffering for the sake of a good cause, either. 'The best thing to do is to keep your cake shut and send a few bob. That St Francis of Assisi bit of whipping off your knickers and joining a leper colony doesn't work for most people, 'I remember him saying.

But the film worked – and I like to think my book did, too.

People always ask me who would I have most wanted to write a book about, but so far never have. There is one name that stands out among all the others, that of the only star with whom I wanted to contemplate working on an authorised edition: Walter Matthau, an actor I have always admired, whose humour I have loved and whom I got to know quite well. We almost had a deal, but just almost.

The idea first came to mind at about at the time I was working on my biography of Jack Lemmon. This was one of my favourite books and was republished in 2002 under the brilliant title of *Some Like It Cool*. At least I thought it was brilliant. The man who wrote and directed the film with a title remarkably similar to that of my book, Billy Wilder, and I spent hours talking about the actor with whom he had spent so many of his happiest hours.

Jack was one of my favourite subjects, as he was many people's favourite stars. He was a wonderful actor who was marvellous both in comedy (like, of course, *Some Like It Hot*, which was almost my book title, and in serious dramas like *Glengarry Glen Ross* and *Save The Tiger*).

What really came through when the new book was in gestation were the agonies he experienced in his sixties and seventies. There had been clues that all was not totally well in the Jack Lemmon household long before. In 1974, I had interviewed him on the eve of the American Film Institute's presentation of its Life Achievement Award to James Cagney. He told me of the speech he was going to make at the celebration. He would refer to the older actor's powers of observation – how he met him when they made the movie *Mister Roberts*, for which Lemmon won an Oscar. 'Are you still using your left hand?' he asked. Lemmon said he was overwhelmed that 'Jim' remembered that from an earlier outing on the screen.

When it came to the ceremony itself, Lemmon told the story – and then rambled for more than 30 minutes. In the end, he had to be helped off the podium. I was there that night and heard Shirley MacLaine say, 'What happened to Jack?'

What had happened was that Jack was under the influence. He claimed it was because he had to go into hospital the next day for a minor operation and had been taking some preparatory drugs. The real truth was that he was drinking and smoking. He had claimed to have given it all up years before. But in 1985, a friend revealed, he had told him: 'You'll pardon my language, but you're a fucking alcoholic.' It was then that it struck home. He stopped smoking – he had been going through four packs a day – and went on the wagon. Lemmon had gone to a drying-out clinic in Arizona, 'but I stopped before I got there and haven't had a drop since'.

We talked for hours in his Hollywood office and dozens of his friends talked about him, too. Inevitably, we got round to talking about that other member of the *Odd Couple* partnership, Matthau. 'You know,' he told me, 'he's my wife.'

So I rang Matthau. Of course he'd talk about his pal Jack. 'Come for lunch tomorrow,' he said. 'You know The Bistro?' I didn't know The Bistro, but I was happy to find out. With my brother Geoffrey I made the discovery.

The Bistro turned out to be one of those swanky places where the beautiful people gathered and hoped that nobody noticed that they chose dishes not exactly made to conform to the latest dietary fad. You could see them look round and about them as they ordered, *sotto voce*, French fries or steaks that had to ooze with fat. It was as if they were requesting sex toys or serious pornography. Mr Matthau was much more circumspect. He had just visited his dentist and had experienced all the glories of root canal treatment. When the young blond waiter, the one with the German accent, asked him his choice, he said: 'Vichyssoise – followed by minestrone.' I don't remember what I ordered – it is not quite as ingrained in my memory as the look on the face of the waiter. 'Lovely fellow,' he said. 'Did you know he used to be a lieutenant in the Gestapo?'

We were off to a good start. We talked about Lemmon and we talked about himself, about his early days on Broadway, about his films – 'This is not real acting; it's retirement acting; I say a few lines and look important and then go off for the rest of the day' – on which he started working when he had a heart attack. We discussed that. 'You can't say to God, "I haven't finished this movie. So I can't go now." But you *can* go.' He confessed about his gambling – about the fact that he could bet an entire film's salary on a single football game.

We talked about making *Hello, Dolly* with Barbra Streisand, whom he described as 'the most incredible...dreadful boring person I have ever had the misfortune to work with'. He was a lot older than Ms S. and had been in the business rather longer than she had. He had no patience with her 'pretentiousness' or her determination to lay down the law. Once having got that off his chest, he proceeded to tell me about his mother – who used to throw things at the television set when she didn't like the movie being screened.

We did a recorded interview for the *Late Night Extra* programme. On the way back, we stopped in his Mercedes at traffic lights. While we waited for the lights to change, a woman looked his way. 'Gee, aren't you somebody famous?' she asked. 'Sure,' replied Walter. 'Don't you know Michael Freedland from the BBC?'

How could you not love a man like that? When I got home, I wrote to ask what seemed a very reasonable question: 'Why don't we do a book?' He replied instantly: 'A good idea,' he said. 'But let's wait seven years.' I thought it sounded very biblical. 'We'll have much more to talk about.'

I waited seven years, and wrote again. Once more, he replied by return: 'We should wait another ten years. Think what more stories we would have to tell . . .'

After those 10 years, 17 years after our first meeting, I wrote again. By then, I had a publisher's agreement to offer him $1 million. I rang. 'Do I owe you any money?' he asked. 'No? Well, let's have lunch tomorrow.' We fixed a time. I went to his house, one of the more tasteful and beautiful semi-mansions in a neighbourhood of Los Angeles called Pacific Palisades (the area where I had seen Nanette Fabray for that now famous talk about Fred Astaire). 'Pleased to see you,' he said, now bent and craggy with a face like one of those maps on a car satellite screen. 'We've been pen pals for a long time, haven't we?' I didn't spell out for how long. We went, along with his film producer son, to a small Chinese restaurant – this time he ate more than I did – and talked about the book. He seemed to be ready to do it, but wanted much more than the $1 million on offer.

It was the start of negotiations, I reasoned. Except that, in just a couple of weeks, he had been struck with cancer, lost the use of his legs and then died. I mourned him – as I mourned, almost exactly a year later, when Jack Lemmon died, too. Yes, I miss him, and not just for the book that never was.

All along, there had been other books about other people. I liked most of them, but there is one that I never list in the 'Also by Michael Freedland' pages of my biographies. It started at lunch in the not terribly salubrious neighbourhood of Clapham Junction. My host was David Roberts, by now the chief editor of Weidenfeld and Nicolson. 'I've got an idea for you,' he said. They have always been words of music to my ears. 'You know that luscious girl with the big shoulders in the soap, *Dynasty?*' 'Joan Collins, you mean?' I asked. 'No, not her, the other one – Linda Evans.'

That was not the sort of tune I wanted to hear. Something discordant was ringing in my ears. I didn't see Linda Evans in the same list as Al Jolson, Irving Berlin or even Sophie Tucker. 'The money won't be bad,' said Roberts.

He was right. It wasn't bad. It would be a quickie book that no one would be asked to consider as literature, but it was likely to sell well. I told him that I had a friend who would do it very well, by the name of Stephen Reynolds – a byline I had used on certain newspaper stories that I didn't think fitted into my image as a serious journalist.

'No,' he said. 'we want you, Michael Freedland.' I more or less said I'd do it if he promised there would be no publicity, but that wouldn't have been very clever. So I signed up, went to America, spoke to her former husband John Derek (husband by then of the sex symbol Bo Derek) and a number of people from her show. I spoke to people who knew her when she was so high – and so nicely wide. One of them revealed that she had had an abortion, still newsworthy at that time in the late 1980s. It was enough to sell lots of books and get serialisation in the *National Enquirer* – not a journal I'd buy very often, but one that was willing to spend more money than I had previously ever seen on serialisation rights – and there were paperback editions in both Britain and America. There was even an edition in Norwegian.

My bank manager was pleased, and at least I didn't have to list it at the front of the books that came later on.

# 27   A *duet and a trio*

Then there was a book that I called *Words and Music by*... The 'by' in the title alluded to a gentleman called Walter Scharf. I had met Scharf a number of years before when he, like Astaire and Chevalier, was one of the subjects of my Radio Four series *Be My Guest*.

Scharf was one of the backroom boys of Hollywood movies. Of musical movies, principally. On the programme, we spoke about the people with whom he had worked – including, and it was this that got the juices going, Al Jolson and Irving Berlin. He was musical director on more than a hundred films. These included Jolson's *The Singing Kid* – 'he was the cruellest man I know' and Irving Berlin's *Holiday Inn*, when he was the very first person ever to play 'White Christmas'. He had conducted the orchestra for Danny Kaye's *Hans Christian Andersen*, for Frank Sinatra's *The Joker Is Wild*, and for Gene Wilder's *Willie Wonka and the Chocolate Factory*. He had taught Elvis Presley how to perform on *Lovin' You*, *Tickle Me* and *King Creole*, and had suffered the problems of working with that arch-perfectionist Barbra Streisand when he had been musical director on *Funny Girl*.

He helped me in my research for the Berlin book. What intrigued me about him was the collection of names with whom he had worked, which was why he made such an interesting *Be My Guest*... well, guest. I now thought he would make a good book subject. Frank Cass agreed and so did Walter. I spent weeks with him at about the time I worked with Chris Hunt, a talented director who became a very talented businessman with his own company making arts films. The project was my first TV show, *The Real Al Jolson* on the ITV *South Bank Show*. Scharf was in that and, a few years later, in a programme Chris and I made on Irving Berlin, too.

Walter and I became close friends, even though he was more than 25 years my senior. His book was not so much about his own life, but about the show people with whom he had worked. Once more, I met Alice Faye and got the requisite peck on the cheek. But what was really exciting was to find stories that wouldn't necessarily have made books on their own, but, put together in this volume, told a story about Hollywood and Hollywood music and music people not known before.

There was, for instance, an insight into the process of writing 'White Christmas', which in recent years has come to be thought of as just one of a string of Irving Berlin songs that he kept in his trunk, ready to be dusted down for use in some future time. Like 'God Bless America' and 'Easter Parade' (which had started out as a ditty called 'Smile and Show Your Dimple', but when it was first published, not a smile was seen, nor a dimple creased). Scharf always said that was not true. 'White Christmas', he told me, 'was new. There was, I think, an old Christmas song that Irving had written years before. I should know. I was the first to play the tune properly. I had heard him thumping it out as though he were playing it with boxing gloves, sitting at his strange piano – the one with a lever underneath to change keys – and with him it was always as though he were giving birth to a baby. Finally, he appeared. 'I said, "Well, Irving, what have you got?" "Let me play it for you," he replied. He started thumping again. No one imagined at that moment they were present at the birth of an institution. Then he said, "Will you play it for me?" So I did. The first to play it – properly, that is.'

If Berlin was an institution already, like his most successful song, you couldn't say that yet about the young Hillbilly who was retained by Paramount after scoring huge successes with his first albums. Scharf was the man who prepared Elvis Presley for the movies, working with him on three films, *Lovin' You*, *King Creole* and *Tickle Me*. 'He treated me as a father,' said Scharf. 'Always so respectful.'

Barbra Streisand was somehow more difficult. 'She tried to get round me by schmoozing, pretending to be a baby. She stuck her tongue out. She did everything but suck her thumb.'

The film they worked on together was the first Streisand vehicle and probably the best, *Funny Girl*. Scharf had known the original

Funny Girl, Fanny Brice. 'She wasn't the crude caricature of herself that Barbra made her.'

What *was* like a caricature was the relationship between Dean Martin and Jerry Lewis. The verbal fights were so extreme, said the musical director of five Martin and Lewis films (including their last, *Hollywood Or Bust*) that he told the producer Hal Wallis, 'As long as they don't kill each other, I'll be happy.' I discovered others felt much the same thing when I wrote my Dean Martin biography – although it turned out that both felt more for each other than most people now remember.

It was the first time I had shared a credit on a book. I did it again soon afterwards with a Q and A biography called *There's No Answer To That*. My subjects and co-authors (as the Public Lending Right Office would have it when it came to annual payments for library lendings) were Morecambe and Wise, by far the most successful comedy act British TV has ever known.

They were known as Eric and Ernie. Eric Morecambe and Ernie Wise, both now dead, but still names to conjure with, as the juggler might have put it. Actually, it didn't take any juggling to know that they were, as a team, the funniest people on the box. It is true, also, that should there have been a poll to find the best-loved couple in television, they would have come on top.

It started with a magazine story on Ernie, the one – as the act would have it – with the wig and the short hairy legs. I could testify that the bit about the wig was as false as the alleged headpiece. I never looked at his legs, although since he was a little man they were undoubtedly short. I'll have to take his partner's word about them being hairy.

They were an unusual pair. Eric, the obvious clown, was the one with the silly expressions, who only had to move his spectacles sideways to get laughs – but not laughs through slapstick, not laughs through sophisticated jokes either, and that was his true genius. When André Previn came on their TV show and complained that Eric was playing all the wrong notes of Grieg's piano concerto, Mr Morecambe, via his brilliant writer, Eddie Brayben, had the answer that has gone down in history: 'I am playing all the right notes – but not necessarily in the right order.' The line was funny in itself, the way he put it over... that was the true genius.

Ernie, on the other hand, was a superb sidekick, the straight man who wanted to be seen as funny and to be as well loved as his partner. That was the subject of our chat for the magazine piece – countering the traditionally accepted view that it was Eric who was the funny one and ensuring that we knew he himself was as comical and as well loved as his partner. I suggested the book there and then. Within days, Weidenfeld accepted the idea that there was a Q and A biography in their story.

I had to see Eric first. It took about ten seconds to realise that he was as funny and as loveable off the box as he was on it. This was a time when documentary police programmes were almost as big on television as Eric and Ernie – at least people did tune in to them. One of the big ones was called *Police Five*, in which for five minutes a broadcaster called Shaw Taylor asked viewers for help in tracing known criminals.

Eric and I met at the London studios of Thames Television. As we were introduced, a police car, siren blaring, passed by. Without taking a moment to think, Eric jumped in: 'That's Shaw Taylor going to lunch.' How could you resist that sort of man?

I found Ernie much easier to resist. I also realised that Eric and Ernie, the buddies of the small screen who had been together since old-time variety, could resist each other, too. They admitted that the two rarely met from one TV series to another and the rumour was that their wives didn't get on, and there was a certain tension between them that was difficult not to spot. Ernie was always trying to prove that he was the funnier one. Eric didn't have to try at all.

We met day after day at the rehearsal rooms in Richmond, where they planned their shows so meticulously that they could have been working on a second invasion of the beaches of Normandy. What they were actually doing was invading people's homes and making sure that they were welcome.

I once brought the then 13-year-old Jonathan to meet them. They had no objection to his sitting in on our conversations about the show and their guests – Yehudi Menuhin being asked if he was free to come and play his banjo, Shirley Bassey looking exquisite in a sequined gown – and army boots. I thought that was extraordinarily generous. As we left that day, Eric called out, 'Regards to the wife, Jonathan.'

Later, Eric happened to come into the Radio London studios to do an interview with someone else. He spotted me as I walked into reception, 'Michael,' he called, 'how great to see you' and gave me a big hug. My stock at the station had never been higher.

Ernie was the one whose stock in trade was his literary pretensions – 'the plays what I wrote'. The mock seriousness suited him brilliantly, but he needed a foil in Eric. If that seems like a reverse of their roles, you have to realise that Eric could have gone out there on his own and been a sensation just the same. When Eric died, Ernie tried to work alone, and sadly failed. When he himself died a few years later, it was as if he had had to give up because there was no one there to joke with.

Every now and again the name Maurice Chevalier cropped up in our talks. Eric and Ernie had appeared with him at a Royal Variety Performance. 'The strangest thing was when we passed his dressing room,' Ernie told me. 'He had finished his act, had been presented to the Queen Mother and yet there he was standing in front of the mirror, going over it all again – when the show had finished.'

It was a gesture of insecurity that fitted in perfectly with what I knew about Chevalier when I researched my biography of the French entertainer. Yes, that word again – it fitted like one of those straight-edged jigsaw pieces (or was it part of a house?).

When I had met him in London, we talked about his accent – 'just a little too much sometimes,' he admitted. Alan Jay Lerner told me that when Maurice made *Gigi*, he asked him, 'Is the accent all right?' Lerner said it was. 'No, I mean was it *strong* enough?'

What we didn't talk about was that insecurity. A few trips to France underlined it in big red letters – such insecurity that, mixed with a hefty dose of depression, resulted in at least two attempts at suicide.

It was one of those research expeditions that revealed much more than I could have expected. I learned about his mistresses – which didn't surprise me. I found a previously unknown poem to Mistinguett, the dancer with whom he had spent whole performances wrapped in a rug – they were supposed to spend just a few minutes on the routine, but they were so enamoured with each other that every night, it got longer and longer (the routine, that is). The poem contained the line: 'You are my girl, my mistress, my greatest woman friend. You loved my mother.'

His mother, I found out, was the real love of his life and when she died, he tried suicide for the first time. Failing that time only seemed to inspire him to do it again. François Vals, his secretary, told me of taking away a knife from him at the time when he realised that neither his voice nor his energy were as good as they had been.

Then there was the question of his collaboration with the Nazis during the war. Or did he collaborate? I remembered that when I was working at Woburn Abbey I had suggested that we invite Chevalier to the house. The French-born Duchess of Bedford wouldn't hear of it. 'He was a collaborator. I was in the Resistance.'

So I met Resistance people. One by one I had the same answer: 'He was no hero, but he wasn't a collaborator.' There had been angry complaints when Chevalier took part in the Paris victory parade – even from some of the people in the crowd who welcomed De Gaulle but had cheered the Vichy French leader Marshal Pétain just a few months before.

The main point was not just that Chevalier had lived and worked in France during the occupation, but that he had gone to Germany. That was not a heroic thing to do – especially when he was photographed by Nazi soldiers as he stood by a German railway station sign at Alten Grabau, site of a prisoner of war camp. However, there was no evidence that he had done more than sing to French prisoners – and only those from his home suburb of Menilmontant.

'We wished he hdn't done it,' said Henri Amouroux, a leading Resistance figure.

The Germans ordered him to make jokes about Churchill. He refused. And that could have saved him, I learned when I spoke to members of the Maquis, the secet Resistance army. But his answer to the Nazi order was not as brave as it might have seemed. 'I won't do it,' he said, 'because I don't make political jokes.'

Chevalier himself told me: 'If I had deserted my people and gone to America I could have made 20 times more than I earned at home during the war.'

There were other mitigating factors, which helped to clear him at a hastily arranged post-war tribunal. He had had a Jewish mistress, Nita Rayer, whom he had secreted along with her mother in what proved to be a safe haven in the south of France. He also had the backing of his friend Marlene Dietrich, who was everyone's heroine after the liberation. She, after all, was German, but had stayed in America during the war and had entertained Allied soldiers. She demonstrated her support for Maurice by driving with him in the 'peace parade' down the Champs Elysées.

And then there was Ginette Spanier, the couturier, head of the house of Balmain, socialite friend of Noel Coward and Danny Kaye. She was British, Jewish – and worked for the Resistance. 'He wasn't a collaborator,' she told me.

But he did collaborate with women – in every way possible. His mistresses, I discovered, regarded themselves as his wives. One of them was Janie Michels, who was the Contesse de la Chapelle. 'I was really married to him,' she told me as we sipped calvados on the terrace of her lovely home at Deauville. 'In every other sense. Seeing a priest doesn't change anything. When you're not young, it makes no difference.' She went to live with Chevalier – with her daughter – at his home, which he had called after the name he gave his mother, La Louque. Janie recalled him saying: 'I am strong and I am weak.'

So weak that he would admit to her: 'Today, I have been a little devil.' The contesse was important to him, and not just for the comfort she offered. He talked about his wife, Yvonne Vallée, from whom he had been divorced, although the documents had not been recognised by the Church, and that was something which worried him. 'When Yvonne was in my bed,' Janie told me he said, 'I felt poison all over me. I've had some very bad adventures, but this was the worst.'

These were exclusives, the blood and guts of a biography. Yet there was more to come – not just other stories from other women, like his publisher, Thérèse de Saint-Phalle, who talked about stroking his ego, or Jacqueline Cartier, the Paris journalist, who recalled several evenings with an elderly man who would take her out to eat, but never drink the glass of wine he ordered. 'Wine is now for the nose,' he told her. It was a typical Chevalier statement.

The fact that he actually bought the wine was something of a revelation in itself. Another fact uncovered in my researches was that Maurice didn't exactly enjoy spending money. In Beverly Hills, I went to see the by then nonagenarian movie director Rouben Mamoulian, who had produced as well as directed one of Chevalier's biggest Hollywood films, *Love Me Tonight*, in which he starred with Jeannette MacDonald.

It was good to hear about Chevalier before the cameras, but what really struck home was when we got round to talking about the star's culinary habits. 'Every day we used to go to a restaurant. But Maurice would never come with us. I asked him why, and he said he had other arrangements.' One day he saw what those arrangements were. Chevalier was sitting outside the sound stage – eating out of a brown paper bag.

Hermione Gingold, the British character actress who had starred with him in *Gigi* (and told me about the panic caused by clicking noises on the soundtrack – which turned out to come from the then 70-year-old Chevalier's loose-fitting false teeth) recalled the time he had asked her to come to visit him at his suite at London's Savoy Hotel. Quoting their most famous song routine, she remembered it well. 'He said "Come at One". I thought, "Great, lunch." I got there at one and we talked and talked. At 2.15, I looked at my watch and told him, "You know, I'm getting hungry." "Are you?" he said. "Yes," I said, "I think I'll be going."' At that point, Maurice replied, "Well, you must come again some time." Not a coffee or a Coca-Cola or anything.'

Ginette Spanier knew all about that. 'He would come to my apartment, always on the exact second that he said he would come, and he always worried about spending a franc. However, he was wonderful, so kind, considerate and charming that you forgot that pecadillo of his.'

A man with plenty of pecadillos was Kenneth Williams, whom most people would think of as being full of jokes – a fellow who made men and women laugh until it hurt. He did it in the famous *Carry On* films, he did it on Radio Four's *Just A Minute* programme and on *Round The Horne*. He did it, too, on countless TV shows. But if Chevalier was a depressive, this was a mountain of insecurity – one who was shy about his sexuality, who confided everything to his diaries, adored his mother and had an uneasy relationship with other members of his family.

I was grateful to enjoy the friendship of his sister Pat, who unburdened herself with wonderful stories about her strange, frequently depressed brother. There were incredibly revealing talks with people who spent teatimes with him at Lyons corner houses, people like Andrew Ray who knew about Kenneth's relationships with guardsmen, writers like Simon Brett who told the lovely story of the time Williams – who lived the simple life in a flat bereft of all furniture except a table and chairs, a hard bed and a toilet which he never allowed anyone else ever to use – queued at a bank. He was recognised by the bank clerk, who called a colleague to come and say hello. 'Ooh, it's Kenneth Williams,' she called to others behind the counter. 'What can we do for you, Mr Williams?' asked the first clerk. 'May I call the manager?' 'Of course,' said Kenneth in his most imperious manner. The manager came. 'Mr Williams,' he said. 'It's so nice to meet you. What can we do for you?' 'Will you cash a cheque?' he asked. 'Certainly,' said the first girl, who couldn't get over the privilege of serving such a distinguished customer. 'Do you have any identification?'

That lovely actress Sheila Hancock talked about his depressions, so overpowering that his sudden death resulted in an open verdict at the inquest. Most people took that as meaning he committed suicide, even though the doubts have to remain.

I had met Williams twice before. The first time was when I was on the *Daily Sketch*, and called to discuss the 'disgusting' state of theatre green rooms. 'Come in here,' said Williams in his most gushing voice, 'you can see the chorus girls – they've got no clothes on.' I made my excuses and left – with a smile on my face. Many years later, we were both at a book fair. He not only ignored me. He turned his face rudely away from me when the organisers tried to effect an introduction. While working on the book, I got to realise that that was only typical. He was a man who would go to a restaurant, demand a quiet table behind a curtain – and then complain that no one came to ask for his autograph. When a little girl did brave the other side of the curtain, he could turn on her with a curt 'f∗∗∗ off.'

I am pleased to say that my Williams biography had some of the best reviews I ever achieved. But humour was not the overwhelming reaction to the story.

That was not the problem I had with André Previn. We talked and laughed and joked for nearly two years. Despite myself, this was yet another authorised biography that I did with him at the end of the 1980s. He, too, had read the Astaire book and was kind enough to say that he liked it. He liked, too, my Bernstein biography, for which he had given me an interview. Every day, week after week, I went to his Surrey house near Dorking. With him I went to Vienna (again!) where he was conducting the famous Philharmonic. In Los Angeles, I saw him on the podium with that city's Philharmonic Orchestra and spoke to its musicians – who loved him (one woman called him 'Bubbelah'). I went with him to concerts conducted by other people (neither of us was too complimentary) and we laughed some more. We talked about our childhoods. 'We had the same mother,' he joked to his then wife Heather (she was his fourth; there is now a fifth), who told me lovely stories, too.

We talked about his days in Hollywood, when he was the wunderkind of MGM in its glory days, when there was a resident symphony orchestra on the premises, about the films like *My Fair Lady* and *Gigi*, for which he won Oscars. We talked about his early days as a refugee from Germany, about his decision to abandon the world of movies for the concert hall – which he did seamlessly and brilliantly successfully. Other musicians, like David Raksin, talked about him and how much they admired him. Dame Janet Baker talked about him as an accompanist, which is an understatement of what he did, conducting the world's greatest orchestras while she sang.

Where we had disputes it was over his Jewish background. He did not want to talk about it. 'It is not a tradition that concerns me,' he said.

But it was Hollywood that brought the good stories, the best tales. He told me of the classic party at which he played the piano, a 16-year-old, brilliant in music but less experienced in other ways of the world. Ava Gardner was at the party and came to sit next to him on the piano stool. After he had played and she had toyed with the back of his neck, she said, 'How would you like to take me home?' His reaction wasn't that of the sophisticate he later became. 'Haven't you got a car of your own?' he asked – at which point she told him to do something that was anatomically very difficult, if not impossible. Then there was the comedian Lennie Bruce, who was together with him in the early fifties in San Francisco. One night they were standing outside a bookshop, in the window of which was a set of books that André said he would have given a small fortune to own, but he didn't actually have a small fortune with which to buy it. The next day Bruce knocked on Previn's hotel room door, and handed a parcel to André. It contained the books the musician wanted so badly. 'Lennie,' he said, 'how could you ever afford this?' 'I didn't buy them,' said Bruce. 'I stole them.'

I was pleased with the book and sent it off to Previn, who was kind but asked for changes – mainly to the Hollywood stories. 'Please, Michael, for the sake of friendship, please don't use the Ava Gardner story or the Lennie Bruce story' or a whole mass of other stories. 'I want to talk about my music, not about Hollywood.' For the sake of friendship, I took out the stories and for the sake of friendship, I sent him a Christmas card and a note of congratulations when he received an honorary knighthood. And for the sake of friendship, André ignored them both and then brought out another book of his own – about his life in Hollywood.

It was a pity because I really had thought we had a kind of lasting friendship going there. But, I am pleased to say, there were others which, thanks to book projects, really were genuine and, best of all, lasting.

# 28  *The Cincinnati Kid*

None of those friendships was better than that with the man whose name will not instantly roll out of many people's memory banks, David Simon. David is a retired doctor living in Cincinnati, Ohio, and our friendship began with a letter that I am truly ashamed to say I put on what agents call the slush pile. On the other hand, it was resurrected over a bottle or two of champagne and cemented over a labour of love for which I shall for ever be grateful, if that isn't an understatement.

It was in 1990 that David, then a busy general practitioner in his home town, sent me a letter out of the blue. He had read my Bernstein biography on a cruise ship and wondered if I would like to write a book about his father. Now, I was flattered and grateful for his comments, but I had had letters like that before, asking me to write books about people I knew nothing about – one from a millionairess with sexual problems, another from a Las Vegas stripper. I always wrote back in what I hope were courteous terms, but neither was really my cup of tea and I knew they weren't going to amount to anything. I like to think I have an antenna for such things. Dr Simon's letter was rather more serious, I realised, and, of course, I would reply.

Somehow, the letter got lower and lower on the pile and I did nothing about it. Exactly six months later, he wrote to me again – actually, he re-sent the same letter with the same enclosures. His father, Frank Simon, it turned out, was an eminent cornet player. At one time he had been the deputy to the 'March King', John Philip Sousa. Of course that interested me, but I knew the chances of getting a publisher for such a venture were precisely nil. However, the letter was kind and I appreciated it. Also, I was slightly (no, extremely) ashamed of myself for not acknowledging the letter in the first place.

This time, I wrote apologetically and I hope courteously, but intended to say no, I didn't think it was on. I said that I loved the idea of the book – which I did – but I didn't believe it could ever be a commercial proposition. Sorry, but...It was the sort of letter I had received a thousand times and which I never thought I would ever write myself.

To my amazement, David Simon rang me when my letter arrived. He understood the problems, he said, but he was going to be in London the following week. Would I have lunch with him? Of course I would. At the Savoy? Naturally. At the Grill? I got even more interested.

We met in the Savoy lounge. A smallish, bespectacled, dignified man, older than I, tapped me on the shoulder while I looked at some exhibit or other in a glass case (I had to convince Sara that it wasn't the menu).

We walked into the Grill. I ordered Dover sole, which put me in a good mood. He ordered champagne, which put me in an even better one. He spoke about his home, about his father and about his family and that put me in an even better mood still. Somehow this was love, or at least deep friendship, at first sight. What was more, he wanted the book and so did I. He would sort out the financial arrangements.

Meanwhile, the trusty Frank Cass came on board and agreed to publish a book which became *Music Man*.

I couldn't have known how rewarding the whole experience would be, and I don't mean just financially. David welcomed me into his home like a long-lost cousin, and he and his lovely wife Jane pulled out all the stops to make the visit worthwhile. Daily, I went to his office where there were stacks of books, papers and other memorabilia about the man who after leaving Sousa had founded the Armco Band – Armco was a steel company – in Frank Simon's home town of Middletown, about an hour's drive from Cincinnati.

I hadn't known much about brass bands, except that my dear old dad loved sitting in a deckchair listening to them. When I realised the love that David had for his father, I understood that there were now two very strong bonds between us – we both adored our dads, who both loved the same sort of music. It didn't matter that one had played it and the other had just listened.

Not for the first time, I learned about other people's lives when writing the *Music Man* book. When David Simon told me about the visits from Ferde Grofe to Middletown, I have to say I scratched my head. 'Fred who?' was not, I still think, a stupid question. 'Not Fred,' the doctor replied, 'Ferde. He came to help with the orchestrations.'

So what? Again, a not unreasonable question – except when he explained that it was an historic moment. Grofe wasn't just working on *The Armco Hour*, the name of Frank Simon's show – Armco, the steel company employing his musicians. Grofe's friend George Gershwin had asked him for help, too. Gershwin was writing a little piece no one yet knew about – called 'Rhapsody In Blue' – at the time and needed an opening. It was Grofe who arranged the clarinet chords at the beginning of the piece, perhaps the most recognisable part of the work. At least, that was what I was told. I did some checking. Grofe *was* known to have written the chords – and at that time.

I went to New Orleans to meet the trumpeter Al Hirt, one of the best-known jazz names in the States. 'I owe everything to my teacher, Frank Simon,' he told me. 'He sounded wonderful. I heard him and remember saying to him once, "How the hell do you do that?" He answered: "Son, It's a question of breathing. It won't last long because the muscles in your lips won't be supple enough. So learn to do it now.'

Five times I stayed with David, and five times he took me to meet band aficionados and not a few of Frank Simon's old students, who remembered him with great love. This was apparently a man whose dream was that he could train other musicians to play as well as he could himself. I also met David's brother Joe, another lovely man who, when he read the first draft of the book declared it to be a 'masterpiece' – well, who couldn't love a man like that?

Don't let anyone say that human relations are not important. They are as vital in the world of books as anywhere else on the planet. Certainly, money is not everything, although it is always nice and David Simon was perfectly generous. He was generous with his time, too. We would talk at home in the evenings. I would go with him as he moved from one hospital to another. I'd wait in the doctors' room, drinking coffee while he attended to his patients. I am not sure the other doctors appreciated my diagnoses of their own cases as I waited – you would be surprised how many appendectomies I recommended while I contemplated one Simon concert after the other.

## 29 Sean, Frank and Dino – and not forgetting Michael

My biography of Sean Connery was very different, but what a story! This was the man who in old age was still voted the most sexy man alive. 'I can't imagine a man being sexy who was not alive,' he commented. His 'Pussy Galore', Honor Blackman, told me that being with him in a haystack was the most exciting thing that ever happened to her. Ken Adam, the amazing designer of the James Bond sets, recalled the heavy rows between Sean and his first wife, Diane Cilento. 'It was like a scene from *Who's Afraid of Virginia Woolf?*' he said.

That was one offbeat story I was pleased to pick up. There were others when I went back to Connery's Edinburgh childhood, when he was living in a tenement in Fountainbridge, the kind where the tin bath hung on a wall outside.

I heard there about his father, Joe Connery, who worked very hard lifting glasses of beer in the pubs of Rose Street – a thorough-fare which boasted of having more hostelries to the acre than any other road in Britain.

He was the noted champion of what was known locally as the Rose Street Run – scoring points as he entered each pub and then gave them the benefits of his non-existent wealth. The pubs were operated by the brewers Campbell, Hope and King. On one notable occasion, Joe completed the run – and ended up between the tram lines of nearby Princes Street, where he was picked up by the local constabulary. In court, he was asked to explain. 'There were three big fellows who knocked me doon,' he said. The sheriff asked if he knew who they were. 'Oh, I do ken,' he said. 'They were three big fellers by the name of Campbell, Hope and King.'

Craigie Veitch, an eminent Edinburgh journalist, remembered Sean as a boy – 'Big Tam' as he was known, the fellow who got jobs on a milk round, delivering coal and working as a coffin polisher. Then there was Alex Kitson, who was to become deputy general secretary of the Transport and General Workers' Union, who grew up with him. 'Tam used to say, "Can I chum you?"'

Later he 'chummed' with the Welsh actor Victor Spinetti – who helped Sean over a lost love affair. Sean's mother Effie, always a strong influence in his life, adored the girl, Carol Sopel, whom he had taken back to Edinburgh, where she even drank in one of Joe's pubs. But her Jewish mother thought she could do better. When it was all over, Sean was difficult to console. But Spinetti took him to his flat. 'Carol', said the half-Italian actor, 'was absolutely beautiful. Sean was very much in love and totally heartbroken when it all ended.'

Love would always be an important part of Connery's life – almost as big a part as his golf. I heard a lot about his golf – and the fact that there were some people who thought he had, like Chevalier in another generatioin, rather short arms and deep pockets. Among them, the New York limousine driver who spent a whole day taking him round the city looking for an apartment and was given a four-dollar tip for his trouble. That wasn't, however, the time when Sean went hunting for trousers in a Manhattan store and came back with a pile of them – which he had bought for three dollars a pair.

Desmond Llewellyn, probably the most famous Bond player apart from 007 himself – 'Q', allegedly the inventor of the Aston Martin and its ejector seat and every other gimmick, who grew old in the part, told me of the time Connery and Ted Moore, the director of photography, were talking about the adoration Sean had for golf. Moore asked him if he was playing that weekend. 'No,' he answered. 'Well, how about a game on Saturday?' 'No,' said the multi-millionaire superstar. 'I only really enjoy playing at Wentworth and I can't play Saturdays.' There was a good reason for that, he explained. He was a member of the Stage Golfing Society and they didn't have their concessionary rates at weekends.

I met a woman recently who told me about the Caribbean hotel where she and her husband would go to spend anniversaries. They always had the same suite, overlooking the white beaches and the surf. They booked as usual in the late 1990s, only to be greeted by a crestfallen manager. Sean Connery was staying in the hotel, he explained, and he insisted on having their suite. Would they mind giving it up for him? Yes, the woman said, she did mind. But after much persuasion, she and her husband agreed. Shortly afterwards, they bumped into Connery on the staircase. 'Good morning,' she said politely. 'We gave up our honeymoon suite for you.' According to her: 'He just looked at me as if I were some creature he didn't care to meet and walked past us. We saw him several times after that. He never even acknowledged us.' What was it I said about stars being spoilt?

Women loved him, that was a given. But it was a little strange to hear other actors sing his praises. Like Charlton Heston, whom I had met before in a luxurious penthouse suite at London's Grosvenor House hotel – 'Call me Chuck,' he insisted. (At that first meeting, he had talked about his own acting – serious, concentrated, much like Gregory Peck; and his politics, the mirror opposite of Peck's, although they both regarded taking part in national and international affairs as one of the vital ingredients of life. Peck was so left-wing that Richard Nixon had him on his famous 'enemies list', Heston, the head of the American National Rifle Association, might have regarded Nixon as a dangerous pinko.) He had the utmost admiration for Sean Connery. 'He spent his early years with his career focused on one role and so didn't get used up in anything else.' That was the first kind thing I had heard about the wisdom or otherwise of being known as James Bond from a fellow actor. But Heston noted: 'Other actors who do one part become chained to it. Not Sean. He went on to other things. I admire him as an actor and as a fellow Scot. I have great pleasure in his skills and his talents.'

I am sure Sir Sean, as he later became, appreciated that. Acting, he said, was 'nineteen weeks of swimming, slugging and necking'. There were those Scots, however, who had their doubts. When I scouted the streets of Edinburgh for comments about the man who, by standing order, regularly gave a virtual fortune to the funds of the Scottish National Party (the SNP), the folks were less than enthusiastic. One man summed it up: 'Oh, he can talk about being a Scot and a Nationalist but he dinnae be one. I dinnae ken why he doesn't come and live here.' That was a constant cry about a man who claimed on a number of occasions to be trying to buy something suitable – and then went off to his home in Marbella. Before long, he was to sell the Spanish house, but home was still outside Scotland and outside Britain, mostly in America.

My reward, however, was a project about one of the most interesting movie phenomena of the past 40 years, from his first film to the most recent.

Few careers matched that of one of the most significant entertainers of the last 60 years – a project which was in many ways the most important book in my career to date. In 1998, Frank Sinatra died – at virtually the precise moment that my Sinatra biography was published. (The Americans, who had decided to await his imminently expected demise before bringing out their version, published their edition a few weeks later.)

It was a good time to write a book which has, I am grateful to say, been regarded as the definitive biography of the man whom I am sure we have to regard as the world's greatest entertainer of the second half of the twentieth century, virtually taking over where Jolson had left off. As is probably obvious by now, I like big important entertainers who have a story to tell. It was why I liked Jolson and why I wanted to write a Sinatra biography.

The question of titles is always a sticky one. All too often, I had got away with the mere name of the subject – which, in many ways, is good enough. But Sinatra, I felt, needed something more. My editors at Weidenfeld and Nicolson wanted to call it 'Sinatra – Sixty Years A Star'. I had a better idea – *All The Way*. For one thing, it was a fair follow-up to *His Way*, the surprisingly good Kitty Kelley book of a decade or more before. Second, it said exactly what I wanted it to say – that this was all the Sinatra story. Third, and not least of all, it was the title of my favourite Sinatra song.

If, as I learned in my first lesson, you have to make sure that the facts fit, you also need to be able to find a thread. With Sinatra, it was easy and much more complicated: I quickly discovered that he was the most generous and selfish, loyal and womanising, cruel and kindest man in American show business. It was obvious from the stories I picked up in a trawl of Sinatra places, beginning in his home town of Hoboken (taxi rides from one end to the other, $4), crossing the Hudson River to New York and then flying off to Las

Vegas and Los Angeles, with stops at Palm Springs in between. As he said, all the stops along the way.

In Hoboken, I met people who knew the young Sinatra, notably the Spaccaventos, Joe and his son Patty, who ran an Italian restaurant there. In their kitchen, Joe rolled meatballs and threw them to Patty as they talked about the early days of the Sinatra family, particularly about Frank's mother, Dolly, the local ward healer, interpreter for Italian stevedores in trouble in the police courts, midwife and abortionist. Joe used to deliver groceries to her and heard the stories of her love for her son, her language (not the kind she used in the courts), which was colourful enough to make any of the sailors docking at Hoboken feel at home (or on deck) and her influence. It was through her that the kid dressed in velvet Little Lord Fauntleroy suits had a baseball team – she supplied the uniforms – and was able to join a singing group called The Three Flushes and begin his entire career.

I saw Johnny Marotta, who had been to school with him. He never expected Frank to be a sensation. 'There were a lot of better singers in Hoboken,' he said. I saw an ex-fireman who remembered when his father, Marty, became a captain. He was only the fire station cook, but Dolly fixed it so that he became a captain – the one who rode with his son in an open limousine through the main drag in Hoboken, with cabbages thrown in their direction by jealous youngsters who resented Frank's progress and his failure to join the armed services. It was, after all, World War Two.

In New York, I found great-grandmothers who had been teenagers in bobby sox, ones who had been among the thousands who crowded into the Paramount Theatre on Broadway from 10 a.m. until midnight (with terrible effects on the sanitary arrangements there) to hear the skinny Frankie wow them with his strong lyrical voice singing the hit songs of the day. They were the ones who caused riots in the streets and brought on visits from the truancy brigade.

In Hollywood, I met 'em all, the people who had worked with Frank, 'The Voice' who eventually became chairman of the board – although that was before he became Ol' Blue Eyes. It was the time when he had his pick of all the women around, but he had just one real love, the statuesque Ava Gardner. I heard stories of his bursting into tears when she made it clear that she wanted no more of her role as Mrs Sinatra.

It was there that Dan Taradash, the man who wrote *From Here To Eternity*, graphically described Sinatra's search for the role that gave him one of the most remarkable comebacks in the history of showbiz – and how Ava had been responsible for that, by begging Joan, the wife of Harry Cohn, head of Columbia Pictures, to persuade her old man to give him a screen test.

I made my statutory journey to the North Bedford Drive home of Sammy Cahn in Beverly Hills while researching the book. It was a hot summer's day and he was sitting at his desk, writing a new lyric (he had to do at least one a day) and I happened to ask him if he had attended the Palm Springs wedding of his pal Mr S. and Barbara Marx. 'No,' said the man who regarded himself as one of Sinatra's favourite people. After all, he had created a mass of Sinatra hits like 'Come Fly With Me', 'Love and Marriage', 'My Kind of Town' and my own favourite, 'All The Way'. 'I never like the desert in summer and the then Vice-President Spiro Agnew was there – and I've always hated the man. And there was another reason.' 'What was that?' I asked, breath bated. 'I wasn't invited,' he said.

The great clarinettist and the last of the big band leaders Artie Shaw told me of the time the gentlemen in long overcoats and twisted noses called on him – because Sinatra had heard that Ava had gone back to Shaw, her previous husband, after leaving him.

I heard about his Mafia connections and came to the conclusion that he didn't need to be part of the Mafia because he had his own. Nobody ever said 'No' to Sinatra.

I discovered that this was a man who could arrange to rub out someone who offended him, could cut close friends like Sammy Davis Jr and Dean Martin out of his life for years for some 'crime' they themselves could never remember, but could also provide a home to an actor like Lee J. Cobb when he was recovering from a heart attack (and pay for his hospital bed) and give clothes and toys to a poverty-stricken family he heard about when their youngest child incredibly wandered on to his film set in Utah. 'Is Santa Claus bringing you lots of gifts for Christmas?' he asked her. 'No,' she said. 'We don't get presents.' Sinatra went to the house and found that none of the family had any decent clothes and that there was no furniture in their house – all of which he provided, together with a truckload of decorators, in time for the holidays.

Gene Kelly told me about the time that Sinatra was sacked from MGM. 'We were sitting in the commissary when I happened to mention that Louis B. Mayer had broken his arm, falling off his horse. Frank was heard saying something like, "Oh, I thought he fell off his mistress".'

In Palm Springs, I met his butler, George Jacobs, and went round the restaurants and bars that he attended as if it were part of a religious ritual. In one, I heard that he was the world's greatest tipper – $100 for being served a glass of his favourite tipple, Jack Daniels. In another establishment known as Melvyns, the proprietor, Mel Haber, told how he hosted the dinner held on the eve of Frank's wedding to his fourth and last wife, Barbara Marx – the woman Sinatra called 'the dumbest broad I've ever known'. Most of that evening was spent trying in vain to fend off the photographers from the *National Enquirer*. Mel himself told me he had tried to escape every time Sinatra came to the fashionable eaterie – he was so afraid of complaints from the man who would throw ice cubes at hangers-on, the face of one of whom was so badly scarred from that regular experience that Frank called him 'Mr Lump Lump'.

Then there was the Sinatras' neighbour living close to them on Frank Sinatra Drive, who one day drove past what they thought was a bag lady, a woman in rags with what looked like blood streaming from her matted hair. They stopped the car as the man's wife said, 'That's Barbara.' They helped her into a seat and she told them: 'The bastard threw me out of the car.' Alas, that story doesn't appear in my book. It was told to me after I had given a lecture on Sinatra on a cruise ship.

(One of the great joys of recent years has been to travel on cruises fairly regularly, and I'll never cease to be grateful for the opportunity; Sara and I have seen some wonderful places on equally wonderful ships. We have been to India and to Hong Kong, to Vietnam and to Petra. We have travelled through the Panama Canal and seen the pyramids. But it gets a little frustrating when, invariably, someone will come up with a story I would have loved to have featured in a biography already written and published.)

One of the most revealing interview was with Juliet Prowse, who had been engaged to Sinatra for two years, but had never married him because she didn't want to give up her own career.

I had met her in London many years before when she was starring in the British stage version of *Sweet Charity*. She had never spoken about Sinatra before, but had decided that it was about time that she did so. What I didn't know was that she was dying of cancer. 'Can you come to Las Vegas?' she asked. 'Tomorrow?' What she didn't know was that, for reasons I have never been able to understand, my travel agent had routed me home via Vegas – and on the very day that she suggested for our interview.

We talked for hours, about Sinatra and Sam Giancana, the Mafia don with whom he was plainly deeply involved, and about his own generosity, jealousy and violence. She told me how he had given her a 12-carat diamond engagement ring while sitting in the car in which he had driven to Los Angeles airport to meet her – an open Cadillac – as crowds gathered around to witness the event; how he had her followed and asked why she had been doing cartwheels down Wilshire Boulevard the night before; and worse, why she had a man in her apartment. 'We had an open sort of relationship and I knew he had other women. On this night, he came banging on the door of my apartment and I wouldn't let him in. A little later on, there was a call from Frank's secretary, telling me to get out of the apartment because Frank was coming along any moment to blow up the building. The man and I sat on the sidewalk outside until about 3 a.m. and then I thought, he is not going to start threatening me, so we went back inside. We never heard any more about it.' The lawyers wouldn't allow me to use that story in the first edition of my Sinatra biography – because he was still alive and could sue us for libel if we accused him of attempted murder. He was actually much too ill and too far gone to have done any such thing.

Ask Sinatra who he most admired among other singers, and Ella Fitzgerald was at the top of his list. I could understand it. She had a velvet voice and when she sang one of Sinatra's own standards, like Gershwin's 'Someone To Watch Over Me', a complicated piece, she was one of the very few singers who could phrase the lyrics properly – rhyme the line 'He may not be the man-some...girls think of as hand...some' the way it should be sung and not lose the verse somewhere in the middle.

But there was another reason. She was a real lady. I wrote a piece about her in *The Times*. She not only liked the interview – she wrote to tell me so. There are not too many stars who have done that.

Mind you, Alice Faye kissed me – perhaps she didn't often get the chance to do that to a man 30 years her junior, as I was.

The Sinatra book remains one of my favourites, even though others followed that I enjoyed, too – like my biography of Michael Caine. With that, there was perhaps the best situation of all. In Los Angeles I rang Jerry Pam, Caine's American publicist. He said that he couldn't talk to me unless Michael himself gave permission. I was to ring him the following morning, which I did. 'Yes,' he said, 'Michael has agreed we can talk.'

So we lunched and spoke about this British boy-made-good in a very big way indeed – just before he received his knighthood. By the time I got home to Elstree, Jerry was on the phone. 'Michael says he will talk to you. But he wants to see some of your books.' I sent a parcel the same day. A week later, as requested, I phoned again. Caine spoke to me. 'I haven't read your books, so I'm sending them back. I've decided I'd be too bored speaking about myself yet again, but go ahead with it.'

It was indeed the perfect situation. Appointments could be made with people to whom I could say that Michael knew about the book and had no objection to my writing it – and yet feel free from all the problems of 'authorisation'. Again, I spoke to dozens of people, not least June Wyndham Davies, the woman who gave Caine his first stage kiss in repertory. It might have been more exciting for her if the jacket he was wearing hadn't smelt of fish. It was the only one that the son of a Billingsgate fish market porter owned, the one he had worn when, briefly, he went to work with his dad before deciding he would rather be an actor. Then there was Jackie Collins, with whom I had first come into contact back in my *Luton News* days. That was when I had seen her at a performance given by a singer with whom she was at the time 'friendly'. I wrote that it was nice that she wanted to be with her boyfriend, but 'a lady should never look bored'. She just about remembered the evening, and we laughed about it. She also provided me with some nice inside information from Hollywood. I spoke, too, to Angie Dickinson, who had never been sexier than when she was with him in *Dressed To Kill*. She called him 'an English Humphrey Bogart'.

He and Sean Connery were close friends – and never more friendly than when they worked together on the John Huston movie, *The Man Who Would Be King*, about two British soldiers on the north-west frontier in the days of the Raj. And Angie

Dickinson's comparison truly came into play in that film – a movie with several incarnations, none of which until then had actually got to the screen. Caine wasn't so sure about taking a role that had originally been earmarked for someone else. 'Who was going to play my part?' he asked Huston. 'Humphrey Bogart,' the director replied. 'OK,' said Caine, 'nothing more to be said.'

Caine's first big role, of course, had been as the cheeky Cockney *Alfie*. I spoke to the director, Lewis Gilbert, who virtually discovered the boy born Maurice Michael Micklewhite. (His name changed when his agent said there was a small part for him, perhaps too small for such a big name. So he altered it to Michael Scott, which sounded better than the 'Tiskletight' he had been called in repertory. But when his first named bit part came up, the agent pointed out that there was another Michael Scott on the Equity books. There was an urgent need for the second name change, the agent insisted. At that moment, Michael was standing in a Leicester Square phone box. He looked around him, Gilbert told me, and saw that the Odeon cinema was showing *The Caine Mutiny*. 'Call me Michael Caine,' he said. 'Right,' said the agent.

Gilbert recalled the preparations for *Alfie*. Actually, those began when Caine played a tiny part in the wartime epic *Carve Her Name With Pride*. He was one of a group of prisoners-of-war in a train. He had one line to say: 'Water, water, water.' Gilbert told me: 'That was his part. He got between £5 and £10 for the role. If he got £10, that was bloody good pay.'

It took some time before he was able to put into play his hunch that Michael Caine would prove to be a discovery to remember. Before that, others could claim responsibility for his success – like Cy Endfield, the American director of *Zulu*, who met the young actor at a restaurant, intent on casting him as a Cockney in his film based on the Battle of Rorke's Drift – except that he didn't think he made a very good Cockney. Caine walked out, feeling desolate. It was then that Endfield had a brainwave. Could Caine play a foppish officer? As I discovered, Caine could play anything and did, right up to the time that he starred in *Little Voice* and the movies that followed, showing him for what he is – a man in his seventies. What becomes very clear when researching biographies is that people who have played parts in the success of stars are happy to talk about it. Lewis Gilbert, now an octogenerian, recalled taking Michael to a

tailor in the actor's own home territory of the Elephant and Castle
to be fitted out in suits for the part. 'He started to walk around like
Alfie would walk around. He had the sort of walk that Cockneys
had, a sort of arrogance. And it was wonderful. As I saw him
swagger, my worries left me and I thought, "My God, you're going
to be fantastic." Suddenly, I saw how it would all be.'

Caine remembered almost wrestling with Shelley Winters, one of
his co-stars, in the film. Officially, it was a love scene. Shelley, by
then even bigger than the way she looked playing the matronly
figure in the 1966 movie, recalled for me working with the young
star: 'She's practically killing me,' he cried out while the cameras
were still turning – in a scene interrupted by the pinging of a
whalebone in her corset.

She wasn't sure about the competition she suffered. 'There were
always these young girls on the set. Very cool little numbers, none
of them talking much. They just stood around sending out waves to
Michael.' So why? Ms Winters had her theories: 'I think the basis of
his appeal is a certain narcissism, an attitude that suggests, "You
will have the best time of your life with me, even if it's only for one
hour."'

With one failed marriage behind him – he married too young, had
a daughter, but divorced soon after her birth – I heard about the
way Caine met his second wife Shakira. He saw her in a television
coffee commercial and spent the next day searching for her. He
thought she was Brazilian and was on his way to Rio to meet her.
Then he found out she lived in Fulham. It was sort of love at first
sight (for him certainly; for her it took a little longer), and within a
year they were married and parents of a baby girl.

Caine, it became very obvious to me, was a family man. He
adored his mother although his father, Maurice Micklewhite Senior,
the fish porter, thought he was going into a 'Nancy' profession. It
was at the end of his mother's life, I discovered, that he found out
about his mother's big secret – for decades, quite secretly, she had
been visiting a mental hospital every week, where her retarded elder
son lived. Michael knew nothing of his existence until the very end
of his mother's life – and took on the visiting routine for her, as well
as the financial responsibilities.

I have also managed to revisit previous books, an opportunity
allowed few biographers – all of us regret what we have missed

when so much happens to a subject after the work is published. *Some Like It Cool* was worth doing for reasons I would have preferred not to have occurred – Jack Lemmon's death – but there was so much new to say about him, an assessment after two decades and so many wonderfully deep films.

Writing about Doris Day involved getting beyond the blonde who showed a great deal of fashion sense and a lot of white teeth, while she sang 'Che Sera Sera'. When the wit Oscar Levant – no, not Groucho Marx – said, 'I knew Doris Day before she was a virgin,' he may not have known how near the truth he was. No, not literally, but the untouchable Doris of those films with her friend Rock Hudson was far from the truth. This, I heard from friends, had been a very normal woman – a woman who faced tragedy and abuse. She married while still in her teens and then was punched in the stomach when pregnant. Her second marriage failed through apparent incompatibility – although she and her ex-husband slept together frequently after their break-up. Her third husband, whom she thought loved her deeply, died and left her with debts of millions of dollars, and their financial adviser was found to have cheated her of more millions. Her fourth husband said she was more in love with her dogs than with him.

Now that struck a chord when Doris and I spoke. She was much loved in the community of animal-lovers – and her supporters in what became the Doris Day Pet Foundation. She ran, she said, a 24-hour animal rescue service. 'If I hear of a cat or dog wandering in the streets or hit by a car,' she told me, ' I rush round in my van to try to rescue them, I then take them home, feed them and tuck them up in the cots I have for them here.' Plainly, this was more interesting – and more important – to her than singing. By the time she reached the age of 80 in 2004, there were still fans wanting her to do just that. They might also have wanted her to make a new film.

Had she done so, I guarantee nobody would have rung the film's distributors as I had when I contacted Warner Bros. from my desk at the *Luton News*. She had just made *Love Me Or Leave Me*, in which, for the first time, she actually appeared in her underslip. 'I'd like a cheesecake picture of Doris Day,' I said. 'Miss Day does not do cheesecake,' I was told brusquely. Of course, she might have made some in her kitchen.

Liza Minnelli didn't do cheesecake either, but the best pictures of her are in that scene in *Cabaret*, in which she appears wearing a very brief outfit indeed and exhibiting lots and lots of thigh – and suspenders.

I had first visited for what seemed at the time to be a potboiler in the late 1980s. In a new edition in 2003, thanks to help given by an assortment of her friends and colleagues, I was able to piece together the torrid life she had experienced in the years since.

*Liza With A 'Z'* was now subtitled 'The Triumphs and Traumas of Liza Minnelli'. The triumphs were as notable as the traumas, but the latter seemed to be what people would remember. The book was written, proofs marked and corrected and at the printers ready to go when the clebrated divorce action between Liza and David Gest was revealed. Following on what New York liked to call the wedding of the century – the wedding list at Tiffany's, Elizabeth Taylor heading a pack of superannuated black-dressed bridesmaids – which was the biggest show of her life, this was a gift to any biographer, and happened just in time to add a new chapter.

'I believe in grabbing at happiness,' Liza said. 'If you have to pay later for a decision you've made, that's all right. That, too, is part of living.'

Few people would totally agree with that. Knowing Liza's attitudes as I do and knowing the behaviour of someone who never seemed to care much about the reality of life – as anybody who has ever read a newspaper or watched a TV newscast can testify – it seemed to say a lot. However, I doubt if even she would have said it was 'all right'. When I met her, she insisted that she was always in full control of her emotions. It was no more true than the stories put out by her PR people that her voice and her body were back to the way they were. It wasn't true in either case.

When I have spoken about Liza in lectures on Hollywood, there is always someone who sympathetically comments that her story is simply a repeat of that of her mother, Judy Garland. The similarities are there, certainly, but they begin and end with drugs.

Judy was forced into drug dependency by her cruel bosses at MGM, who gave the teenage Garland uppers to wake her up for work in the early mornings and downers to make her sleep at night. Liza seems to have been born with a self-destruct button. Her drug dependency and her fondness for the bottle were not forced on her by anyone. She did it all to herself.

I met Judy Garland, too. This was a frail, frightened woman who had been exploited all her life. Liza is not frail and gives no indication of being frightened. Indeed, the one word that most of the men in her life could justifiably use about her is 'threatening'. The lawsuits that followed her breakup with Gest involve tales of a woman who was extraordinarily violent. Believe them or not, a frail frightened woman would not be accused – as her chauffeur has since alleged – of beating up men and demanding sex from them with menaces. She has never denied that she has a violent temper, although she would probably prefer to call it temperament.

What struck me about her is that for all the thousand-odd guests at her famous wedding show and the offers of love and devotion from people like Michael Jackson (a dubious recommendation, if ever there were one) and Elizabeth Taylor, this was a woman without real friends and yet who craved friendship, perhaps the sort of friend who would not just wrap arms around her, or cry with her, but would give advice – the kind that she would be willing and able to accept.

Her hangers-on were people who thought they could get something our of her and from whom she thought she could get something, too – deep friendship, if not sex. And she doubtless needed both. Like her mother, she had a coterie of homosexual fans. That's another question people always ask about her: why? I put that to a group of 'gays' and one gave me what I think was a tenable answer. It wasn't the usual one of the women wearing clothes that were vaguely masculine – according to their own lights. No, said one man. 'She is just the sort of woman we'd like to be.'

I don't know whether George Abbott would have felt the same. Mister Abbott, as some of the most outstanding stars of Broadway knew him – they were never allowed to call him 'George' – was 106 when I met him. He was the man who had directed Broadway shows since the days of World War One, among them Liza's first appearances in her big Broadway break, *Flora, the Red Menace*, which won her a Tony. At that age of 106, Mister Abbott had just directed a revival of his hit show *Damn Yankees* and was bright as the buttons he could still press to get his way on what went on the stage and what did not. 'Liza,' he said, 'what a gal! And what a waste.' Her stepfather, whom she called 'Pop', Sid Luft, who had been her mother's husband during her growing-up years, told me how distressed he was at the situation in which she now found herself.

'I thought and hoped that she was back on form. She looked so wonderful at her wedding.'

What struck me when I met her and when I spoke to the people who knew her well was that she was forever living the life of Sally Bowles from *Cabaret*, trying to be the 'kookie' she liked to play in that film and in *Arthur*, long past the age when it might have been considered respectable.

None of this takes away from her the fact that she has always been a fighter of a different kind. She recovered from the most appalling illnesses, not least a viral encephalitis, which appeared to cripple her – she was unable to walk for weeks, and for a time there was the fear that she never would again. The trouble, as I discovered during the long haul of interviews for the book, was that so many of her troubles were due to her drugs and her drink.

'When I go, I want to go like Elsie,' she sang in that *Cabaret* number. The fear is that she might just do exactly that.

I followed that with a new biography of Dean Martin, telling the story of one of the nicest people in the business, much maligned for a drinking problem that, most of the time, he didn't really have. I had had an inkling of what the story would be in 2004, when I did a BBC Radio Two series on him.

The book, *Dean Martin, King of the Road*, like the Liza biography, was serialised in the *Sunday Express*, which did a great deal for publicity and book sales.

I had interviewed Dino, as the Rat Pack called him (I hate all the emphasis constantly put on his Rat Pack days – as sometime member Joey Bishop told me, 'After all, what was it? Five guys having fun') and enjoyed his frankness and his amazing sense of humour. 'I only drink moderately,' he said. 'In fact, I have a case of Moderately in the dressing room.'

Apart from Fred Astaire, Dean was the only book subject of mine about whom, on the whole, I heard only good things. He was the most popular star of his day, about whom there was none of the dichotomy of views expressed about Frank Sinatra.

There was Jeanne Martin, the woman he had married, who had given him four children and looked after the three born to his first wife as well, divorced and with whom he then spent the last 10 years of his life without marrying again. She didn't like the comparisons with Sinatra. He was a womaniser who spent as much time drinking as he could fit into his schedules. Dino in those last years was loyal to her and actually *didn't* like to drink.

He most definitely was not a womaniser, she insisted. Not that Dino was short of female admirers. One of the scoops in the book was to discover that Shirley MacLaine called at the Martin house and was received by Jeanne, who thought she had come on a business errand. It turned out she was there to express her undying love for Dean. To cool matters down, the Martins offered her a drink and a snack – in the midst of consuming which, she started to choke. So they turned her upside down (a view of Ms MacLaine not usually on view) and thumped her back. It was, as I said in *King of the Road*, an embarrassing end to an embarrassing experience.

I would have liked my Shirley MacLaine book itself to have included that incident, but at the time people were very wary of saying anything about her that she might not have liked. However, I did provide some information about her last life, a couple of centuries before. Shirley was just getting into her first excursions on the reincarnation plane and no one before me had revealed the information.

I spoke to Greg Garrison, later to be producer of Dean's TV shows, who described how Dean would perpetuate his image as a drunk. He would stand on stage and pour himself a drink – and then sway. Take another drink and sway some more. He then would hiccup. All in about a minute on stage, a very long time indeed before a live audience. When he left the stage, he said to Garrison, who hadn't at that time seen the act before, 'Fooled you, didn't I?' 'I thought,' said Garrison, 'son of a gun.' The booze was simply apple juice.

There was one other factor in Dean's way of life that actually was true. He didn't like to rehearse. Greg Garrison would stand in for Dean during the week and provide him with tapes of the songs he would sing on Saturday nights, which he would then play in his car to and from his morning religious experience – at the golf club. As Dean told me: 'Why rehearse in the studio when I can rehearse on the golf course? I did more rehearsing than anyone else on the show.' But it could throw those others – like Gene Kelly, who wasn't totally happy with the idea. 'We dancers knew that there would be no rehearsal,' he said. 'So what did we do? We winged it. There were times when he preferred to just sit and sing and let someone else do the work.' (I met Kelly shortly before his died. Naturally, we also talked about *Singin' In The Rain*. He said he was suffering from flu when he did the celebrated routine, which was not only the best dance experience in movies but was perfect acting. The scene told the story of a man falling in love better than any consisting of perfect dialogue. After two days of warm water pouring on him, the dancing got better, but his health didn't. Neither did his wardrobe, he told me. He went through two blue suits, both of them badly shrunk.)

It's always good to find background information like that. It was the epitome of the jigsaw theory, being able to find a piece that would fit, but also surprise. Dozens of people told variations of Dean and the apple juice story.

If that fact was a scoop of sorts, the real discovery was one that had to wait until both Dean and his 'brother' Sinatra (who wouldn't tolerate the Martin way if it didn't suit him) died. When Dino left a Rat Pack return show with Frank and Sammy Davis Jr., because he was ill and still suffering from the effects of his son's death, Sinatra was so angry that he didn't speak to him for two years. Those who knew would say that was just par for the Sinatra golf course.

A bigger exclusive came from the Hollywood old-timer Dick Quine, a staff director at Columbia Pictures. It was there that the landmark film *From Here To Eternity* was made. Legend has it that Sinatra got the role largely as a result of interference by the Mafia. This was the story alluded to in *The Godfather* movie, a tale embroidered by the notion of the Mafia placing a horse's head in the producer's bed.

The horse's head incident never happened. But, as Quine, who was around at the time (he later shot himself when he discovered he was suffering from an incurable illness) said, much of the story was true. 'The Mafia came to Harry Cohn [the iron dictator of Columbia] and told him to give a job to this Italian-American singer who was down on his luck. But it wasn't Sinatra. It was Dean Martin they had in mind.'

There were variations on Dean Martin's last years, the unknown tales that brought tears to the eyes – sad, sad stories of his nightly visits to the Italian restaurant, where he would sit in a corner, hiding behind a menu. Shekky Greene, one of the last of the old-style Jewish comedians, was a friend of Dino's. 'He would sit at the table and take his teeth out,' Greene recalled. A shocking insight into the lifestyle of the man who had once been known as the most attractive guy in Hollywood.

But that is what happens to a man who loses a son in an air crash.

The idea of a biography is to try to alter people's perceptions – the drink, the hard work and the womanising. Jerry Lewis, for ten years Dino's partner, was interviewed for me by the LA-based British journalist Barbra Paskin and described him as 'an Adonis'.

I met Lewis myself when he was in London to star in *Damn Yankees* at the Adelphi Theatre. We talked about his ex-partner. 'I loved Dean,' he told me. 'He was wonderful. You have no idea how much I missed him when we broke up.'

The fascinating 'fitting' discovery in this part of the story was that both partners in their comedy act, the successors to Laurel and Hardy and then Abbott and Costello, claimed to have ended the partnership. As Dino said: 'The two greatest things that happened to me were meeting Jerry and then...leaving Jerry.'

Dean said he couldn't bear being the patsy to Jerry's comedy routines, with virtually nothing to say. Jerry – who revealed that he used to buy Dean's comic books for him; the 'Adonis' would look bad buying them himself – said that he couldn't stand it either and insisted that his partner pack it in. Even though they had what he called 'lightning in a bottle'.

(Jerry has had a bad reputation with journalists in recent years. I have to say I found him delightful – but maybe that was because we both loved Al Jolson, whom his own father would imitate in his Catskill Mountains act. How could we not get on – especially when Jerry made his own recordings of Jolson songs like 'Rockabye Your Baby With A Dixie Melody'? We left the hotel room where the interview took place and travelled downstairs in the same lift. He gave a one-man vaudeville act for my pleasure in that elevator.)

The other great thing in Dean's life was Jeanne. Inevitably, there had to be talk about Dean Paul, killed in that air crash. We knew that. What we didn't know before the research began was that it wasn't just grief that broke up her former husband. It was guilt. The two men, father and son, had not been on speaking terms before Dean Paul's death and the weight of that thought could not be lifted.

The lives of other people remains a subject that will forever entice me. If I have demonstrated that enthusiasm, I shall be entirely grateful.

# 30 ...Like show business

Ask me the most exciting night of my professional life and it has to be the one at which Sara, our children, other close friends and family waded through the crowds at London's Victoria Palace Theatre. Dani looked at the smile on my face and said: 'It just shows you, Dad. Dreams can come true.'

This dream had first entered my consciousness on the night I went to a Broadway show at the time I was 'schlepping' the Jolson book in New York in the early seventies. As I sat in what the Americans love to call the 'orchestra', one thought kept running through my mind: if Jolson was the king of Broadway, as he had undoubtedly been, this is where I should go next. There ought to be a Jolson show – based on my book, of course.

The idea stuck and Sara, who I am sure believes that it is unlucky to be optimistic about such things, kept saying I shouldn't give it a further thought. 'There have been the two films. Why should anyone want to put on a Jolson show?'

Perhaps unkindly I said something to the effect that her defiance was even more of a reason to pursue the notion. And it seemed there were others who agreed with me. This was 1973, and show business had never been a better business. Almost immediately after my return home, a producer rang me and asked if I had ever thought of putting on a Jolson musical. 'Ever thought?' I asked. 'I have thought of nothing else.' We had a long lunch and I was convinced he wanted to do it. I never heard another thing about it.

Then a young impresario from Australia came to see me. He wanted to do a Jolson show. Very badly. We talked and we exchanged letters. Again, nothing happened.

In 1977, a magnum of champagne arrived at our house in Elstree.

It came from a complete stranger. He was an entrepreneur, he explained, and business had been lousy for him. So bad he had been on the verge of suicide – until, that is, he had read my Jolson biography. So I had saved his life. Had I ever thought of saving it a little bit more by putting on a Jolson show? Again, we had a meeting – and nothing happened. A lovely London family asked us for dinner and talked about wanting to put on a show. How about Al Jolson? *How about it?* Nothing came of that either.

Nine years later a family friend, Brenda Cooper who, with her husband Brian, had dabbled in the angel business – investing in theatrical productions – was keen on producing a show. Jolson? Of course, I said. She had a consortium of friends who wanted to do the same thing. We signed a contract. We had photographs taken of the signing. And then . . . nothing. I had never got as close before, but it still didn't look as though it would happen.

Until 1994. The year that saw the end of *You Don't Have To Be Jewish* quite surprisingly had a new bounce to it. It had all started when I was commissioned by the *Sunday Telegraph* to do a major feature on pantomimes. My very close friend Roger Filer was running the Stoll Moss theatrical empire. (He, too, had had thoughts about a Jolson show and thought it might work at Drury Lane, but it wasn't to be.) He was the obvious man to go to. 'No,' he said. 'The man you should see about pantomime is Paul Elliott. He really *is* the panto king.'

So I went to see Eliott at his office, atop a great staircase over London's Strand Theatre. We talked and it was a good story, a man who produces and writes dozens of pantos each year, a man who says his greatest joy is hearing 'Good evening boys and girls . . .' Oh yes, it is. He also produces other shows. As we talked, I looked around the walls of his office with its views of the West End. Then I saw two posters – one for the show *Elvis*, the other for *Buddy*, the Buddy Holly story.

'What about', I asked, going into the old routine, 'a show on Al Jolson?' I knew the answer and was about to go straight on to *Mother Goose* at Cheltenham. 'Al Jolson?' he said. 'Sounds like a good idea.' He wasn't ready to talk yet, but asked me to get in touch the following February, at the end of the pantomime season. I decided to do so but wasn't any more optimistic. After two months, any interest he might have had would surely have disappeared by then. Yet in February, I rang him. 'Lunch on Tuesday?' he suggested. 'Lunch on Tuesday will be fine,' I said.

We talked in greater detail than I had with anyone before. I outlined my ideas. He liked them – particularly my insistence that there should be a runway slicing the theatre in two, just as in Jolson's day. As Al had said, 'That way you lose seats, but your show runs twice as long.'

Elliott said he liked it. There were more lunches, more phone calls. Finally, on 3 July 1994 (a date I remember: it was our wedding anniversary) he phoned me to say: 'I've just signed the contract . This very day next year, we begin rehearsals of *Jolson* at the Theatre Royal, Plymouth.' (My original title of *Jolie*, one of the book's later titles and what Jolson used to call himself, had now given way to the more commercial *Jolson*. I understood the commercial arguments.)

A year went by. The star of the show would be Brian Conley. I must say I didn't take to that idea very much. Conley was a TV comedian, and not the Jolson I imagined. And there wouldn't be a runway. Fire regulations ruled it out.

Sara and I went to Plymouth in the early summer of 1995 and couldn't believe it. Conley was not just good, he was very good. The audience thought so. There was a standing ovation that night. And there would be in Liverpool and in Southampton, where there were more previews. The show sold out virtually every performance and the showbiz paper *The Stage* couldn't get over the figures it was achieving.

Finally, it opened at Victoria Palace. The crowds were huge. Everyone who anyone was there – other show people, journalists and writers, the odd politician. The critics loved it. And so did I. What was amazing about Conley was that he didn't impersonate Jolson, yet he sounded like him. When a scene from *The Jolson Story* was shown – with, of course, the real Jolson voice – you couldn't see (or hear) the seams. Somehow, the voices didn't jar. They both sounded right.

Right enough to last for 18 months, a year and a half when my name was on the posters outside one of London's biggest and most important theatres. It would have run longer, but Conley wanted out so that he could do a new TV series. The trouble was that he had been too successful. The critical raves were about his performances (much better than when he did extracts on television, which were, frankly, terrible) and without him, there were no audiences.

Nevertheless, the show then had a glorious six months in Canada, went on tour in America for a year and was featured in Sydney, Australia, for three months.

Excited? You ain't heard nothin' yet.

# 31 Finale – No, not quite

It is perhaps difficult to explain one's life without mentioning dependence on those of other people. If I hadn't demonstrated that dependence throughout my professional career, there would have been no career.

People ask for lessons that I have learned. Probably, the best has to be to live a life outside of the professional one. I have seen too many people, in journalism as much as in show business, for whom their business is everything – with no time for others, no time for a family.

That may be all right for them, but not for me. My greatest gift has been my family. Sara, who has survived two devastating episodes of serious bad health, most recently in the spring of 2004, and, with great courage, has continued life as though nothing has happened, is an example that deserves to be shouted from the mythical rooftops, but she is far too modest to do so.

My three children, Fiona, Dani and Jonathan, have all married happily and given us two grandchildren each. I have discovered in grandparenthood a delight I could never have imagined before the first, Beth, arrived. She, her sister Ellie and their cousins, Ben and Jamie, Jacob and most recently Sam, are the apples of my eye – and my pears and my peaches, too.

Our children have all managed brilliantly successful careers that have helped to enhance their happy marriages, not spoil them. Fiona, now a highly respected lawyer in the field of medical ethics, sitting on numerous committees that affect the health of the nation, is married to the barrister Robin Oppenheim, whom I am more than just proud to regard and love as a son. Dani, who never believed she would succeed, runs the famous Stella Artois tennis tournament and annually receives the plaudits of all the people for whom she makes life easier. She is married to Dave Sewell, a writer. Jonathan, whom people still call a chip off the old block – I still prefer to call myself the block for the young chip – is a journalist, author and broadcaster of international repute whom I am never allowed to forget (as if I would want to) whenever I am introduced to anyone. His wife Sarah, a TV and radio producer, is a delight, too.

As for me, being dangerously close as I write this to the biblical span of three score years and ten, I still look forward. As Frank Sinatra said, the best is yet to come.

# Index of Names

Simmonds, Jeffrey, 210, 213, 246
Simon, David, 295–8
Simon, Frank, 297
Sinatra, Frank, 302–7
Skelton, Red, 209
Skelton, Tom, 32, 33
Skolsky, Sidney, 213, 216–17
Slovo, Joe, 194
Smallman, George, 28–9
Soper, Reverend Lord, 114–15
Spanier, Ginette, 291
Spinetti, Victor, 300
Steel, David, 182
Stein, Saul, 244
Stewart, James, 224
Stoloff, Morris, 227
Streisand, Barbra, 6, 281, 284, 285
Sunshine, Gerald, 26
Suzman, Helen, 194
Swift, Maurice, 48
Sykes, Dennis, 210, 226

Tallel, Crown Prince Hassan bin, 164–6
Taylor, Elizabeth, 312
Taylor, Rod, 276
Thatcher, Margaret, 66, 81, 181–3, 200
Thurber, James, 65
Topol, 273
Tucker, Richard, 108
Tucker, Sophie, 210, 269
Turner, Lana, 217

Unterman, Abraham, 133

Ustinov, Peter, 68

Vadim, Roger, 275, 276
Vogel, Rabbi Feivish, 111

Wallfish, Asher, 153, 163
Wallis, Hal, 265–6
Walsh, Raoul, 271
Warner, Jack Jr, 260, 265
Wayne, 127
Webb, Kenneth Burgess, 24
Weidenfeld, George, 270
Weisman, Malcolm, 194
Weizmann, Chaim, 138, 157, 160
West, Timothy, 278, 278
Weston, Bernice, 122
Wiesel, Elie, 104
Wigoder, Devorah, 118
Wigoder, Geoffrey, 118
Wilder, Billy, 267
Williams, Kenneth, 291–2
Wilner, Izzy, 48
Wilson, Harold, 35, 66, 179–81
Wilson, Michael, 120
Winters, Shelley, 309
Wise, Ernie, 145, 286–8
Wolfson, Sir Isaac, 93

Yarrow, Tommy, 74
Yidel, Yehuda, 4
Yitzhok, Levi, 5
Yoelson, Moses, 219

Zalmondson, Sylva, 126
Zletovski, Michel, 154